Minimum Viable Product for Startups

Mastering the MVP lifecycle from strategic market research to sustainable product scaling

Saurabh Gupta

www.bpbonline.com

First Edition 2026

Copyright © BPB Publications, India

ISBN: 978-93-65893-335

To View Complete
BPB Publications Catalogue
Scan the QR Code:

Dedicated to

My mentor

J.B. Mall, *Defence Psychologist*

About the Author

Saurabh Gupta is a seasoned tech entrepreneur, product leader, and published author with over two decades of experience in building scalable, data-driven, and customer-centric products. He holds a master's degree from BITS Pilani and is an alumnus of Harvard Business School. Throughout his career, he has led high-impact product teams, launched digital platforms across diverse industries, and authored multiple books on technology, product strategy, and startup innovation. Recognized for his clarity of thought and hands-on leadership, Saurabh is a strong advocate for Lean methodologies, MVP-driven development, and outcome-focused product thinking. In 2018, he was honored with the NEXT100 CIO Award for his contributions to technology leadership. A frequent speaker at conferences and community events, he shares his perspectives on product mindset, data-driven culture, and ethical AI. Based in Bengaluru, India, he is the co-founder of FroGo, where he is building a next-gen digital supply chain experience. He also actively advises startups on technology and product strategy, writes about the evolving product landscape, and contributes to India's dynamic tech ecosystem.

About the Reviewer

Dr Tariq Ahmad, PhD CEng MIET, has over 30 years of experience in the IT industry, specializing in .NET, Python, **artificial intelligence (AI)**, **natural language processing (NLP)**, and **large language models (LLMs)**. He has worked for global organizations, including KPMG and Sybase, and is now based in England, working for a leading consultancy. In his current role, he helps clients unlock the value of AI by applying advanced NLP and LLM techniques, guiding them through the challenges of adoption, assurance, and integration of AI-driven solutions. His work spans technical development, research, and consulting, with a focus on delivering impact in complex and safety-critical domains. Prior to this, he was a senior developer for a company providing software solutions and services to the public sector.

Acknowledgement

I would like to express my sincere gratitude to everyone who contributed to the completion of this book. Writing Minimum Viable Product for Startups has been as much of a personal journey as a professional one, and I am deeply thankful to all who made it possible.

First and foremost, I want to thank my parents, Neha, my wife, and Vidhi, my daughter, for their unwavering belief, support, and encouragement. Your patience and faith gave me the strength to pursue my passion with clarity and confidence. Thank you for reminding me to stay grounded while always aiming high, and for believing that this book would eventually see the light of day.

I am also profoundly grateful to the many industry leaders, mentors, and fellow product thinkers whose ideas, conversations, and generosity in sharing knowledge kept my curiosity alive. Your insights helped shape the perspective from which this book was written, and your impact on the world of product development continues to inspire me every day.

A special note of thanks to BPB Publications for turning my work into reality. Thanks for the professionalism and trust throughout the publishing process.

This book is a reflection of both shared wisdom and lived experience. To everyone who has challenged my thinking, offered guidance, or simply asked the right question at the right time. Thank you!

Preface

We operate in an age where products are expected to launch fast and scale even faster. Yet behind every successful launch or graceful failure lies something fundamental, a well-crafted **minimum viable product (MVP)**.

In today's startup landscape, speed is the new currency, and validation is survival. Investors are cautious. Customers are unapologetically sharper. Markets evolve at breakneck speed. The expectations are higher than ever, but so is the potential for focused and high-velocity product builders.

Every week, dozens of products debut with fancy landing pages, feature sets, and engagement models, only to disappear quietly because they fail to connect with real customer problems. Meanwhile, there are Lean MVPs that are tested early and iterated often, go on to become iconic brands and billion-dollar ventures.

What sets them apart? The product mindset. Top entrepreneurs do not obsess over perfection. They prioritize traction over theory, feedback over assumptions, and real-world usage over internal applause. To them, a product is not a deliverable but a live experiment. And the MVP is the fastest and most reliable way to test that hypothesis.

Minimum Viable Product for Startups is a practical guide for turning ideas into actionable products, while navigating through the critical stages like market research, customer feedback, iterations, and launch. Whether you are a first-time founder or a seasoned product leader, this book is designed to help you move with clarity, learn with speed, and build without losing sight of what matters.

This book takes you through the complete journey of MVP development, from the foundational principles to real-world execution. It begins by exploring what an MVP truly is and why it matters in the startup landscape, then guides you through understanding market needs, setting clear goals, and mapping out the stages of MVP creation. You will explore how to build efficiently with the right tools and teams, execute with agility, and test with purpose. As your MVP evolves, the book offers strategies for scaling, overcoming common barriers, and maintaining the right mindset throughout. It concludes with an essential discussion on ethical considerations, ensuring that speed never compromises integrity. Whether you are validating your first idea or refining your product strategy, this playbook is your hands-on companion at every step.

Chapter 1: Understanding Minimum Viable Products - This first chapter sets the foundation by unpacking what a minimum viable product truly is and, importantly, what it is not. It walks through the philosophy behind MVPs, emphasizing why they are not just scrappy prototypes but strategic instruments for learning. We explore core principles of the Lean Startup methodology, the role of validated learning, and how MVPs evolve through various startup stages. The chapter also dives into the importance of focusing on essential features, building fast with purpose, and fostering a culture of experimentation and iterative delivery from day one.

Chapter 2: Market Needs for MVP - This chapter equips you with tools to decode consumer behavior, uncover unmet needs, and identify pain points worth solving. It emphasizes the importance of market research, customer interviews, and competitive analysis to validate whether your product is addressing something real. You will also learn how to leverage empathy maps, early adopter feedback, and beta testing to sharpen your product-market fit before investing heavily in development.

Chapter 3: Defining MVP Goals and Objectives - The chapter helps you define what success looks like before you write a single line of code. Learn how to set measurable goals that align with your startup's mission, define **key performance indicators** (**KPIs**), and establish the right guardrails to keep your MVP focused. We also explore how to link MVP objectives to broader business outcomes and long-term vision, ensuring you are not just building features, but building directionally with purpose.

Chapter 4: MVP Development Stages - In this chapter, we walk through the essential stages of MVP development. Starting with ideation, you will learn how to translate ideas into prototypes, prioritize features using proven frameworks like MoSCoW and Kano, and move quickly through feedback-driven iterations. The chapter provides actionable tips for setting timelines, managing scope creep, and building feedback loops that fuel rapid learning and improvement throughout the process.

Chapter 5: Building Blocks for MVP Development - In this chapter, we focus on the infrastructure behind fast, flexible MVPs. You will explore how to assemble the right team, choose a Lean tech stack, and adopt tools that accelerate progress without compromising quality. We also discuss the role of low-code platforms, cloud services, and AI-powered development assistants. This chapter offers practical guidance on balancing speed with scalability and introduces techniques to future-proof your MVP from the start.

Chapter 6: MVP Execution - This chapter covers how to move from prototype to live MVP, with a strong focus on user-centered design and Agile development. You will learn about effective design patterns, UX strategies, and prototyping tools that help validate your assumptions quickly. We also cover key aspects of launch planning, user onboarding, and customer acquisition strategies tailored for MVPs. Real-world case studies highlight what successful MVP execution looks like in action.

Chapter 7: MVP Testing Strategies - In this chapter, we will learn how to define clear testing objectives, set up feedback loops, and use techniques like usability testing, A/B testing, and performance validation to gather actionable insights. We also explore lightweight analytics tools and testing frameworks that help you make informed product decisions without slowing down your velocity.

Chapter 8: Scaling MVP to Success - This chapter lays out strategies for evolving your MVP into a more complete, stable, and widely adopted product. From incorporating user feedback to expanding feature sets and solidifying infrastructure, we explore the tactical and strategic moves that help you grow. You will also learn how to align your scaling roadmap with go-to-market strategies, growth loops, and retention metrics to build long-term success.

Chapter 9: Common Barriers and the Mindset - This chapter focuses on cultivating the mental models and cultural mindset needed to navigate uncertainty, manage pivots, and embrace experimentation. You will learn how to deal with fear of failure, how to rally your team around progress (not perfection), and how to stay resilient through the highs and lows of product building.

Chapter 10: Ethical Considerations in MVP Development - The final chapter explores the responsibility founders have while building fast, particularly around user privacy, data security, accessibility, and long-term societal impact. Learn how to embed ethical thinking into your product development process and why trust and transparency are critical currencies in today's tech ecosystem.

Coloured Images

Please follow the link to download the
Coloured Images of the book:

https://rebrand.ly/536901

We have code bundles from our rich catalogue of books and videos available at https://github.com/bpbpublications. Check them out!

Errata

We take immense pride in our work at BPB Publications and follow best practices to ensure the accuracy of our content to provide with an indulging reading experience to our subscribers. Our readers are our mirrors, and we use their inputs to reflect and improve upon human errors, if any, that may have occurred during the publishing processes involved. To let us maintain the quality and help us reach out to any readers who might be having difficulties due to any unforeseen errors, please write to us at :

errata@bpbonline.com

Your support, suggestions and feedbacks are highly appreciated by the BPB Publications' Family.

At www.bpbonline.com, you can also read a collection of free technical articles, sign up for a range of free newsletters, and receive exclusive discounts and offers on BPB books and eBooks. You can check our social media handles below:

Instagram　　　*Facebook*　　　*Linkedin*　　　*YouTube*

Get in touch with us at: business@bpbonline.com for more details.

Piracy

If you come across any illegal copies of our works in any form on the internet, we would be grateful if you would provide us with the location address or website name. Please contact us at business@bpbonline.com with a link to the material.

If you are interested in becoming an author

If there is a topic that you have expertise in, and you are interested in either writing or contributing to a book, please visit www.bpbonline.com. We have worked with thousands of developers and tech professionals, just like you, to help them share their insights with the global tech community. You can make a general application, apply for a specific hot topic that we are recruiting an author for, or submit your own idea.

Reviews

Please leave a review. Once you have read and used this book, why not leave a review on the site that you purchased it from? Potential readers can then see and use your unbiased opinion to make purchase decisions. We at BPB can understand what you think about our products, and our authors can see your feedback on their book. Thank you!

For more information about BPB, please visit www.bpbonline.com.

Join our Discord space

Join our Discord workspace for latest updates, offers, tech happenings around the world, new releases, and sessions with the authors:

https://discord.bpbonline.com

Table of Contents

CHAPTER 1
Understanding Minimum Viable Products

Introduction

In the fast-paced startup landscape, the ability to swiftly adapt and respond to market demands can determine the success or failure of a business. At the heart of this agility is the concept of the **minimum viable product** (**MVP**). An MVP is not just a product development strategy; it is a mindset focused on learning, iteration, and efficiency. It is about building a product that is good enough to attract early adopters and validate your idea early in the development cycle.

Creating an MVP starts with identifying your core value proposition and understanding the minimum features needed to deliver that value to your customers. It means focusing on what is essential and stripping away anything unnecessary. This approach allows startups to test their assumptions, gather valuable user feedback, and make informed decisions about the product's future direction.

Structure

In this chapter, we will cover the following topics:

- Historical perspective and evolution of MVPs
- MVP practices for startups
- Understanding MVP

- Lean Startup methodology

- Importance of MVP in startup success

- Demystifying MVP myths

- MVP development amidst emerging trends

- Stages of MVP development

- Evolution of MVP through startup stages

- Culture of experimentation at startups

Objectives

Remember that the goal is not to create a perfect product right from the start. Instead, it is to build a viable product that allows you to start learning from users and iteratively improve based on their feedback. This chapter will equip you with the knowledge and insights needed to implement MVP strategies effectively, laying the foundation for your startup's success in a competitive landscape. You will learn how to identify the core features necessary for your MVP, engage with early users, collect and analyze feedback, and iteratively refine your product. By adopting this approach, you can navigate the challenges of early-stage product development with agility and confidence, setting the stage for long-term success.

Historical perspective and evolution of MVPs

The origins of the MVP concept can be traced back to the early days of software development, where the predominant approach was the Waterfall model. This linear and sequential methodology required detailed planning, extensive documentation, and strict adherence to predefined stages. Each phase, from requirements gathering to design, implementation, testing, and maintenance, had to be completed before the next one began. While this approach provided a clear structure, it often led to lengthy development cycles and significant delays in delivering products to market.

The rigidity of the Waterfall model meant that any changes to requirements or design had to be meticulously managed, often leading to scope creep and increased costs. By the time a product was finally delivered, market conditions and customer needs might have shifted, resulting in products that were outdated or misaligned with user expectations.

Agile Manifesto and Lean manufacturing influence

The turn of the millennium brought a revolutionary shift in software development practices with the introduction of the Agile Manifesto in 2001. The Agile Manifesto transformed how we approach development by emphasizing the importance of people and their interactions over rigid processes, focusing on creating functional software rather than getting stuck in excessive documentation. It encourages close collaboration with the customers instead of sticking to contracts and promotes adaptation and flexibility over a fixed plan. Agile methodologies, such as *Scrum* and *Kanban*, emerged, promoting iterative and incremental development, continuous feedback, and adaptive planning.

Parallel to the rise of Agile, Lean principles from manufacturing, particularly those started by *Toyota*, began to influence software development. Lean manufacturing focused on optimizing processes, eliminating waste, and delivering value to customers efficiently. Key concepts included just-in-time production, continuous improvement (Kaizen), and respect for people. These principles resonated with the emerging Agile methodologies, creating a foundation for more flexible, responsive, and customer-centric product development practices.

Rise of MVP

In this evolving landscape, *Eric Ries* introduced the concept of the MVP in his groundbreaking book, *The Lean Startup*, published in 2011.

As per *Ries*, MVP is a version of a new product that enables maximum learning about the customers with the least effort. He is often considered the pioneer of the MVP concept and Lean Startup methodology.

The MVP approach emphasized rapid experimentation, hypothesis testing, and iterative development, aligning closely with both Agile and Lean principles.

Ries's MVP concept was born out of his experiences in startups, where he observed that many companies failed because they invested heavily in building fully featured products without first validating whether there was a market need. By focusing on building only what was necessary to test key assumptions, startups could minimize waste, reduce time to market, and make more informed decisions based on real user feedback.

Evolution of MVP

Since its introduction, the MVP concept has continued to evolve, adapting to various industries and contexts beyond software development. The principles of MVP have been applied to hardware startups, service-based businesses, and even large enterprises seeking to innovate and stay competitive.

MVP practices for startups

By focusing on developing an MVP, startups can validate their ideas quickly, minimize risks, and gather essential feedback from real users. This iterative approach enables entrepreneurs to refine their products based on actual market needs, ensuring a stronger product-market fit. Let us explore top practices at startups for MVP development.

Rapid experimentation

Modern MVP practices emphasize rapid experimentation and learning. Startups use MVPs to test different aspects of their business model, such as pricing strategies, marketing channels, and customer acquisition tactics. This approach allows startups to pivot quickly based on validated learning, reducing the risk of pursuing unviable paths.

Integration with Design Thinking

The integration of MVP with Design Thinking has further refined the approach. Design Thinking emphasizes empathy, ideation, and prototyping to solve complex problems and create user-centered solutions. By incorporating Design Thinking principles, startups can create more effective MVPs that address real user needs and provide meaningful value.

Application across industries

The application of MVP principles has expanded beyond software to include hardware startups, where building physical prototypes can be costly and time-consuming. In such cases, MVPs might involve creating low-fidelity prototypes or using 3D printing to test key assumptions before committing to full-scale production. Service-based businesses also leverage MVPs by testing new service offerings or delivery methods with a small group of customers to gather feedback and refine their approach.

The historical perspective and evolution of MVPs highlight the shift from rigid, linear development models to more flexible, iterative approaches that prioritize validated learning and customer feedback. By understanding the origins and evolution of the MVP concept, startups can better appreciate its significance and apply its principles effectively to build products that meet market needs, minimize risks, and drive sustainable growth. As we move forward, we will explore the fundamental principles of MVPs, their role in startup success, and practical strategies for implementing MVPs in your own ventures.

Understanding MVP

Understanding the concept of an MVP is essential for any startup aiming to navigate the uncertain waters of product development. The MVP is a strategic approach that helps startups validate their ideas with minimal resources while maximizing learning from real customer interactions. To bring this concept to life, let us explore it through anecdotes and industry examples.

Definition

MVP is a product with the minimum set of features necessary to gather validated learning about customers and their needs. The goal is to launch quickly, gather feedback, and iterate, ensuring the product evolves based on real user input rather than assumptions.

The following figure showcases the characteristics of MVP:

Figure 1.1: *MVP characteristics*

Case studies

Let us examine three cases to understand how the MVP approach not only validated their ideas but also generated initial traction for their products.

Dropbox

Drew Houston, the founder of Dropbox, faced a common startup dilemma, to validate a product idea without building a full-blown product. Houston knew that building a file synchronization service would be resource-intensive. Instead, he created a simple explainer video showcasing Dropbox's core functionality, seamlessly syncing files across devices.

The video resonated with potential users, generating thousands of sign-ups almost overnight. This overwhelming response validated the market demand and gave Houston the confidence to proceed with development. By focusing on the MVP, a video that communicated the value proposition, Dropbox minimized initial costs and gathered critical user interest.

Airbnb

Airbnb's founders, *Brian Chesky* and *Joe Gebbia*, faced a different challenge. They had an idea for a platform that allowed people to rent out their spare rooms or homes, but they needed to test whether there was a market for it. They decided to start small by creating a basic website listing their own apartment during a design conference in San Francisco.

The MVP was simple but effective. They hosted their first guests and used the experience to gather feedback and understand user needs. This initial success demonstrated the viability of their concept and attracted early users and investors. The Airbnb MVP was not just about technology; it was about testing a new business model in a real-world setting.

Buffer

Joel Gascoigne, the founder of Buffer, wanted to build a tool for scheduling social media posts but needed to validate the idea first. He created a minimal landing page explaining Buffer's concept and included a sign-up form to gauge interest. When visitors signed up, they were directed to a pricing page, providing insights into their willingness to pay.

This Lean approach allowed Buffer to validate demand and gather valuable data on pricing without building the actual product. The feedback and interest from potential users gave Gascoigne the confidence to move forward with development. Buffer's MVP was not about the technology itself but about understanding market demand and pricing strategy.

Value proposition of MVPs

The value proposition of MVPs lies in their ability to quickly validate a product idea with minimal resources. By focusing on core features, startups can test market assumptions, gather user feedback, and iterate rapidly, ensuring alignment with customer needs and maximizing resource efficiency.

Power of starting small

The essence of an MVP is to start small and learn quickly. Think you are a chef with a new recipe idea. Instead of opening a restaurant right away, you might host a dinner party with friends and family to experiment with your dishes. Their feedback helps you refine the recipes before you invest in a full-scale restaurant. Likewise, an MVP allows startups to test their ideas on a smaller scale, gather feedback, and iterate before making significant investments.

Building trust with early users

Early adopters play a vital role in the success story. They are the ones who provide honest feedback, helping you identify strengths and weaknesses. Building trust with these users is essential. By engaging with them, addressing their concerns, and iterating based on their feedback, you create a loyal user base that feels invested in your product's success.

Learning from failure

Not all MVPs succeed, but even failures provide valuable learning opportunities. The goal is to learn, not necessarily to succeed on the first try.

Failure is not the end but a step towards understanding what works and what does not. Each iteration brings you closer to a product that truly meets user needs. The examples of Dropbox, Airbnb, and Buffer reflect that starting small does not mean thinking small. These companies began with simple MVPs that allowed them to validate their ideas, understand their users, and build successful products that have transformed their industries. Embracing the MVP approach means committing to a journey of continuous learning and improvement, where every iteration brings you closer to a product that resonates with your users and achieves market success.

Lean Startup methodology

The Lean Startup methodology has transformed the way startups tackle product development and market entry. By emphasizing validated learning, iterative development, and a scientific approach to building businesses, the Lean Startup methodology provides a framework that helps startups navigate uncertainty and increase their chances of success.

Core principles of Lean Startup

The core principles of Lean Startup revolutionize how we build products by emphasizing validated learning, rapid experimentation, and iterative development. These principles focus on creating an MVP to test hypotheses, using customer feedback to guide improvements, and ensuring efficient use of resources to achieve sustainable growth.

Validated learning

At the heart of the Lean Startup methodology is the concept of validated learning. This involves testing assumptions about a business idea through experiments and learning from the results. Instead of relying on intuition or traditional business planning, startups create hypotheses about their product, market, and customers, then design experiments to validate or invalidate these hypotheses.

Build-Measure-Learn feedback loop

The Build-Measure-Learn feedback loop is a core process in the Lean Startup methodology. It consists of three key steps:

1. **Build**: Create an MVP that includes only the essential features needed to test the core assumptions.

2. **Measure**: Collect data on how the MVP performs in the market. This involves tracking user interactions, gathering feedback, and analyzing metrics.

3. **Learn**: Analyze the data to determine whether the assumptions are valid. Based on this learning, decide whether to pivot (make a fundamental change to the product or strategy) or persevere (continue with the current path and iterate further).

Innovation accounting

Innovation accounting is a way of measuring progress in a startup context. Traditional financial metrics are often not suitable for early-stage startups because they do not capture the learning and experimentation that are crucial at this stage. Innovation accounting focuses on actionable metrics that drive validated learning and help startups track their progress in terms of customer acquisition, engagement, and retention.

Key components of a Lean Startup

In a Lean Startup, key components include developing an MVP to quickly test hypotheses, utilizing validated learning to iteratively improve the product, and leveraging rapid experimentation to pivot or persevere based on feedback. This approach minimizes waste, accelerates learning, and boosts the chances of achieving product-market fit.

Hypothesis-driven development

In Lean Startup, every new idea or feature is treated as a hypothesis that needs to be tested. This approach encourages a mindset of experimentation and learning, where failure is seen as an opportunity to gain valuable insights.

Customer development

Customer development involves engaging with potential customers early and often, understanding their needs, preferences, and pain points. This approach ensures that startups build products that truly solve customer problems and provide value.

Agile development

Lean Startup integrates Agile development practices, which emphasize flexibility, collaboration, and rapid iteration. Agile methodologies, like Scrum and Kanban, align well with the Lean Startup approach, enabling teams to respond quickly to feedback and changes in the market.

Significance of Lean Startup methodology

The Lean Startup methodology is transformative, enabling startups to build products efficiently through validated learning, rapid experimentation, and customer feedback.

Let us understand how Lean Startup methodology minimizes risk and maximizes the chances of achieving product-market fit:

- **Risk reduction**: The Lean Startup methodology helps reduce the risks associated with launching new products. By validating assumptions early and iterating based on real user feedback, startups can avoid costly mistakes and ensure they are building something that customers want.

- **Cost efficiency**: Building an MVP and iterating based on feedback allows startups to use their resources more efficiently. Instead of investing heavily in a fully featured product upfront, startups can focus on developing the most critical features and expand gradually based on validated learning.

- **Faster time to market**: The Lean Startup approach enables startups to launch their products faster by focusing on the essential features needed to test their hypotheses. This rapid deployment allows startups to gain early traction, gather feedback, and make necessary adjustments before scaling.

- **Customer-centric development**: Engaging with customers throughout the development process ensures that the product evolves to meet their needs. This customer-centric approach increases the likelihood of product-market fit and long-term success.

- **Adaptability and resilience**: The iterative nature of the Lean Startup methodology fosters adaptability and resilience. Startups learn to pivot when necessary, adjusting their strategies based on validated learning. This ability to adapt quickly to changing market conditions and customer feedback is crucial for survival and growth.

Industry references

Let us see how Lean Startup methodology has enabled startups to optimize resources while building customer-centric MVPs.

Zappos

Zappos, the online shoe retailer, tested its business model using a Lean Startup approach. Instead of investing in a large inventory upfront, the founder took pictures of shoes from local stores and listed them online. As soon as he received a customer order, he would purchase the shoes from the store and deliver them. This MVP allowed Zappos to validate demand for online shoe shopping without significant upfront costs.

IMVU

Eric Ries co-founded IMVU, a social network and virtual world, where he applied Lean Startup principles. IMVU launched a simple product that allowed users to create avatars and interact in a virtual environment. The team used the Build-Measure-Learn feedback loop to iterate rapidly, testing new features and making data-driven decisions based on user feedback.

Validated learning, iterative development, and customer-centric practices can be instrumental in reducing risks, optimizing resources, and increasing the chances of a startup's success. The principles of Lean Startup provide a robust framework for navigating the uncertainties of the entrepreneurial journey, ensuring that every decision is informed by real-world data and customer insights.

Importance of MVP in startup success

Startups have the trajectory of a rollercoaster. The highs can be exhilarating, but the lows can be devastating if not navigated wisely. One of the key tools for an entrepreneur is the MVP.

Understanding and effectively leveraging MVPs can be the difference between a thriving startup and a failed venture.

Let us understand how a stable MVP can help startups assess their product while staying Lean:

- **Hypothesis validation**: Startups operate under conditions of extreme uncertainty. By focusing on the most critical features needed to validate your business hypothesis, an MVP allows you to test your core assumptions with minimal resources.

- **Cost efficiency**: Developing a fully-fledged product is expensive and time-consuming. An MVP allows you to launch with just the essential features, significantly cutting down on initial costs. This Lean approach ensures that you're not pouring money into features that customers might not even use.

- **Faster time to market**: Speed is crucial in the startup world. An MVP enables you to launch your product quickly and start gathering user feedback. This rapid deployment can give you a competitive edge, helping you capture market share before others do.

- **Validated learning**: An MVP is a powerful tool for learning. By putting a basic version of your product into the hands of real users, you can gather invaluable insights into how they interact with it, what they like, what they do not, and what they are willing to pay for. This validated learning is crucial for refining your product and business model.

- **Building customer relationships**: Engaging with early adopters through your MVP helps build a loyal customer base. These users are often more forgiving of initial imperfections and are willing to provide the feedback necessary to improve your product. By involving them in the development process, you create a sense of community and loyalty that can be a powerful asset as you grow.

- **Facilitating pivoting**: Startups often need to pivot, that is, change direction based on market feedback. An MVP provides the flexibility to pivot without significant sunk costs. If your initial hypothesis proves incorrect, you can adjust your product or strategy based on real data rather than speculation.

Demystifying MVP myths

Despite its proven benefits, the concept of the MVP is often misunderstood. The following figure showcases some of the top myths that entrepreneurs need to be aware of:

Figure 1.2: Common MVP myths

Understanding the true nature and benefits of an MVP is essential for any entrepreneur aiming for startup success. By debunking common myths and embracing the principles of the MVP, you can navigate the uncertainties of the startup journey more effectively. The MVP is not just a product development strategy; it is a mindset that prioritizes learning, agility, and customer-centricity. As you move forward with your startup, keep these principles in mind to build a product that truly resonates with your market and sets the foundation for sustainable growth.

MVP development amidst emerging trends

Staying abreast of the latest technology trends is not only about leveraging new tools and techniques but also about understanding how they can transform the planning and execution of MVPs. These trends offer both opportunities and challenges that can significantly influence the success of your MVP strategy.

Artificial intelligence and machine learning integration

Artificial intelligence (**AI**) and **machine learning** (**ML**) are revolutionizing MVP development by enabling more intelligent and data-driven decision-making processes. Let us find out how deep tech is making it possible:

- **Personalization**: AI allows for the creation of highly personalized user experiences. According to a 2021 McKinsey report, companies that leverage AI for personalization can achieve a 10 to 15% increase in revenue.

- **Predictive analytics**: ML helps startups predict user behaviour and optimize MVPs. GenAI is shifting to multimodal models, handling text, images, audio, and video together. By 2027, 40% of GenAI solutions will be multimodal, says *Gartner*. This is up from just 1% in 2023. This evolution unlocks richer human-AI interactions and new ways to differentiate.

- **Processes automatio**n: AI-driven automation can streamline various aspects of the MVP, reducing manual intervention and operational costs. For instance, customer service bots can handle routine inquiries, while ML algorithms can automate data analysis tasks, freeing up human resources to focus on more strategic activities.

- **Data-driven decision making**: AI and ML facilitate data-driven decision making by processing vast amounts of data and extracting actionable insights. For a startup, this means making informed decisions about product features, marketing strategies, and user engagement tactics based on empirical evidence rather than intuition alone.

- **Real-time adaptation**: One of the standout benefits of integrating AI and ML is the ability to adapt in real-time. An MVP equipped with AI capabilities can learn from user interactions and continuously improve its performance. For example, an e-commerce platform might use ML to adjust pricing strategies dynamically based on user behavior and market conditions.

No-code and low-code platforms

The rise of no-code and low-code development platforms is democratizing software development, allowing non-technical founders to build MVPs quickly and cost-effectively. Let us explore how these platforms are beneficial for startups, especially when faced with constraints like limited resources and elementary technological setups:

- **Rapid prototyping**: These platforms enable rapid prototyping and iteration, significantly reducing time to market. Forrester estimates that by 2028, the market for low-code development platforms will increase to $50 billion.

- **Accessibility**: These tools make it possible for anyone to develop and test their ideas, fostering innovation across various industries.

Remote and distributed teams

The shift towards remote work, accelerated by the COVID-19 pandemic, has impacted MVP planning and execution. Startups are increasingly relying on distributed teams and leveraging remote collaboration tools.

- **Global talent pool**: Access to a global talent pool allows startups to tap into diverse skill sets and perspectives. According to the *World Economic Forum's Future of Jobs Survey*, 47% of employers recognize the potential of expanding talent pools through diversity, up from just 10% in 2023.

- **Productivity tools**: Tools, like *Slack*, *Trello*, and *Asana*, facilitate seamless communication and project management, ensuring that remote teams remain productive and aligned.

Customer-centric development

Customer-centric development approaches, such as Design Thinking and **user experience** (**UX**) research, are becoming integral to MVP planning. These methodologies emphasize understanding user needs and designing solutions that deliver exceptional value. Let us explore how they contribute to successful MVPs:

- **User feedback integration**: Continuous integration of user feedback helps in refining the MVP and ensuring it meets customer expectations.

- **Empathy in design**: Design Thinking promotes empathy and a deep understanding of user pain points, leading to more user-friendly and successful products.

- **Iterative improvement**: By embracing iterative development cycles, startups can quickly test and refine MVP features based on real user data, leading to faster product evolution and increased user satisfaction.

Lean and Agile methodologies

The adoption of Lean and Agile methodologies continues to grow, emphasizing iterative development, continuous improvement, and responsiveness to change. Let us learn how these methodologies are making a difference:

- **Agile adoption**: Agile practices enable startups to iterate quickly, respond to user feedback, and pivot when necessary. Despite the rise of AI, new-age buzzwords, and talks of Agile losing momentum, 95% of professionals still consider it essential to their work.

- **Lean Startup principles**: Lean Startup principles, such as the Build-Measure-Learn loop, remain foundational for MVP development, promoting a cycle of rapid experimentation and learning.

- **Flexibility and responsiveness**: These methodologies enable startups to adapt quickly to market changes, customer needs, and emerging opportunities, enhancing their ability to stay competitive in dynamic environments.

Focus on sustainability and ethical practices

There is a growing emphasis on sustainability and ethical practices in product development. Customers expect transparency and responsibility from the brands they support. Let us find out how it helps the startups:

- **Sustainable development**: Startups are integrating sustainability into their MVP planning, ensuring that their products are environmentally friendly and socially responsible. A *Nielsen* report indicates that 81% of global consumers feel strongly that companies should help improve the environment.

- **Ethical AI**: As AI becomes more prevalent, ethical considerations, such as bias mitigation and data privacy, are becoming crucial. Accenture claims that 62% of customers expect companies to take a firm stand on issues like sustainability, transparency, and fair employment practices.

The latest trends in MVP planning and execution highlight the importance of leveraging cutting-edge technologies, fostering a customer-centric approach, and adopting flexible methodologies. By staying informed about these trends and integrating them into your MVP strategy, you can ensure that your startup remains Agile, innovative, and responsive to market needs. Embrace these trends as opportunities to enhance your MVP development process, delivering products that not only meet but exceed user expectations, and driving long-term success in an ever-evolving landscape.

Stages of MVP development

The journey from idea to market-ready product involves several key stages, each critical to the development of a successful MVP. Understanding these stages helps ensure that your product evolves based on validated learning and meets the needs of your target audience. Here is a brief overview of the MVP stages.

Ideation

Ideation is the first stage of the MVP development process. This is where the initial idea for your product is conceived and refined.

The key activities of ideation are:

- **Market research**: Conduct thorough research to understand the market landscape, identify gaps, and validate the need for your product.

- **Problem definition**: Clearly define the problem you aim to solve. Understanding the pain points of your target audience is crucial.

- **Hypothesis formulation**: Develop hypotheses about how your product will solve the identified problem and benefit users.

- **Value proposition**: Articulate the unique value your product offers and why users would choose it over existing solutions.

Prototyping

In the prototyping stage, you create a preliminary version of your product to visualize and test the concept. This is about bringing your idea to life in a tangible form.

The key activities of prototyping are:

- **Wireframing**: Create basic sketches of the product layout and interface to visualize the UX.

- **Mock-ups**: Develop more detailed visual representations to refine the design and functionality.

- **Interactive prototypes**: Build interactive versions of the product to test user interactions and gather early feedback.

Testing

The testing stage is critical for validating your hypotheses and ensuring that the MVP meets user needs. This is where you start engaging with real users.

The key activities of testing are:

- **Usability testing**: Observe how users interact with the prototype, identify usability issues, and gather feedback.

- **A/B testing**: Compare different versions of the product to determine which performs better in terms of user engagement and satisfaction.

- **Beta testing**: Release the MVP to a small group of users (beta testers) to gather feedback and identify bugs or issues before the broader launch.

Iteration

Based on the feedback received during the testing stage, the iteration stage involves making improvements to the MVP. This is a cyclical process of refining the product to better meet user needs.

The key activities of iteration are:

- **Feedback analysis**: Analyze user feedback to identify common themes and areas for improvement.

- **Prioritizing features**: Determine which features to add or enhance based on user needs and business goals.

- **Implementing changes**: Make the necessary updates and improvements to the product, ensuring it evolves iteratively.

Launch

The launch stage is when you release the MVP to the broader market. This is a crucial step that involves marketing, monitoring, and ongoing support.

The key activities of launch are:

- **Marketing and promotion**: Create awareness and generate interest in your product through various marketing channels.

- **Monitoring and analytics**: Track user behavior and product performance using analytics tools to gather ongoing feedback.

- **Customer support**: Provide support to users, address any issues that arise, and continue to collect feedback for future iterations.

Each stage of the MVP development process plays a vital role in ensuring that your product is viable, valuable, and aligned with market needs. From ideation to launch, every step involves critical activities that contribute to the product's success. By following these stages, you can systematically develop an MVP that resonates with your target audience, minimizes risks, and sets the foundation for continuous improvement and growth.

Evolution of MVP through startup stages

Understanding how the MVP evolves through the different stages of a startup's lifecycle is crucial for sustained growth and success. The MVP is not a static product; it adapts and improves as your startup matures, responding to market feedback, customer needs, and business objectives.

To illustrate this process, consider a conversation between Arjun Mehta, a startup founder, and Priya Sharma, the product head:

Arjun Mehta: Good morning, Priya! Do you have some time to go over our product planning over the next few quarters?

Priya Sharma: Good morning, Arjun! Of course, let us dive in. It is very crucial for our roadmap. Where should we start?

Arjun Mehta: We are currently in the ideation and validation phase. What should our focus be with the MVP here?

Priya Sharma: At this stage, our goal is to validate our core value proposition. We need to focus on identifying the essential features that address our target users' primary problem. This involves conducting thorough market research and forming a hypothesis about what our users need. The MVP at this stage is all about proving that there's a real need for our solution with minimal effort.

Arjun Mehta: Right, and we have focused on the essential features to test our assumptions. As we start gaining traction, how should we refine our MVP?

Priya Sharma: Exactly. Initially, we should resist the urge to add extra features. The goal is to release a basic, functional version and start gathering feedback. Usability tests and feedback from early adopters will be invaluable for this.

Arjun Mehta: Okay, so let us say we get some initial traction and validation. What comes next as we move into the next stage?

Priya Sharma: In the growth stage, we start refining the MVP based on the feedback we received. This means improving the UX, enhancing the core features, and maybe adding a few more features than users have requested. Our focus shifts to scaling and ensuring our product can handle more users.

Arjun Mehta: How do we balance adding new features with maintaining a Lean product?

Priya Sharma: It is a delicate balance. We need to prioritize features that provide significant value and set us apart from competitors. At the same time, we should continue iterating based on user feedback to improve usability and performance. Scalability becomes a key consideration here.

Arjun Mehta: What about performance optimization? When should that come into play?

Priya Sharma: Performance optimization becomes crucial in the maturity stage. At this point, we focus on optimizing the product's performance and reliability. Any issues that were acceptable in the early stages need to be ironed out.

Arjun Mehta: And what about differentiating from competitors? When does that become a priority?

Priya Sharma: Differentiation is ongoing but particularly important in the maturity stage. By then, we should have a solid product that users love. The next step is to add unique features that set us apart from competitors and solidify our market position.

Arjun Mehta: How does the MVP mature post growth stage?

Priya Sharma: By the maturity stage, our product should be robust and feature-rich. Our focus will be on optimizing performance, enhancing customer satisfaction, and maintaining our competitive edge. Continuous innovation is critical; we should introduce advanced features that keep us ahead of the market.

Arjun Mehta: And customer support becomes even more important, right?

Priya Sharma: Definitely. Excellent customer service and support systems are crucial for maintaining and growing our user base. Engaging with our customers to understand their evolving needs will help us refine the product further.

Arjun Mehta: That makes sense. Now, let us talk about the expansion stage. How do we handle the MVP here?

Priya Sharma: In the expansion stage, our MVP should support broader market penetration. We might look at entering new geographical markets or customer segments. This could involve adapting the product to meet different market needs and developing complementary products or services to diversify our offerings. It's also a good time to explore strategic partnerships that can help us scale faster.

Arjun Mehta: So, continuous market research and adaptation are key?

Priya Sharma: Absolutely. Continuous customer feedback is key. We must keep an eye on market trends and user feedback and remain flexible to adapt our product strategy accordingly. Forming strategic partnerships can also help us enhance our market reach and product capabilities.

Arjun Mehta: Awesome! How do we ensure that our team is aligned with this evolutionary process?

Priya Sharma: Stay Agile. The market changes rapidly, and so do customer expectations. Regular communication and updates are vital. We need to ensure that everyone understands our current focus and future goals. Agile methodologies can help us remain flexible and responsive to changes. Plus, fostering a culture of continuous learning and experimentation will drive innovation at every stage.

Arjun Mehta: Great points, Priya. Thank you. Let us ensure our roadmap reflects these layers of evolution and keep our team aligned with this vision.

Priya Sharma: Absolutely. I will get started on refining our roadmap and scheduling a team meeting to align everyone. We are on a solid path forward!

The following figure shows the evolution of an MVP through the startup stages as a dynamic and continuous process:

MVP Evolution Through the Startup Stages

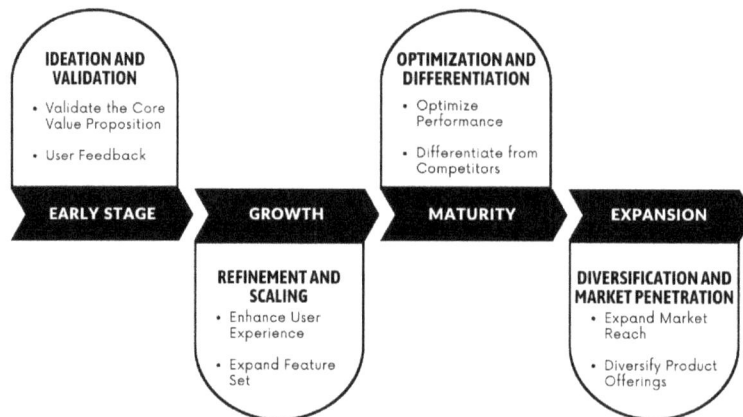

Figure 1.3: *Summary of MVP evolution through the startup stages*

From the initial ideation and validation phase to the growth, maturity, and expansion stages, each phase presents unique challenges and opportunities. By understanding and embracing this evolution, tech entrepreneurs can ensure that their product remains relevant, competitive, and aligned with market needs.

Culture of experimentation at startups

Fostering a culture of experimentation within your startup is not just beneficial, but essential for the success of your MVP. This cultural element empowers your team to explore, innovate, and adapt, driving continuous improvement and ensuring that your product evolves in response to real-world feedback and market dynamics.

Essence of a culture of experimentation

A culture of experimentation is characterized by an environment where team members are encouraged to test new ideas, take calculated risks, and learn from both successes and failures. It involves a mindset that values curiosity, open-mindedness, and a relentless pursuit of knowledge and improvement.

Importance of experimentation for MVPs

Experimentation plays a crucial role in MVP development, allowing startups to test hypotheses, gather real-world feedback, and validate assumptions before scaling their products or services.

Validating hypotheses

At the heart of an MVP is the concept of testing and validating hypotheses. Whether it is a new feature, a marketing strategy, or a pricing model, experimentation allows you to gather empirical evidence to support or refute your assumptions. This scientific approach minimizes guesswork and helps you make informed decisions.

For instance, when Dropbox first launched, they used an explainer video as an experiment to validate the demand for their file synchronization service. This simple yet effective experiment provided clear evidence that there was a significant market interest before they invested heavily in product development.

Iterative development

Experimentation aligns perfectly with the iterative nature of MVP development. Each experiment provides insights that inform the next iteration of the product. This continuous feedback loop ensures that your MVP evolves based on real user interactions and preferences.

Buffer, the social media scheduling tool, started with a basic landing page to test the concept. They continuously iterated on their product based on user feedback from these early experiments, refining the functionality and UX incrementally.

Encouraging innovation

A culture of experimentation encourages team members to think creatively and come up with innovative solutions to problems. It fosters an environment where new ideas are welcomed and unconventional approaches are explored. This innovation is critical for differentiating your product in a competitive market.

Airbnb's initial MVP was a simple website listing the founders' own apartment. This unconventional approach allowed them to test the market demand for short-term rentals and gather valuable insights, leading to the innovative platform they are today.

Reducing fear of failure

In a traditional business setting, failure is often stigmatized. However, in a startup with a culture of experimentation, failure is seen as a learning opportunity. This shift in mindset reduces the fear of failure, encouraging team members to take bold actions and explore new ideas without the paralyzing fear of making mistakes.

At *Amazon, Jeff Bezos* has long championed the idea that *failure and invention are inseparable twins.* This philosophy has led to a culture where experimentation is part of the company's DNA, resulting in groundbreaking innovations, like AWS and the Kindle.

Data-driven decision making

Experimentation is inherently data-driven. By running experiments and analyzing the results, startups can make decisions based on data rather than intuition. This leads to more accurate, reliable, and scalable solutions.

IMVU, the social network and virtual world co-founded by *Eric Ries*, utilized A/B testing extensively to make data-driven decisions about features and UX. This approach allowed them to optimize their product based on quantitative evidence rather than subjective opinions.

Implementing a culture of experimentation

A culture of experimentation promotes continuous testing, learning, and iteration, which are essential for developing a successful MVP. This mindset allows startups to rapidly validate ideas, uncover market needs, and optimize products based on real-world feedback.

Let us understand how it fosters creativity, adaptability, and sustainable growth, making it the engine that drives long-term success:

- **Leadership support**: For a culture of experimentation to thrive, it must be supported by leadership. Founders and executives should model experimental behaviors, celebrate learning from failures, and provide the resources needed for experimentation.

- **Empowering teams**: Empower your teams to take ownership of their experiments. Encourage cross-functional collaboration and provide them with the autonomy to test new ideas and approaches.

- **Establishing processes**: Develop clear processes for designing, conducting, and analyzing experiments. Use frameworks, like Lean Startup, Design Thinking, and Agile, to structure your experimentation efforts.

- **Celebrating learning**: Celebrate both successful and unsuccessful experiments. Recognize the effort and learning derived from each experiment and share these insights across the organization to foster a collective knowledge base.

- **Investing in tools and training**: Provide your team with the tools and training needed to conduct experiments effectively. This includes data analytics platforms, A/B testing tools, and educational resources on experimental design and analysis.

A culture of experimentation is a cornerstone of successful MVP development. It encourages innovation, validates hypotheses, reduces the fear of failure, and enables data-driven decision making. By embedding this cultural element into your startup, you create an environment where continuous learning and improvement are the norm. This not only enhances your product development process but also positions your startup for long-term success in an ever-changing market. Embrace experimentation as a strategic imperative, and watch your MVP evolve into a product that truly resonates with your users and drives sustainable growth.

Conclusion

Understanding MVPs is a cornerstone for any startup aiming for success in today's fast-paced market. The MVP approach emphasizes validated learning, iterative development, and a customer-centric mindset, allowing startups to create products that truly meet user needs. By starting with a core value proposition and essential features, entrepreneurs can mitigate risks, optimize resources, and bring their products to market more quickly. This chapter has explored the evolution of MVPs, the benefits of a Lean Startup methodology, and the latest technological trends that influence MVP planning and execution. Embracing these principles and staying adaptable ensures that your MVP evolves in alignment with customer feedback and market demands.

In the next chapter, we will explore the critical process of identifying and addressing the specific needs of your target market. This involves comprehensive market research, customer segmentation, and competitive analysis. You will learn how to gather and interpret data to discover unmet needs and pain points, ensuring that your MVP is well-positioned to deliver value. Additionally, we will discuss strategies for building strong customer relationships and leveraging their feedback to refine your product. By understanding your market deeply, you can create an MVP that not only meets but exceeds customer expectations, paving the way for long-term success.

Points to remember

- **Definition of MVP**: We explored what an MVP is, highlighting its purpose as a version of a product that has enough features to satisfy early adopters and gather feedback for future iterations.

- **Importance of experimentation**: We learnt the critical role of experimentation in MVP development, allowing startups to test hypotheses, gather feedback, and validate assumptions before scaling their products.

- **Focus on core features**: We discussed the importance of focusing on core features in an MVP, prioritizing functionalities that solve a specific problem for users rather than building a full-featured product from the start.

- **Iterative development**: We learnt the concept of iterative development in MVPs, where continuous feedback loops and incremental improvements drive product evolution based on real-world usage and user feedback.

- **Validation and learning**: We understood the goal of an MVP to validate assumptions and learn from user interactions, guiding startups in making data-driven decisions and pivoting when necessary to align with market needs and user preferences.

Join our Discord space

Join our Discord workspace for latest updates, offers, tech happenings around the world, new releases, and sessions with the authors:

https://discord.bpbonline.com

CHAPTER 2
Market Needs for MVP

Introduction

In the previous chapter, we explored the foundational principles of building a product mindset, a crucial shift for any entrepreneur or tech founder aiming to productize the ideas. As we move forward, it is essential to understand that the product mindset is only effective when it is deeply rooted in the understanding of market needs. This chapter will guide you through the process of identifying, researching, and validating these needs, providing you with a strategic advantage in a competitive landscape. In addition, it will equip you with the insights and tools necessary to ensure that your **minimum viable product** (**MVP**) aligns perfectly with the demands and pain points of your target audience.

Structure

In this chapter, we will cover the following topics:

- Identifying market needs
- Conducting market research
- Customer research and segmentation
- Understanding customer pain points

- Competitive analysis

- Hypothesis development and testing

- Leveraging feedback for MVP iteration

- Case studies

Objectives

By the end of this chapter, you will be able to identify market needs and market research. Moreover, you will be able to understand how to pinpoint unmet needs within target markets to create products with real customer value. The chapter helps you build skills to gather and analyze market data to inform product decisions.

Next, we will tackle customer research and competitive analysis. This will help the readers learn to categorize customers based on behaviors, needs, and demographics to tailor solutions effectively. Additionally, you will discover how to assess competitors' strengths and weaknesses to uncover opportunities for differentiation.

Finally, we will discuss hypotheses testing and MVP iteration. We will explore how to formulate, test, and refine assumptions about the product's value and market fit. In addition, we will explore how to use customer insights and test results to enhance and evolve the MVP.

Identifying market needs

The success of your MVP hinges on your ability to accurately identify and address the true needs of your market. Let us walk through the essential process of distinguishing between market needs and wants and understand the effective techniques for uncovering these critical insights.

Defining market needs versus market wants

Understanding the difference between market needs and wants is fundamental to creating a product that connects with the target audience.

Market needs are the essential problems or pain points that your target customers must solve. These are non-negotiable requirements that your product must address for it to be valuable and relevant. For example, a grocery shop owner might need an efficient way to manage their finances, while a food delivery product might need the exact location for pickup and delivery.

Market wants are the desirable features or enhancements that customers would like to have but are not essential for solving their primary problems. These are often nice-to-have features that enhance user experience but are not critical to the product's core functionality.

Importance of focusing on genuine needs

From an MVP standpoint, focusing on genuine needs rather than wants is crucial for several reasons.

Firstly, it ensures resource optimization. Startups often operate with limited resources, and prioritizing needs ensures that efforts and investments are directed towards solving the most pressing issues, maximizing the impact of your MVP.

Secondly, it enhances market fit. Addressing genuine needs increases the likelihood of achieving product-market fit, as customers are more likely to adopt and remain loyal to a product that effectively solves their core problems.

Lastly, it supports scalability. By focusing on essential needs, you create a solid foundation that can be scaled and built upon. Wants can be addressed in later iterations, ensuring your product evolves in alignment with user feedback and market demands.

Techniques for identifying market needs

To accurately identify market needs, you must employ various techniques that provide deep insights into your target customers' lives, behaviors, and pain points.

Empathy interviews

Empathy interviews are in-depth, qualitative conversations with your target customers aimed at understanding their experiences, motivations, and challenges. This technique involves:

- **Preparation**: Develop a set of open-ended questions designed to explore the customers' daily routines, challenges, and how they currently address those challenges.

- **Engagement**: Engage in a conversational manner, allowing the interviewee to share their stories and insights without leading them to specific answers.

- **Analysis**: After conducting several interviews, analyze the common themes and pain points that emerge. This qualitative data provides valuable insights into the genuine needs of your market.

Observational studies

Observational studies involve watching and analyzing how your target customers interact with their environment and existing solutions. This technique provides an unfiltered view of their behaviors, habits, and challenges. Moreover, you will also get to gauge the willingness to adopt a new solution. Let us explore some of the common techniques for conducting observational studies:

- **Natural setting**: Observe customers in their natural settings, such as their workplace or home, to gain insights into their daily routines and pain points.

- **Non-intrusive**: Maintain a non-intrusive presence to ensure that your observations reflect genuine behaviors rather than influenced actions.

- **Documentation**: Document your observations meticulously, noting any recurring issues, inefficiencies, or frustrations that your MVP could address.

Data analytics and trends

Leveraging data analytics and trends is a crucial practice for understanding market needs on a larger scale, particularly from a technical standpoint. This technique has three essential steps:

1. **Data collection**:

    - **Sources**: Gather data from a variety of sources, including customer feedback, usage analytics, and comprehensive market research reports.

    - **Tools**: Employ advanced tools like Google Analytics for web traffic analysis, social media insights tools (e.g., *Hootsuite, Sprout Social*), and CRM systems (e.g., *Salesforce, HubSpot*) for customer relationship management. Additionally, consider using data aggregation platforms like *Tableau* or *Power BI* to consolidate and visualize data from multiple sources.

    - **APIs and integrations**: Utilize APIs to pull data from various platforms into a central database for more seamless analysis. This can include integrating data from e-commerce platforms, email marketing software, and user behavior tracking tools.

2. **Trend analysis**:

    - **Descriptive analysis**: Basic analytics to understand the data, sample size, and basic know-how.

    - **AI-driven analysis**: Implement machine learning algorithms and **natural language processing** (**NLP**) techniques to analyze large datasets and identify emerging trends and patterns. These technologies can help sift through social media discussions, search trends, and industry reports to detect subtle shifts in market needs.

    - **Sentiment analysis**: Use sentiment analysis tools to understand the emotional tone of customer feedback and social media conversations. This can provide deeper insights into customer satisfaction and pain points.

    - **Predictive analytics**: Leverage predictive analytics to forecast future market trends based on historical data. This can involve using time series analysis, regression models, and clustering techniques to predict customer behavior and market movements.

3. **Insight extraction**:

 - **Advanced data mining**: Apply data mining techniques to uncover hidden patterns and correlations within your data. Tools like *SQL, R,* and *Python* can be used for more in-depth statistical analysis and modeling.

 - **Customer segmentation**: Use data segmentation to categorize your audience into distinct groups based on behavior, demographics, and other variables. This can help in tailoring your MVP features to specific customer segments.

 - **Market gap analysis**: Conduct a thorough market gap analysis by comparing your data against industry benchmarks and competitor offerings. Identify areas where customer needs are not being met and where your product can provide a unique solution.

By employing these techniques, you can gain a comprehensive understanding of your market's genuine needs, ensuring that your MVP is not only relevant but also indispensable to your target audience. This foundation will guide the subsequent stages of your product development, enabling you to build a solution that truly resonates with your customers and sets the stage for long-term success.

Empathy interview guide template and questionnaire

A structured template for conducting empathy interviews to gather qualitative insights from users is given as follows:

Section	Questions
Context	Brief introduction. Explain the purpose of the interview. Assure confidentiality and ask for consent to record.
User background	1. Tell me about yourself and your role.
	2. Introduce the problem statement.
Experience	1. Exchange views.
	2. Any product that they used to solve the problem.
	3. How was their overall experience?
Pain points and emotional impact	1. What challenges has the user faced during the problem?
	2. How did the challenges make you feel?
	3. What impact did they have on your work/life?
	4. How did you handle the impact?
Desired improvements	1. What do you wish was different or better?
	2. How would you like to face and overcome the situation?

General feedback	1. Is there anything else you would like to share?
	2. Do you have suggestions for improvements?
Closing	1. Thank you, and next steps.
	2. Incentives (if any).

Table 2.1: Empathy interview questionnaire template

Demystifying TAM, SAM, and SOM at startups

When you are in the startup world, it is easy to get overwhelmed by the plethora of acronyms and jargon thrown around. Among these, TAM, SAM, and SOM are crucial terms that can significantly impact your understanding of the market and your MVP strategy. Let us demystify these terms and explore their importance.

Total addressable market

Total addressable market (**TAM**) refers to the total revenue opportunity that is available if your product or service achieves a 100% market share. It is the broadest measure of market size and indicates the maximum potential market demand for your product.

It is important for several reasons, listed as follows:

- **Vision setting**: TAM helps in setting a grand vision for your startup. It shows the maximum potential scale of your business.

- **Investor attraction**: Investors often look at TAM to gauge the long-term potential and growth prospects of your startup.

- **Strategic planning: understanding**: TAM helps in strategic planning and prioritization of resources to tap into this potential.

Serviceable available market

Serviceable available market (**SAM**) is the portion of TAM that your product or service can address with its current capabilities and scope. It considers the market segments you are targeting and the geographical areas you can reach.

It is important for several reasons, listed as follows:

- **Realistic targeting**: SAM provides a more realistic picture of the market size you can serve, considering your current business model and product features.

- **Market penetration**: It helps in setting achievable targets for market penetration and growth.

- **Focused marketing**: SAM guides your marketing efforts by focusing on the segments that are most likely to convert into customers.

Serviceable obtainable market

Serviceable obtainable market (SOM) is the portion of SAM that you can realistically capture, considering your resources, competition, and market constraints. It represents your short-term market opportunity.

The reasons why it is important are as follows:

- **Operational planning**: SOM is critical for operational planning and setting sales targets.

- **Resource allocation**: It helps with the efficient allocation of resources to areas where you have the highest chances of success.

- **Performance measurement**: SOM provides a benchmark for measuring your market share and performance over time.

Importance of TAM, SAM, and SOM

Let us consider a startup developing a new fitness app. The total global market for fitness apps is estimated to be $20 billion (TAM). Within this, the market for fitness apps catering to yoga enthusiasts in the US is $5 billion (SAM). Given your startup's resources and current reach, you can realistically capture $500 million of this market in the first few years (SOM).

Figure 2.1 depicts how these terms help startups grow up the ladder:

Figure 2.1: *A clear view of the target audience/market is vital to planning the MVP and product iterations*

Demystifying TAM, SAM, and SOM equips startup founders and product managers with essential tools for market analysis and strategic planning. These terms are not just buzzwords but powerful metrics that can guide your startup towards sustainable growth and success. As you continue to develop your MVP, keep these market sizes in mind to ensure that your efforts are aligned with realistic opportunities and goals.

Conducting market research

Understanding your market is a critical component of developing a successful MVP. Effective market research helps you identify your target audience, understand their needs, and position your product to address those needs effectively. Let us explore both primary and secondary research methods, commonly used tools, and highlight tools specifically useful for early-stage startups.

Primary research methods

Primary research involves collecting firsthand data directly from your target audience. This approach provides specific insights that are highly relevant to your product and market.

Surveys and questionnaires

Surveys and questionnaires are a cost-effective way to gather quantitative data from a large audience. Here is how to craft them effectively:

- **Define objectives**: Clearly outline what you want to learn from the survey. Your objectives will guide the questions you ask.

- **Design questions**: Use a mix of open-ended and closed-ended questions. Open-ended questions provide qualitative insights, while closed-ended questions yield quantitative data.

- **Keep it short**: Respect your respondents' time by keeping the survey concise and focused on essential questions.

- **Incentives**: Build a compelling narrative by offering incentives to encourage participation, such as discounts, shopping vouchers, free trials, or a prize draw.

In-depth user interviews

Interviews allow for deeper exploration of individual user experiences and insights. Effective techniques include:

- **Preparation**: Develop a structured interview guide with key questions and topics.

- **Active listening**: Listen actively and empathetically, encouraging the interviewee to elaborate on their experiences and perspectives.

- **Follow-up questions**: Use follow-up questions to probe deeper into interesting or unexpected responses.

- **Recording and notes**: Record the interview (with permission) and take detailed notes to capture valuable insights.

Focus groups and communities

Focus groups gather diverse perspectives through moderated group discussions. To conduct productive focus groups:

- **Select participants**: Choose a diverse group of participants who represent your target audience.

- **Set clear objectives**: Define what you aim to achieve from the focus group.

- **Prepare a discussion guide**: Outline key topics and questions to guide the discussion.

- **Moderate effectively**: Ensure that all participants have an opportunity to speak, and that the discussion stays on track.

- **Analyze results**: Identify common themes and insights from the group discussions.

Secondary research methods

Secondary research involves analyzing existing data from various sources to gain insights into your market.

Industry reports

Industry reports provide comprehensive analysis and data about market trends, key players, and growth opportunities. They utilize these reports to:

- **Understand market size**: Gain insights into the overall size and growth potential of your market.

- **Identify trends**: Stay updated on emerging trends and shifts in your industry.

- **Benchmarking**: Compare your startup against industry standards and best practices.

Market analysis

Market analysis helps you understand the broader market dynamics affecting your industry. The key steps include:

1. **SWOT analysis**: Conduct a **strengths, weaknesses, opportunities, and threats (SWOT)** analysis to identify your startup's SWOT.

2. **PEST analysis**: Use **Political, Economic, Social, Technological (PEST)** analysis to evaluate external factors impacting your market.

3. **Trend analysis**: Monitor trends in consumer behavior, technology, and regulatory changes.

SWOT analysis template

Use the template in the following *Table 2.2* to analyze the internal and external factors impacting your startup or product. The SWOT analysis is divided into four quadrants: strengths, weaknesses, opportunities, and threats. Fill in each quadrant with relevant points based on your market research and internal assessments.

Strengths	Weaknesses
Internal positive attributes	**Internal negative attributes**
What does your startup do well?	What areas need improvement?
What unique resources or advantages do you have?	What resources or capabilities do you lack?
What do your customers see as your strengths?	What feedback have you received about shortcomings?
Opportunities	Threats
External factors that could benefit you	**External factors that could harm you**
What market trends can you capitalize on?	What market trends could negatively impact you?
Are there gaps in the market you can fill?	Who are your competitors and what threats do they pose?
What innovative technologies or partnerships could help you?	Are there regulatory or economic challenges you face?

Table 2.2: SWOT analysis matrix

Table 2.3 is an example of SWOT analysis for a tech startup:

Strengths	Weaknesses
Innovative product features	Limited marketing budget
Strong team with diverse skills	Lack of brand recognition
High user satisfaction and loyalty	Underdeveloped customer support processes
Opportunities	Threats
Growing demand for tech solutions in the market	Increasing competition in the tech industry
Possible potential for international expansion	Rapid technological changes requiring adaptation
Partnerships with established companies	Economic downturn affecting customer spending

Table 2.3: Sample SWOT matrix

This SWOT analysis template can be a powerful tool for startups to understand their strategic position and make informed decisions. By regularly updating your SWOT analysis, you can stay Agile and responsive to market changes.

Competitor analysis

Competitor analysis helps you identify gaps and opportunities in the market. To conduct a thorough competitor analysis:

- **Identify competitors**: List both direct and indirect competitors.
- **Analyze competitor products**: Evaluate competitors' products, features, pricing, and customer reviews.
- **Assess market positioning**: Understand how competitors position themselves in the market and identify opportunities for differentiation.

Tools to conduct market research

Startups often deal with limited resources, and therefore, it is essential to leverage cost-effective tools. Here is the list of a few tools that can be leveraged to conduct the market research:

- **Google Forms**: Free and easy to set up for surveys.
- **Social media**: Platforms like *Twitter, LinkedIn,* and *Facebook* can be used to gather insights and engage with your target audience.
- **SurveyMonkey free plan**: Allows for basic survey creation and data collection.
- **Miro**: An online collaboration tool that can be used for brainstorming and mapping user journeys.
- **Statista**: Offers access to a wide range of industry reports and statistics.
- **Quora/Reddit**: Engage in discussions and gather insights from community responses.
- **Mailchimp free plan**: Useful for sending out surveys to email lists and collecting feedback.

By using a combination of these primary and secondary research methods and tools, you can gather comprehensive insights into your market. This research will form the foundation for developing an MVP that genuinely addresses your customers' needs and positions your startup for success.

Market research plan template

A comprehensive template to plan and conduct market research effectively is given in the following table:

Section	Details
Research objectives	Define the goals of the market research
Target audience	Identify the demographic, geographic, and psychographic segments to be researched
Research methods	1 (Primary): Surveys, interviews, focus groups 2 (Secondary): Industry reports, competitor analysis
Data collection tools	List the tools and platforms to be used for surveys, data analytics, etc.
Timeline	Outline the schedule for each research activity
Budget	Estimate the cost of research activities and tools
Key metrics	Define the metrics to measure research success
Analysis plan	Describe how the collected data will be analyzed and interpreted
Reporting	Plan for documenting and presenting research findings

Table 2.4: *Market research plan template*

Customer research and segmentation

Understanding your customers is pivotal to developing an MVP that resonates with your target audience. By conducting thorough customer research and effective segmentation, you can tailor your product to meet the specific needs of different customer groups. Let us understand the importance of customer research, the types of customer segmentation, and how to interpret and synthesize research results to develop accurate customer personas.

Importance of customer research

Customer research is the cornerstone of targeted marketing and product development. By gaining a deep understanding of your customers, you can:

- **Enhance product relevance**: Develop features that address specific customer pain points and needs.

- **Improve marketing efficiency**: Craft targeted marketing messages that resonate with specific customer segments, leading to higher conversion rates.

- **Increase customer satisfaction**: Deliver a product that meets or exceeds customer expectations, fostering loyalty and advocacy.

- **Optimize resource allocation**: Focus your development and marketing efforts on the most promising customer segments, maximizing **return on investment** (**ROI**).

User research versus customer research

It is important to distinguish between user research and customer research. The distinction is as follows:

- **User research**: Focuses on understanding the behaviors, needs, and experiences of the end-users who interact with your product. This involves usability testing, user interviews, and observational studies to ensure the product is user-friendly and meets user needs.

- **Customer research**: Encompasses a broader scope, including user research, but also delving into the purchasing behaviors, preferences, and motivations of the customers who make the buying decisions. This can include market surveys, focus groups, and sales data analysis.

Customer segmentation

Customer segmentation involves dividing your customer base into distinct groups based on various characteristics. This allows you to tailor your product and marketing strategies to each segment effectively. Broadly, we will categorize segments by their demographics, psychographics, and behavioral attributes. However, these categories can be further bifurcated based on product objectives and the industry. Refer to *Figure 2.2* for the attributes included within the segments:

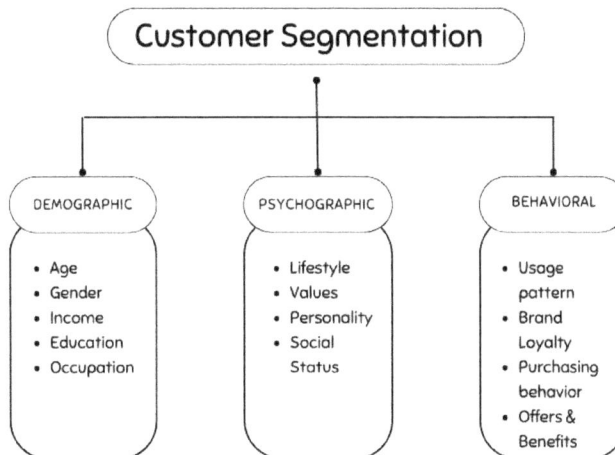

Figure 2.2: Customer segmentation by demographic, psychographic, and behavioral

Interpret and synthesize customer research results

Once you have conducted customer research, interpreting and synthesizing the results is crucial to developing actionable insights and accurate customer personas.

The following are the steps to develop accurate and useful customer personas:

1. **Collect and analyze data**: Gather data from various research methods, including surveys, interviews, and secondary sources. Use qualitative and quantitative analysis to identify patterns and trends.

2. **Identify key segments**: Based on the data, identify distinct customer segments that share common characteristics. Focus on the most relevant segments for your MVP.

3. **Create persona profiles**: Develop detailed profiles for each segment, including:

   • **Demographics**: Age, gender, income, education, occupation.

   • **Psychographics**: Lifestyle, values, personality, social status.

   • **Behavioral traits**: Usage patterns, brand loyalty, purchasing behavior.

   • **Pain points**: Key problems and challenges faced by the segment.

   • **Goals and motivations**: What they hope to achieve using your product.

4. **Validate personas**: Ensure the personas accurately represent your target audience by validating them through further research and feedback from real customers.

5. **Utilize personas in development**: Use these personas to guide product development, ensuring that your MVP addresses the specific needs and preferences of each segment. Tailor your marketing strategies to resonate with the unique characteristics of each persona.

By conducting comprehensive customer research and effective segmentation, startups can develop a more targeted and user-centric MVP. This approach not only enhances product-market fit but also ensures that marketing efforts are efficient and impactful, setting the stage for sustained growth and success.

Understanding customer pain points

A deep understanding of customer pain points is crucial for the successful development of an MVP. Pain points are the specific problems or challenges that customers face, which your product aims to solve. We will identify and analyze these pain points to ensure your MVP addresses the most critical issues effectively.

Analyzing pain points for MVP development

Once you have identified a range of pain points, prioritize them based on their impact and frequency:

- **Impact on user experience**: Determine how significantly each pain point affects the overall user experience. High-impact pain points should be addressed first.

- **Frequency of occurrence**: Consider how often each pain point is encountered by your target audience. Common issues should take precedence.

- **Severity of the problem**: Assess the severity of each pain point. Severe problems that cause significant frustration or prevent users from achieving their goals should be prioritized.

- **Market demand**: Align the pain points with market demand. Focus on pain points that, when solved, offer a competitive advantage or meet a significant market need.

Map MVP features with critical pain points

To ensure your MVP effectively addresses the most critical pain points, follow these steps:

1. **Map pain points to features**: Create a list of potential features that directly address the identified pain points. Ensure each feature provides a tangible solution to a specific problem.

2. **Validate solutions**: Before finalizing features, validate your proposed solutions with potential users. Use prototypes, wireframes, or simple mockups to gather feedback and refine your approach.

3. **Prioritize features**: Based on the impact and feasibility, prioritize features that address the most critical pain points. Focus on delivering maximum value with minimal effort.

4. **Develop incrementally**: Adopt an iterative development approach. Release your MVP with core features addressing the highest-priority pain points, then gather feedback and iterate.

5. **Measure and adjust**: Continuously measure the effectiveness of your MVP in solving the identified pain points. Use user feedback and analytics to make necessary adjustments and improvements.

By thoroughly understanding and addressing customer pain points, startups can create an MVP that genuinely resonates with their target audience. This approach not only enhances the product's relevance and usability but also significantly increases the chances of market success.

Competitive analysis

For startups, understanding the competitive landscape is essential to developing a compelling MVP. Competitive analysis helps you gain valuable insights from competitors and strategically position your product in the market. Let us understand the fundamentals of competitive analysis, techniques for effective analysis, and how to use these insights for your MVP development.

Understanding competitive analysis

Competitive analysis involves researching and analyzing your competitors to understand their strengths, weaknesses, strategies, and market positioning. By doing so, you can identify opportunities and threats, allowing you to make informed decisions about your MVP development. Here are a few of the areas one can dive into to analyze competition.

- **Understand market positioning**: Analyze how competitors position their products in the market. Look at their unique selling points, pricing strategies, and target audiences.

- **Identify best practices**: Learn from the successes and failures of your competitors. Identify what works well in their products and what does not, helping you avoid common pitfalls.

- **Spot market gaps**: Discover unmet needs and gaps in the market that your competitors are not addressing. These gaps can present opportunities for your MVP to stand out.

Dealing with the results of competitive analysis

Conducting competitive analysis is only the first step; effectively dealing with the results is where true strategic value lies. SWOT. Once you have gathered insights into your competitors' SWOT, it is crucial to translate this information into actionable strategies. Start by identifying areas where your product can fill gaps left by competitors or where you can offer superior value. Use these insights to refine your MVP's features, ensuring they address unmet needs in the market. Additionally, leverage competitive benchmarks to set realistic performance goals and align your product development roadmap. Remember, the goal is not to mimic your competitors but to carve out a unique position in the market that resonates with your target audience. By strategically integrating competitive insights, you can enhance your MVP's market fit and increase your startup's chances of success.

Techniques for effective competitive analysis

For entrepreneurs, analyzing the competition now goes beyond relying solely on gut instinct. Several effective methods are available, making it easier to gain insights into competitors. What was once a tedious task has been simplified by the vast amount of data available online, enabling strong estimations with much less complexity. In this section, we will explore SWOT analysis and feature-led comparison methods for effective analysis.

SWOT analysis

SWOT analysis is a powerful tool for understanding your startup's position in the competitive landscape. It helps you identify internal and external factors that can impact your MVP's success. Let us get an understanding of each of these terms:

- **Strengths**: Identify what your competitors do well. This could include their product features, customer service, market reach, or brand reputation.

- **Weaknesses**: Look for areas where your competitors fall short. These weaknesses could be related to product performance, customer satisfaction, pricing, or market coverage.

- **Opportunities**: Spot potential opportunities in the market that your competitors are not addressing. This could be an underserved customer segment, a technological innovation, or a market trend.

- **Threats**: Be aware of external threats that could impact your MVP. These could include new entrants, changing market conditions, or technological advancements.

Product features and performance benchmarking

Product features and performance benchmarking is a critical component of competitive analysis, offering a structured approach to evaluating how your product stacks up against competitors. This process involves several key steps, such as:

- **Feature comparison**: Compare the features of your MVP with those of your competitors. Identify which features are essential, which are nice-to-have, and which are missing in your competitors' offerings.

- **Performance metrics**: Evaluate the performance of your competitors' products. This includes aspects like speed, reliability, user experience, and customer satisfaction.

- **User feedback**: Analyze customer reviews and feedback on competitors' products. Look for common pain points and areas where users are dissatisfied.

Using competitive insights for MVP development

The outcomes of the competitive analysis serve as valuable input for MVP development. Here are the key areas where these insights significantly influence and shape the MVP:

- **Identify unmet needs**: Use your competitive analysis to find unmet needs and gaps in the market. These gaps can become the unique selling points for your MVP.

- **Innovate and differentiate**: Develop innovative solutions to address these gaps. Ensure your MVP offers unique features or benefits that set it apart from competitors.

- **Unique value proposition**: Clearly articulate what makes your MVP different and better than existing solutions. Focus on the unique value you bring to the market.

- **Feature prioritization**: Prioritize features that address the most critical pain points and market gaps identified in your competitive analysis. Ensure these features are prominently highlighted in your MVP.

- **Continuous improvement**: Use feedback and insights from ongoing competitive analysis to continuously improve and iterate on your MVP. Stay ahead of competitors by constantly enhancing your product.

By conducting thorough competitive analysis and leveraging the insights gained, startups can develop an MVP that not only meets market needs but also stands out in a crowded marketplace. This strategic approach ensures your product is well-positioned for success from the outset.

Competitive analysis template

Use the template given in the following table to build your synthesis on the competitive analysis:

Section	Details
Define your objectives	**Objective**: Clearly state what you aim to achieve with this competitive analysis.
Identify your competitors	**Direct competitors**: List companies offering similar products or services.
	Indirect competitors: List companies offering alternative solutions to the same problem.
Collect competitor information	**Company information**: • Name • Website • Founded • Headquarters • Funding • Key executive
Product analysis	**Product/service name**: • Description • Key features • Technology stack • Pricing • Target audience • Market positioning

SWOT analysis	**Strengths**: What does this competitor do well? Unique selling points. **Weaknesses**: Where does this competitor fall short? Common customer complaints. **Opportunities**: Market trends they are not addressing. Potential partnerships or technological advancements. **Threats**: New entrants. Changing regulations or market conditions.
Performance metrics	**User experience**: Website/app usability. Customer journey. **Customer satisfaction**: Reviews and ratings. Customer feedback on social media. **Reliability**: Downtime incidents. Performance reports.
Market position and strategy	**Marketing channels**: • SEO/SEM • Social media presence • Content marketing • Sales strategy • Sales funnel • Key selling point • Partnership and alliance
Customer analysis	**Customer segments**: • Demographics • Psychographics • Behavioral patterns • Customer pain points • Common issues customer face • How the competitors address these issues
Feature comparison	**Features**: • Core functionality • Additional features • User experience
Benchmarking	**Product performance**: Speed and reliability. User satisfaction scores. **Customer support**: Response times. Quality of support.

Summary and action plan	**Key insights**: Summarize the main findings from the competitive analysis.
	Strategic actions: Define clear actions to leverage strengths, mitigate weaknesses, capitalize on opportunities, and prepare for threats.
	MVP development: How will these insights influence your MVP development? Which features will you prioritize or add?
Continuous monitoring	**Plan for regular updates**: Schedule regular intervals to review and update your competitive analysis.
	Tools and metrics: Identify tools and metrics to continuously monitor competitor activities and market changes.

Table 2.5: Competitive analysis template

Hypothesis development and testing

A hypothesis helps validate assumptions and empower decision-making. This section describes how hypotheses are formed based on initial research, user insights, and competitive analysis, and how they are rigorously tested to ensure that the product meets user needs and business objectives.

Formulating hypotheses based on market needs

Before exploring product development, it is crucial to create testable hypotheses that are grounded in your market research. These hypotheses should address the core assumptions about your market, your customers, and the problems your product aims to solve. Let us see the approach to formulating hypotheses based on market needs:

- **Identify assumptions**: Start by listing out the key assumptions that underpin your product idea. These could be related to the market demand, customer behavior, or the effectiveness of your solution.

- **Formulate hypotheses**: Translate these assumptions into clear, testable statements. For example, *Customers will prefer our product over the competition because it offers a faster, more intuitive user experience.*

- **Prioritize hypotheses**: Focus on the most critical hypotheses that, if proven wrong, could significantly impact your product's success.

Designing experiments to test hypotheses

Once you have your hypotheses, the next step is to design experiments that will allow you to test them. This involves choosing the right methodologies and ensuring that your experiments can provide clear, actionable insights.

The following are certain experimentation techniques and methodologies:

- **A/B testing**: Compare two versions of a product or feature to see which one performs better. This is particularly useful for testing different user interfaces or marketing messages.

- **Split testing**: Similar to A/B testing but with multiple variations. This method can help identify the most effective combination of features or design elements.

- **Prototyping**: Create a simple, interactive model of your product to gather early feedback from potential users. This can help validate the usability and functionality of your solution.

- **User surveys and feedback**: Directly ask your target audience for their opinions and preferences. This can provide valuable qualitative data to support or refute your hypotheses.

Validating hypotheses with MVP

Your MVP plays a critical role in testing and validating your hypotheses. By launching a stripped-down version of your product, you can gather real-world data and insights that inform your development process.

The following are the ways you can use MVP to test and validate key hypotheses:

- **Build an MVP**: Develop the minimum viable version of your product that includes only the core features necessary to test your hypotheses.

- **Launch and measure**: Release your MVP to a small, targeted audience and closely monitor how they interact with it. Use analytics tools to track user behavior and gather quantitative data.

- **Analyze results**: Compare the data against your hypotheses to see which ones hold true. Pay attention to both quantitative metrics (e.g., usage rates, conversion rates) and qualitative feedback (e.g., user comments, survey responses).

- **Iterate and refine**: Based on the insights gained from your MVP, refine your product and update your hypotheses as needed. This iterative process ensures that your product evolves in line with market needs and user expectations.

By systematically developing and testing hypotheses, startups can de-risk their product development process and increase their chances of building a successful MVP. This approach not only ensures that you are addressing real market needs but also allows you to make informed decisions based on empirical evidence.

Leveraging feedback for MVP iteration

Feedback gathering and analysis is an iterative process that ensures product evolution aligns with the user's needs and expectations, leading to a successful and market-ready solution. In this section, we will explore how to effectively leverage feedback for continuous MVP iteration, driving the product closer to its final version.

Collecting user feedback

Collecting user feedback is an essential part of the MVP iteration process. It provides direct insights into how your product is being used and perceived by real users, helping you identify areas for improvement and opportunities for enhancement.

The methods for gathering feedback effectively are as follows:

- **Surveys and questionnaires**: Create structured surveys to gather specific information about user experiences and preferences. Tools like *SurveyMonkey, Google Forms,* or *Typeform* can be useful for this purpose.

- **User interviews**: Conduct in-depth interviews with a select group of users to gain detailed insights into their experiences and challenges. This qualitative approach can uncover nuanced feedback that surveys might miss.

- **Feedback forms**: Integrate feedback forms directly into your product, allowing users to provide comments and suggestions in real-time. Make it easy and accessible for users to share their thoughts.

- **Social media and community forums**: Monitor social media channels, online forums, and community platforms where your users are active. Engaging in conversations and reading user-generated content can provide valuable feedback.

- **Usability testing**: Conduct usability tests to observe how users interact with your product. This can reveal pain points and usability issues that might not be evident from other feedback methods.

Analyzing feedback for product improvements

Once you have collected user feedback, the next step is to analyze it effectively. This involves extracting actionable insights that can guide your product development and iteration process.

The techniques for extracting insights from feedback are as follows:

- **Thematic analysis**: Categorize feedback into common themes or topics. This helps identify recurring issues and prioritize areas for improvement.

- **Sentiment analysis**: Assess the overall sentiment of the feedback to gauge user satisfaction and identify areas that evoke strong positive or negative reactions.

- **Prioritization matrix**: Use a prioritization matrix to rank feedback based on factors like impact, feasibility, and alignment with your product vision. This helps in deciding which improvements to tackle first.

- **User journey mapping**: Create user journey maps to visualize the user experience and identify key touchpoints where improvements are needed. This holistic view can uncover critical areas for enhancement.

Iterative development based on feedback

Iterative development is a continuous process of refining and improving your MVP based on user feedback. This approach ensures that your product evolves in line with user needs and market demands. Let us draw clarity on some of the commonly referred terms in Agile methodology:

- **Agile development**: Adopt Agile methodologies to enable flexible and incremental development. Agile sprints allow you to incorporate feedback and make iterative changes quickly.

- **Prototyping and testing**: Develop prototypes of new features or changes and assess them with users before full implementation. This minimizes risks and ensures that new developments align with user expectations.

- **Feedback loops**: Establish regular feedback loops with your users. Continuously solicit feedback, analyze it, and iterate on your product. This ongoing cycle fosters continuous improvement.

- **Metrics and KPIs**: Define **key performance indicators** (**KPIs**) and metrics to measure the impact of your iterations. Track these metrics to evaluate the effectiveness of changes and make data-driven decisions.

- **Engage with users**: Maintain open communication channels with your users. Keep them informed about updates and changes, and show that their feedback is valued and acted upon. This builds trust and encourages ongoing engagement.

By leveraging user feedback effectively, startups can ensure that their MVP remains aligned with market needs and user expectations. This iterative approach not only enhances the product but also strengthens the relationship with users, fostering loyalty and long-term success.

Case studies

Understanding theoretical concepts and methodologies is essential, but nothing illustrates the principles of market-driven MVPs better than real-world examples. While success stories like

Airbnb, Dropbox, and Booking.com often inspire us, understanding the pitfalls of unsuccessful MVPs is crucial for avoiding similar mistakes. Here, we explore five case studies across various sectors, including direct-to-consumer startups, edtech, B2C, and SaaS, to uncover valuable lessons from their experiences.

Juicero

Juicero was a direct-to-consumer high-tech juicer startup that promised to deliver fresh juice at the push of a button using proprietary juice packs. Let us reflect on their product journey to understand key lessons:

- **Product traction**: Juicero's product was a Wi-Fi-connected juicer that used single-serving juice packs, aiming to offer a convenient and healthy alternative to traditional juicing methods. Initially, the concept attracted health-conscious consumers and tech enthusiasts. However, user engagement plummeted after it was revealed that the juice packs could be squeezed by hand, making the $700 juicer redundant.

- **Product reception and feedback**:
  - **Over-engineering**: The juicer was overly complex and expensive, costing $699, which was far more than consumers were willing to pay.
  - **Value proposition**: A journalist demonstrated that the juice packs could be squeezed by hand, rendering the expensive juicer unnecessary.

- **Takeaways**:
  - Ensure your MVP solves a real problem without unnecessary complexity.
  - Validate the core functionality early to confirm that it offers unique value.

Quibi

Quibi was a B2C short-form streaming service designed for mobile devices, founded by Hollywood mogul *Jeffrey Katzenberg* and former HP CEO *Meg Whitman*. Let us reflect on their product journey to understand key lessons:

- **Product traction**: Quibi offered professionally produced, high-quality short-form videos designed for on-the-go viewing, with a unique emphasis on mobile-first content. Despite an initial surge of curiosity, Quibi struggled to retain users. Its content failed to captivate a significant audience accustomed to free alternatives like YouTube and TikTok.

- **Product reception and feedback**:
  - **Misreading the market**: Quibi launched with a focus on premium, short-form content at a time when users were already satisfied with free short-form content from platforms like *YouTube* and *TikTok*.

o **Poor timing**: Launched during the COVID-19 pandemic, Quibi's mobile-first strategy clashed with increased home viewing.

- **Takeaways**:

  o Market timing is critical; understand and adapt to current consumer behavior.

  o Conduct thorough market research to ensure there is real demand for your product.

Knewton

Knewton was an edtech company that aimed to personalize learning experiences using adaptive learning technology. Let us reflect on their product journey to understand key lessons:

- **Product traction**: Knewton offered an adaptive learning platform that adjusted educational content in real-time based on student performance and learning patterns. While the concept attracted initial interest from educators and institutions, user engagement waned due to the platform's complexity and failure to deliver on its ambitious promises.

- **Product reception and feedback**:

  o **Over-promising**: Knewton promised groundbreaking personalization, but its technology often failed to deliver the expected results.

  o **Complexity for users**: Educators and students found the platform difficult to use and integrate into existing workflows.

- **Takeaways**:

  o Avoid over-promising and under-delivering; set realistic expectations.

  o Ensure ease of use for end-users to encourage adoption and integration.

Homejoy

Homejoy was a direct-to-consumer platform connecting consumers with professional cLeaning services. Let us reflect on their product journey to understand key lessons:

- **Product traction**: Homejoy aimed to simplify the process of finding and booking reliable home cLeaning services through an easy-to-use online platform. Initial engagement was positive, with many users appreciating the convenience. However, customer retention was low, and high acquisition costs made it unsustainable.

- **Product reception and feedback**:

  o **High customer acquisition costs**: Homejoy struggled with high customer acquisition costs and low customer retention.

- o **Legal issues**: Misclassification of workers as independent contractors led to numerous legal challenges.

- **Takeaways**:

  - o Focus on sustainable customer acquisition strategies and retention from the outset.

  - o Understand and comply with relevant labor laws and regulations to avoid legal pitfalls.

Jawbone

Jawbone initially focused on Bluetooth headsets before pivoting to fitness trackers and health technology. Let us reflect on their product journey to understand key lessons:

- **Product traction**: Jawbone developed sleek and innovative fitness trackers that monitored physical activity, sleep patterns, and overall health metrics. The stylish design and comprehensive health monitoring features attracted a dedicated user base initially. However, frequent product malfunctions and recalls eroded consumer trust over time.

- **Product reception and feedback**:

  - o **Market competition**: Jawbone entered a highly competitive market dominated by Fitbit and other established players.

  - o **Product quality issues**: Frequent product malfunctions and recalls eroded consumer trust.

- **Takeaways**:

  - o Thoroughly assess the competitive landscape and find a unique value proposition.

  - o Prioritize product quality and reliability to build and maintain consumer trust.

Understanding these failures highlights the importance of thorough market research, clear value propositions, realistic promises, and strong product quality. By learning from these examples, startups can better navigate the complex landscape of developing and launching a successful MVP.

Conclusion

Understanding market needs is not a one-time activity but a continuous process that evolves as your startup grows. The market is dynamic, and so are customer preferences and pain points. For entrepreneurs and product leaders, it is essential to remain Agile, continually learning, and adapting your approach based on fresh insights and feedback.

By focusing on genuine market needs, conducting thorough research, and leveraging the right tools and resources, you can develop an MVP that truly resonates with your target audience. This customer-centric approach not only increases the chances of your product's success but also builds a solid foundation for sustainable growth.

Remember, the journey from ideation to market success is iterative. Embrace the principles of the Lean Startup, prioritize continuous improvement, and stay attuned to the evolving needs of your market. In doing so, you will be well-positioned to create innovative products that meet and exceed customer expectations, driving your startup toward long-term success.

With a solid understanding of market needs, you are now equipped to move forward confidently in developing your MVP. The next chapter will explore the strategies and best practices for creating MVP goals and objectives that align with your market insights and business goals, guiding you through the critical stages of product development and launch.

Points to remember

- **Understanding market needs**: We explored the distinction between market needs and wants, highlighting the importance of addressing genuine needs for product success.

- **Identifying market needs**: Techniques such as empathy interviews, observational studies, and data analytics were discussed as effective methods for identifying market needs.

- **Conducting market research**: We covered both primary and secondary research methods, emphasizing the significance of surveys, interviews, focus groups, industry reports, market analysis, and competitor analysis.

- **Customer research and segmentation**: The chapter outlined the importance of customer research, several types of segmentation, and how to synthesize research results to develop accurate customer personas.

- **Understanding customer pain points**: Techniques for identifying real pain points and prioritizing them for MVP development were discussed, emphasizing alignment with critical user needs.

- **Competitive analysis**: We examined the value of competitive analysis, techniques such as SWOT analysis and benchmarking, and how to use competitive insights to differentiate your MVP.

- **Hypothesis development and testing**: The process of formulating testable hypotheses, designing experiments, and validating hypotheses with an MVP was detailed.

- **Leveraging feedback for MVP iteration**: Methods for collecting user feedback, analyzing it for product improvements, and iterative development strategies were highlighted.

- **Case studies**: Real-world examples of unsuccessful MVPs provided practical insights and lessons learned from market-driven approaches.

- **Tools and resources**: A range of recommended tools for market research and analysis, along with valuable resources such as books and online courses, were presented to equip you with the knowledge needed to understand market needs effectively.

Join our Discord space

Join our Discord workspace for latest updates, offers, tech happenings around the world, new releases, and sessions with the authors:

https://discord.bpbonline.com

CHAPTER 3
Defining MVP Goals and Objectives

Introduction

Embarking on the MVP journey without clear goals and objectives is no different than sailing without a map. While the previous chapter focused on understanding market needs for an MVP, this chapter pivots to the strategic aspect of defining what success looks like for your MVP. Setting well-defined goals and objectives is crucial for navigating the complexities of product development and ensuring your MVP aligns with both your startup's vision and the market's demands.

The primary purpose of setting clear goals and objectives is to provide direction and focus. At startups, where resources are often limited and the stakes are high, having a clear roadmap is non-negotiable. Goals and objectives help in optimal resource allocation and utilization, team alignment, and setting benchmarks to evaluate progress.

Structure

In this chapter, we will cover the following topics:

- Setting clear goals for your MVP
- Defining success criteria
- Translating goals into objectives

- Key metrics for MVP evaluation

- Defining MVP goals and objectives

- Adapting goals based on feedback

- Common pitfalls

Objectives

By the end of this chapter, you will have a comprehensive understanding of how to set and align your MVP goals and objectives, establish clear success criteria, and select the right metrics to track your progress. This approach will enable the readers to create an MVP that not only meets market needs but also drives your startup towards long-term success.

Setting clear goals for your MVP

Goals are the overarching targets that guide the development of your MVP. They must align with the startup's vision and mission, addressing the primary market needs identified in the previous chapter. Let us understand the importance of setting actionable goals, aligning them with your startup's vision and mission, and utilizing the SMART goals framework to ensure effectiveness.

SMART goals framework

The SMART goals framework is a powerful tool that helps in setting clear and actionable objectives. Each goal should be as follows:

- **Specific**: A specific goal must be clearly defined, unambiguous, and should address the what, why, and how of the objective. A good example would be developing an operational prototype of a new app that includes the core feature of task management.

- **Measurable**: A measurable goal is quantifiable, which means it has a clear criterion for success. For example, achieving a beta user base of 500 users within the first three months of launch.

- **Achievable**: The goal must be realistic and attainable with the available resources and constraints.

- **Relevant**: It should be aligned with broader business objectives and relevant to the organization's mission. A relevant goal ensures that the effort invested will have a meaningful impact.

- **Time-bound**: A time-bound goal creates urgency, prompts timely action, and completion.

The following figure shows sample SMART goals for a tech startup:

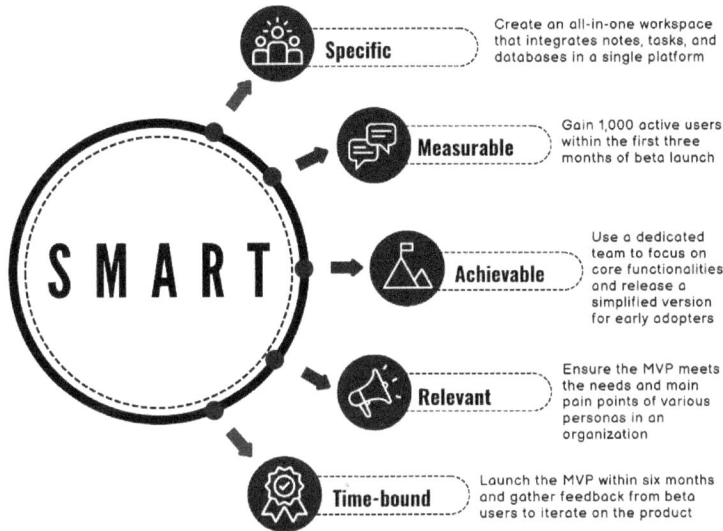

Figure 3.1: *SMART goals for a tech startup*

By setting SMART goals, startups can ensure that their MVP development is focused, efficient, and aligned with their strategic objectives. This structured approach not only enables better planning and execution but also enhances the chances of achieving the product-market fit.

SMART goals framework template for startups

You can use this template to go through the process of setting and refining your goals for your product. For a clear understanding, we will base the template on a goal of increasing user engagement on the MVP:

- **Specific (S)**: What exactly do you want to achieve?
  - o **Answer**: Increase **daily active users** (**DAUs**) on our MVP by enhancing the user experience through new features and engagement strategies.
  - o **Points to consider**:
    - Who is involved? Product team, development team, marketing team.
    - What needs to be accomplished? Increase DAUs by 30%.
    - Why is this goal important? Higher user engagement leads to better retention and customer satisfaction.
- **Measurable (M)**: How will you know when you have achieved the goal?
  - o **Answer:** Track DAU metrics using Google Analytics and in-app tracking tools.

- o **Points to consider**:
  - ▪ **Baseline DAUs**: 500
  - ▪ **Target DAUs**: 650
  - ▪ **Tools for monitoring and measurement**: Google Analytics, Mixpanel
- **Achievable (A)**: Is the goal realistic and attainable?
  - o **Answer**: Yes, with a planned rollout of new features, marketing campaigns, and user feedback iterations.
  - o **Points to consider**:
    - ▪ **Resources**: Additional development hours and marketing budget.
    - ▪ **Potential obstacles**: Technical issues, attrition, or market slowdown.
    - ▪ **Support needed**: Cross-functional collaboration, user feedback collection, and analysis.
- **Relevant (R)**: Does this goal align with your broader business objectives?
  - o **Answer**: Yes, increasing DAUs aligns with our objective of improving user retention and driving long-term growth.
  - o **Points to consider**:
    - ▪ **Business objective**: Enhance user retention and grow the user base.
    - ▪ **Goal relevance**: Directly impacts user engagement and retention metrics.
- **Time-bound (T)**: What is the deadline for achieving this goal?
  - o **Answer**: Achieve a 30% increase in DAUs within the next three months.
  - o **Points to consider**:
    - ▪ Start date and end date.
    - ▪ **Milestones**:
      - ◆ **Month one**: Complete development of new features.
      - ◆ **Month two**: Launch marketing campaign.
      - ◆ **Month three**: Achieve target DAUs.

Action plan: Product teams can use the following table as a reference to monitor actions and assign accountability to the respective teams:

Action	Responsible team	Deadline	Resources needed (Asks)	Tools to be used	Frequency
Develop new features	Product development	Date			
Launch marketing campaign	Marketing	Date			
Monitor user engagement	Product management			Google Analytics, Mixpanel	Weekly
Gather and implement feedback	Product, customer support	Ongoing		Surveys, interviews	Ongoing

Table 3.1: Action plan based on SMART goals framework

Defining success criteria

Success criteria provide a benchmark for evaluating whether the MVP fulfils its objectives or not. Let us explore what criterion looks like, differentiate between short-term and long-term success, and emphasize the importance of customer-centric success metrics.

Key indicators of success

To define success for your MVP, start by identifying **key performance indicators** (**KPIs**) that align with your business goals. The following figure illustrates the indicators that are specific, measurable, and relevant to your MVP's purpose:

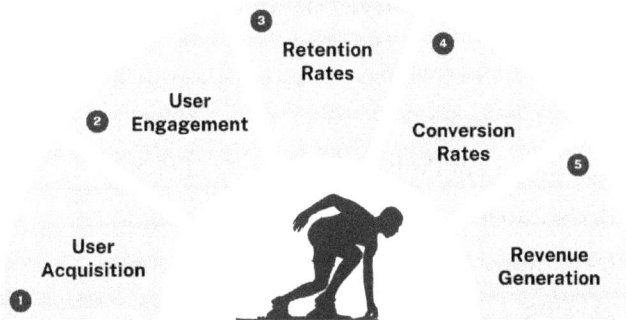

Figure 3.2: Commonly used success indicators of an MVP

Short-term and long-term success

When defining your criteria, it is essential to consider both the short-term and long-term success of the product:

- **Short-term success**: Focuses on immediate goals, such as initial user acquisition, early user feedback, and initial revenue generation. For instance, a short-term success indicator might be acquiring 1,000 beta users within the first month.

- **Long-term success**: Involves sustained growth, scalability, and market penetration. Long-term success indicators include achieving a high user retention rate over six months, expanding market share, and reaching significant revenue milestones.

By setting both short-term and long-term success criteria, startups can ensure that their MVP development is aligned with immediate needs while also paving the way for future growth.

Customer-centric success metrics

For a successful MVP, it must resonate with its users. Customer satisfaction and engagement are critical metrics that reflect how well the MVP meets user needs and expectations. Satisfied customers are more likely to become loyal users and advocates for your product. The following are some of the commonly used industry metrics to measure customer-centricity.

Net promoter score

Net promoter score (**NPS**) measures customer loyalty and satisfaction by asking customers how likely they are to recommend your product to others on a scale of zero to ten. As per the latest trends, AI-powered tools can be utilized to analyze open-ended feedback, providing deeper insights into customer sentiment and areas for improvement.

NPS calculation formula: $NPS = \%\,Promoters - \%\,Detractors$

The following table is the sample NPS survey data:

Metric	Value
Total Respondents	10
(a) Number of Promoters	4 (40%)
(b) Number of Passives	2 (20%)
(c) Number of Detractors	4 (40%)
(d) NPS = (a) – (b)	0

Table 3.2: Sample NPS survey data

The following is the interpretation of this data:

- An equal percentage of Promoters and Detractors results in a neutral NPS. It indicates balanced but not strong customer loyalty.

- With 20% of passive customers, there is an opportunity to convert them into Promoters through targeted engagement programs.

Customer satisfaction score

Customer satisfaction score (**CSAT**) assesses customer satisfaction with a specific interaction or overall experience by asking customers to rate their satisfaction on a scale, typically from one to five. To make the most of this technique, real-time CSAT surveys can be triggered by specific user actions within the product, allowing for immediate feedback and quick response to user needs.

Customer Effort Score

Customer Effort Score (**CES**) evaluates the customers' convenience with your product or service by requesting them to rate the ease of their experience. Modern applications of CES involve using predictive analytics to anticipate future friction points in the customer journey and address them proactively, enhancing overall user satisfaction.

User engagement metrics

User engagement metrics track how actively and frequently users interact with your product, including metrics like **DAU**, **monthly active users** (**MAU**), session duration, and feature usage. By leveraging machine learning algorithms, product managers or analysts can predict user churn and identify features that drive the most engagement, enabling more targeted improvements.

Customer lifetime value

Customer lifetime value (**CLTV**) estimates the total revenue a business can expect from a single customer account throughout its lifetime. Data analytics can help in creating customer segments based on behavior and predict the future LTV for different cohorts, allowing startups to direct their efforts to the most valuable customer segments.

Here is a sample template for calculating CLTV for a startup.

Customer acquisition: The following table calculates the monthly **customer acquisition cost** (**CAC**):

Metric	Description	Value
CAC	The cost incurred to acquire a single customer.	$100
Number of new customers per month	The average number of new customers acquired monthly.	50
Total monthly acquisition cost	CAC × Number of new customers	$5000

Table 3.3: Customer acquisition sample data for LTV demonstration

Customer retention and revenue: The following table derives the net revenue earned from a customer in its projected lifetime:

Metric	Description	Value
Average purchase value (APV)	The average amount spent by a customer per purchase.	$50
Purchase frequency rate (PFR)	Average number of purchases a customer makes monthly.	2
Customer lifetime (months)	The average duration a customer remains active.	24
Monthly revenue per customer	APV × PFR	$50 × 2 = $100
Total revenue per customer lifetime	Monthly revenue × Customer lifetime	$100 × 24 = $2400

Table 3.4: Customer retention and revenue sample data for LTV demonstration

CLV: The following table shows the calculation of **net customer lifetime value (NCLV)**:

Metric	Description	Value
Gross CLV	Total revenue generated by a customer over their lifetime.	$2400
CAC	The cost incurred to acquire a single customer.	$100
NCLV	Gross CLV - CAC	$2400 - $100 = $2300

Table 3.5: LTV calculation demonstration

Churn rate analysis

Churn rate analysis measures the percentage of customers who stop using your product over a specific period. Implementing AI-driven churn prediction models can help startups proactively address potential issues, retain customers, and reduce churn rates effectively.

Sentiment analysis

Sentiment analysis analyzes customer feedback from various sources, such as social media, product reviews, and support tickets, to gauge overall sentiment towards your product. **Natural language processing** (**NLP**) techniques can be handy to automate sentiment analysis, providing real-time insights into customer emotions and potential areas for improvement.

Cohort analysis

Cohort analysis segments users into groups based on shared characteristics or behaviors to track and compare their engagement over time. Applying cohort analysis to A/B testing results helps startups understand how diverse groups respond to changes in the product, allowing for more informed decision-making.

Let us read the following sample cohort analysis of a **Software as a Service** (**SaaS**) product startup in *Table 3.6*. This can help in understanding the user behavior over time by grouping users based on shared characteristics or experiences within a specific timeframe.

Cohort	Signups	Month 1 retention	Month 2 retention	Month 3 retention	Month 4 retention	Month 5 retention	Month 6 retention
January	1000	700 (70%)	600 (60%)	500 (50%)	450 (45%)	400 (40%)	350 (35%)
February	1200	800 (66.7%)	700 (58.3%)	650 (54.2%)	600 (50%)	550 (45.8%)	500 (41.7%)
March	900	600 (66.7%)	550 (61.1%)	500 (55.6%)	450 (50%)	400 (44.4%)	380 (42.2%)
April	1100	750 (68.2%)	700 (63.6%)	650 (59.1%)	600 (54.5%)	550 (50%)	520 (47.3%)
May	950	650 (68.4%)	600 (63.2%)	550 (57.9%)	500 (52.6%)	480 (50.5%)	450 (47.4%)
June	1000	700 (70%)	650 (65%)	600 (60%)	550 (55%)	520 (52%)	490 (49%)

Table 3.6: Sample cohort analysis of a SaaS product

Voice of the Customer programs

Voice of the Customer (**VoC**) programs collect comprehensive customer feedback through surveys, interviews, focus groups, and other methods. Integrating VoC data with customer journey analytics creates a holistic view of customer experiences and preferences, enabling startups to make data-driven improvements. The following figure shows a sample VoC analysis with initial inferences:

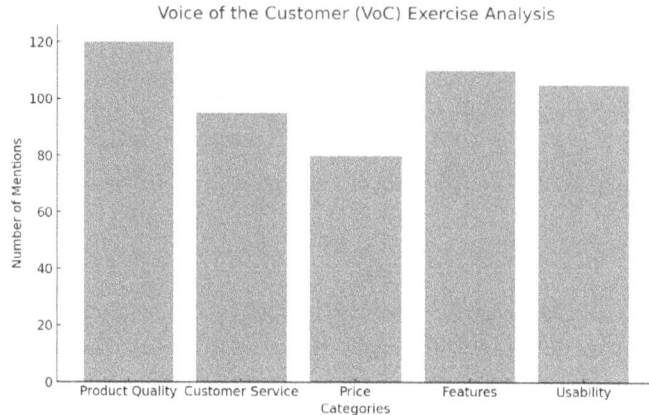

Voice of the Customer (VoC) Exercise Analysis

- **Product Quality** has the most mentions, making it a high priority category.
- **Features** and **usability** important aspects for customer satisfaction.
- **Customer Service** and **Price** are crucial areas for maintaining overall customer satisfaction.

Figure 3.3: *Voice of customer sample analysis*

Customer journey mapping

Customer journey mapping visualizes the steps customers take when interacting with the product, highlighting key touchpoints and pain points. One can use journey mapping tools that leverage the data in real-time to plot the customer journey. Some of the commonly used tools are *Microsoft Visio, Lucidchart, IBM* journey designer, or even *diagrams.net*.

Practical tips for startups

By focusing on customer-centric success metrics, startups can gain valuable insights into how well they are meeting these needs. These metrics enable informed decisions that enhance customer satisfaction and loyalty, ensuring that the products and services offered connect with the target customer base. The following are a few tips that can help startups follow their customers to build customer-centric products:

- **Regularly collect feedback**: Use surveys, interviews, and user testing sessions to gather feedback from your users. This feedback provides valuable insights into user needs, pain points, and areas for improvement.

- **Analyze user data**: Utilize analytics tools like Google Analytics, Mixpanel, or Amplitude to monitor user behavior and engagement. Data-driven insights help refine your MVP and align it with user expectations.

- **Iterate based on feedback**: Continuously improve your MVP based on user feedback and data analysis. Prioritize features and enhancements that address user needs and contribute to a better user experience.

- **Engage with early adopters**: Build relationships with early adopters and leverage their feedback to iterate on your MVP. Early adopters are often more willing to provide detailed feedback and help shape the product.

This template provides a structured approach to track and evaluate customer-centric success metrics, including how to measure each metric, the tools needed, the frequency of measurement, and target values:

Metric	Description	How to measure	Recommended tools	Frequency	Target value
CSAT	Measures the level of customer satisfaction with your product/service	Surveys, feedback forms	SurveyMonkey, Typeform	Monthly	Value
NPS	Gauges customer loyalty and likelihood of recommending your product/service	Surveys, direct feedback	Qualtrics, Promoter.io	Quarterly	Value
Customer retention rate	Tracks the percentage of customers who continue using your product/service over time	Cohort analysis, CRM data	HubSpot, Salesforce	Monthly	Value
Churn rate	Measures the rate at which customers stop using your product/service	CRM data, subscription analytics	Stripe, Baremetrics	Monthly	Value
CES	Assesses the ease of customer interaction with your product/service	Post-interaction surveys, feedback forms	Zendesk, SurveyMonkey	Monthly	Value
User engagement rate	Evaluates how actively customers are using your product/service	Usage analytics, activity logs	Google Analytics, Mixpanel	Weekly	Value
Feature adoption rate	Measures how many customers are using new features	Product usage analytics	Amplitude, Pendo	Bi-weekly	Value

Average response time	Tracks the average time taken to respond to customer queries or issues	Customer support data	Zendesk, Intercom	Monthly	Value

Table 3.7: Track and evaluate customer-centric success metrics

Translating goals into objectives

Once you have defined your overarching goals, the next step is to break them down into specific, actionable objectives. Objectives are smaller, detailed tasks or milestones that collectively help achieve the larger goals. For instance:

- **B2C MVP**: If your goal is to achieve high user engagement, an objective could be to increase DAU by 20% within three months.

- **B2B MVP**: If your goal is to generate initial revenue, an objective might be to secure five pilot customers within the first quarter.

- **SaaS MVP**: If your goal is to ensure product-market fit, an objective could be to achieve a 40% conversion rate from free trials to paid subscriptions within six months.

Prioritizing MVP objectives

Using a systematic approach to prioritize objectives ensures that your team focuses on the most critical tasks that will drive the highest value for your MVP. Let us explore the techniques for prioritizing objectives based on impact and feasibility with the help of a use case.

Consider a hypothetical EdTech startup, *ETPL*, which is developing an MVP for an online learning platform aimed at professional development. ETPL needs to prioritize various objectives to ensure its MVP delivers the maximum value with limited resources. We will explore how the startup can apply different prioritization techniques using specific objectives.

Impact-feasibility matrix

The impact-feasibility matrix helps you categorize objectives based on their potential impact and the feasibility of implementation. The matrix is divided into four quadrants:

- High impact, high feasibility

- High impact, low feasibility

- Low impact, high feasibility

- Low impact, low feasibility

For example, implementing a new user onboarding feature might be high impact and high feasibility if it is a small change that significantly improves user retention.

Let us apply this technique to the ETPL use case. ETPL plots these objectives on an impact-feasibility matrix, as shown in the following table:

	High feasibility	**Low feasibility**
High impact	Enhance mobile app functionality Develop personalized learning paths	Implement an AI-based chatbot
Low impact	Create a detailed analytics dashboard	Add gamification elements

Table 3.8: 2x2 impact-feasibility matrix

Based on this matrix, ETPL prioritizes enhancing mobile app functionality first, followed by developing personalized learning paths.

Weighted scoring model

This technique involves assigning weights to various criteria such as potential revenue, customer satisfaction, alignment with business goals, and ease of implementation. Each objective is scored against these criteria, and a weighted total score is calculated. For instance, launching a new feature that aligns with business goals and has high potential revenue might score high, making it a priority.

In our use case, the ETPL team assigns weights to criteria like potential revenue, customer satisfaction, alignment with business goals, and ease of implementation. The weights are captured in the following table:

Objective	Revenue (0-5)	Satisfaction (0-5)	Alignment (0-5)	Ease (0-5)	Total Score
Personalized learning path	4	5	4	3	16
AI-based chatbot	5	4	5	2	16
Detailed analytics dashboard	3	3	4	4	14
Gamification elements	2	4	3	3	12
Mobile app functionality	5	5	5	5	20

Table 3.9: Weighted scoring model sample

The highest scoring objective is to enhance mobile app functionality, making it the top priority.

MoSCoW method

The MoSCoW method categorizes objectives into must-have, should-have, could-have, and will not-have. For example, a *must-have* might be the core functionality that the MVP cannot succeed without, while a *could-have* might be an additional feature that enhances the user experience but is not essential.

The ETPL product leader categorizes the objectives as follows:

- **Must-have**: Enhances mobile app functionality, implements an AI-based chatbot.
- **Should-have**: Develops personalized learning paths.
- **Could-have**: Creates a detailed analytics dashboard.
- **Will not-have**: Adds gamification elements.

The *must-have* objectives are prioritized first.

Kano model

The Kano model prioritizes objectives based on their ability to satisfy customer needs and enhance customer satisfaction. Features are classified into must-have, performance, delighters, indifferent, and reverse described as follows:

- **Must-haves**: Basic expectations. Without these features, customers are dissatisfied, but having them may not delight.
- **Performance features**: The more you deliver, the more satisfied customers are (e.g., speed, quality).
- **Delighters**: Unexpected features that create high satisfaction and emotional impact.
- **Indifferent**: Features that do not impact satisfaction either way.
- **Reverse**: Features that could annoy certain customers.

For example, integrating a chatbot for customer support might be a great feature that significantly boosts customer satisfaction.

The team at ETPL uses the Kano model to categorize features:

- **Must-have**: Enhances mobile app functionality.
- **Performance**: Implement an AI-based chatbot.
- **Delighters**: Add gamification elements.
- **Indifferent**: Develop personalized learning paths.
- **Reverse**: None identified.

Focus is placed on must-have and performance features.

Eisenhower matrix

The Eisenhower matrix helps prioritize tasks by urgency and importance. Urgent and important tasks are prioritized first, while important but not urgent tasks are planned for next. For example, fixing a critical bug might be urgent and important, while developing a new feature might be important but not urgent.

The ETPL team applies to the Eisenhower matrix:

- **Urgent and important**: Enhance mobile app functionality.

- **Important but not urgent**: Implement AI-based chatbot, develop personalized learning paths.

- **Urgent but not important**: None identified.

- **Neither urgent nor important**: Add gamification elements.

Urgent and important tasks are tackled first.

RICE scoring

The **Reach, Impact, Confidence, and Effort** (**RICE**) method involves scoring each objective based on how many customers it will impact, the potential benefit, the confidence in these estimates, and the effort required. For example, a feature with high reach and impact but requiring moderate effort and high confidence might be prioritized.

The team at ETPL will calculate the RICE scores as shown in the following table:

Objective	Reach	Impact (0-3)	Confidence (0-3)	Effort (0-10)	RICE score
Personalized learning path	3000	3	2	6	1500
AI-based chatbot	2000	3	3	8	1125
Detailed analytics dashboard	1000	2	3	4	500
Gamification elements	1500	2	2	5	600
Mobile app functionality	5000	3	3	6	2500

Table 3.10: Sample RICE scoring model

The objective with the highest RICE score is to enhance mobile app functionality.

Balancing innovation with practicality

While it is essential to innovate, balancing innovation with practicality ensures that your MVP remains feasible and can be developed within the constraints of time and resources. Prioritize objectives that drive significant value and are achievable within your startup's capabilities.

Defining success criteria and translating goals into actionable objectives are key steps in the MVP process. By setting clear goals, prioritizing objectives, and focusing on customer-centric success metrics, startups can ensure that their MVP not only meets immediate objectives but also paves the way for long-term growth and success.

Key metrics for MVP evaluation

Evaluating your MVP involves tracking and analyzing various metrics that reflect how well your product meets its objectives. These metrics provide valuable insights into user behavior, product performance, and overall market fit, guiding further development and improvement.

Identifying relevant metrics

Identifying the right KPIs is crucial for accurately assessing the success of your MVP. Some common KPIs for MVP evaluation include:

- **User acquisition**: Measures the number of new users or customers acquired within a specific period. Key metrics include sign-ups, downloads, and registration rates.

- **User engagement**: Assesses how actively users are interacting with the MVP. Metrics include DAU, MAU, session length, and frequency of use.

- **Retention rates**: Indicate the percentage of users who continue to use the MVP over time. A high retention rate suggests that the MVP meets user needs effectively.

- **Conversion rates**: Tracks the percentage of users who complete desired actions, such as making a purchase, subscribing to a service, or upgrading from a free trial to a paid plan.

- **Revenue generation**: Measures the total revenue generated from the MVP, including sales, subscriptions, and in-app purchases.

KPI template

This template provides a comprehensive framework for defining, tracking, and acting on KPIs to ensure your MVP meets its goals and drives success.

Section 1

Define KPIs: The following table lists the KPIs by categories:

Category	KPI	Description	Target	Measurement frequency	Responsible
User acquisition	User sign-ups	Number of new users registered	1,000 signups per month	Weekly	Marketing

User engagement	Active users	Number of users engaging with the product daily/weekly/monthly.	500 DAUs per 2,000 WAUs	Daily/weekly/monthly	Product
Customer feedback	NPS	Measure of customer satisfaction and likelihood to recommend	NPS of 50+	Monthly	Customer success
Retention	User retention rate	Percentage of users who return to the product over time	40% retention after one month	Weekly	Product
Revenue	**Monthly Recurring Revenu E (MRR)**	Total recurring revenue generated each month	$10,000 MRR	Monthly	Finance
Usage	Feature usage	Frequency of key feature usage	70% of users use the main feature daily	Weekly	Product
Market fit	Churn rate	Percentage of users who stop using the product over a period	Less than 5% churn rate	Monthly	Customer success
Performance	System uptime	Percentage of time the system is operational and available	99.9% uptime	Monthly	DevOps team

Table 3.11: KPI definition

Section 2

KPI tracking plan: The following list must be taken into consideration to build a KPI tracking plan:

- **Data collection methods**: Specify how data will be collected for each KPI (e.g., analytics tools, user surveys, CRM systems).

- **Tools and platforms**: List the tools and platforms used for KPI tracking (e.g., Google Analytics, Mixpanel, HubSpot).

- **Responsibilities**: Assign team members responsible for tracking and reporting each KPI.

- **Reporting frequency**: Determine how often each KPI will be measured and reported (e.g., daily, weekly, monthly).

- **Review and adjustment**: Set up regular meetings to review KPI progress and make necessary adjustments.

Section 3

Plan of action: The following table lists the action plan to track the KPIs:

Task	Description	Deadline (example)	Responsible	Status
Select KPIs	Identify the most relevant KPIs for the MVP.	Jan 15	Product manager	Completed
Set targets	Define target values for each KPI.	Jan 20	Product team	In progress
Implement tracking tools	Set up tools to track the KPIs.	Jan 25	DevOps team	Not started
Data collection	Start collecting data for each KPI.	Feb 1	Product team	Not started
Weekly KPI review meetings	Schedule and conduct regular KPI reviews.	ongoing	Product manager	Not started
Adjustments based on feedback	Make necessary adjustments based on KPI analysis.	ongoing	Product team	Not started

Table 3.12: KPI tracking action plan

The review process involves regularly assessing KPIs to determine the effectiveness and progress of the action plan. The adaptation strategy focuses on using the insights from KPI data to calibrate goals and strategies to ensure continuous improvement of the MVP.

Choosing the goal-driven metrics

Selecting the right metrics depends on your specific goals and objectives. For example, if your primary goal is user acquisition, focus on metrics related to sign-ups and downloads.

If your goal is to enhance user engagement, prioritize metrics like session length and DAU/MAU ratios. Ensure that the chosen metrics are linked to your MVP's objectives and provide actionable insights.

Quantitative versus qualitative metrics

Both quantitative and qualitative metrics are essential for a comprehensive evaluation of your MVP. Let us understand the two types of metrics:

- **Quantitative metrics**: Provide numerical data that can be measured and analyzed statistically. These metrics include user acquisition numbers, engagement rates, retention rates, and revenue figures. Quantitative data helps identify patterns, trends, and overall performance.

- **Qualitative metrics**: Offer insights into user experiences, satisfaction, and perceptions. These metrics are often gathered through surveys, interviews, and feedback forms. Qualitative data helps us understand the reasons behind user behavior and identify areas for improvement.

Various stages, ranging from initial concept and validation to growth and scaling, require distinct sets of metrics to measure progress and make informed decisions. Let us examine a few examples of these metrics.

- **Early stage**: Focus on user acquisition and initial user feedback. Metrics include sign-ups, downloads, and user satisfaction scores from early adopters.

- **Mid stage**: Emphasize user engagement and retention. Metrics include DAU, MAU, session length, and churn rate.

- **Late stage**: Prioritize conversion rates and revenue generation. Metrics include conversion rates from free trials to paid plans, **average revenue per user** (**ARPU**), and total revenue.

Tools for tracking metrics

There are a good number of tools available in the industry that can help startups track and analyze their MVP metrics effectively. The following is a list of a few commonly used tools for metrics tracking:

- **Google Analytics**: Provides detailed insights into user behavior, acquisition channels, and engagement patterns. Ideal for tracking website and app performance.

- **Mixpanel**: Focuses on user engagement and retention metrics, offering in-depth analysis of user interactions and conversion rates.

- **Amplitude**: Offers comprehensive analytics for understanding user behavior and product usage, helping identify key trends and areas for improvement.

- **Hotjar**: Combines heatmaps, session recordings, and feedback tools to provide qualitative insights into user experiences and pain points.

- **SurveyMonkey**: Facilitates the creation and distribution of surveys to gather qualitative feedback from users.

Defining MVP goals and objectives

Defining clear goals and objectives for your **minimum viable product (MVP)** is critical to the success of any startup. These goals provide a roadmap for development, aligning the team, and setting the foundation for measuring success. Here is how to approach this crucial task.

Workshops and brainstorming sessions

Workshops are an excellent way to bring your teams together and collaboratively define your MVP goals. They provide a structured environment for open dialogue, ensuring all voices are heard. Here are the key steps to conduct an effective workshop:

- **Prepare**: Before the workshop, ensure that all participants have a clear understanding of the MVP concept and the overall vision of the startup. Provide pre-reading materials if necessary.

- **Facilitate**: A skilled facilitator can help keep the session focused and productive. They can guide the discussion, ensure everyone participates, and help synthesize ideas.

- **Agenda**: Set a clear agenda that includes introductions, a review of the startup's vision and mission, goal-setting activities, and a summary session.

Brainstorming sessions are crucial for generating diverse ideas and perspectives. Here are some effective techniques:

- **Mind mapping**: This visual technique helps in exploring various aspects of your MVP goals. Start with a central idea (e.g., *user engagement*) and branch out into specific goals and sub-goals.

- **SWOT analysis**: Assessing strengths, weaknesses, opportunities, and threats can provide a comprehensive understanding of what your MVP should aim to achieve.

- **SMART goals**: Use the **Specific, Measurable, Achievable, Relevant, Time-bound (SMART)** framework to refine each idea into actionable goals. For instance, instead of a vague goal like improve user experience, a SMART goal would be increase user retention by 20% within the first six months by enhancing the onboarding process.

Involving stakeholders

Engaging your team and stakeholders in the goal-setting process is vital for ensuring alignment and collective buy-in. These stakeholders can be early investors, angels, advisors, friends, or community members. There are several ways to involve them effectively:

- **Inclusive discussions**: Create an environment where team members feel comfortable sharing their insights and suggestions. This can be facilitated through regular team meetings, one-on-one discussions, or dedicated goal-setting workshops.

- **Cross-functional teams**: Involve members from divergent functions (e.g., development, marketing, customer support) to get a holistic view of the MVP goals. Each team brings unique insights that can shape more comprehensive objectives.

- **Feedback loops**: Establish mechanisms for continuous feedback. This ensures that as the MVP evolves, the goals and objectives can be refined based on real-world insights and team input.

Alignment and buy-in from key stakeholders are crucial for the successful execution of your MVP goals. Here is how to achieve this:

- **Clear communication**: Regularly communicate the defined goals and their progress to all stakeholders. Use tools like project management software, regular update meetings, and detailed reports to keep everyone informed.

- **Align with vision and mission**: Ensure that the MVP goals are clearly aligned with the startup's overall vision and mission. This alignment helps in securing buy-ins as stakeholders can see how their efforts contribute to the bigger picture.

- **Ownership and accountability**: Assign ownership of specific goals to team members or departments. This creates a sense of responsibility and ensures that there is a clear point of contact for each objective.

By following these practical steps, startups can effectively define and align their MVP goals and objectives, setting a solid foundation for product development and future success.

Adapting goals based on feedback

Goal adaptation is crucial for the iterative development of an MVP. By continuously gathering and analyzing user feedback, startups can pivot and refine their goals to better align with market needs and customer expectations, ensuring a more successful product launch.

Continuous improvement

Continuous improvement ensures that your MVP evolves in line with market needs and user expectations. This process not only enhances product quality but also reinforces user trust and engagement. Iterating goals involves the following:

- **Listening to users**: Actively seeking and valuing user feedback to understand their experiences, challenges, and needs.

- **Data-driven decisions**: Using data analytics to identify trends, patterns, and areas for improvement.

- **Flexibility**: Being open to change and willing to adjust your goals and objectives to better align with user needs and market conditions.

To effectively iterate on goals and objectives, you need robust mechanisms for gathering and analyzing feedback, such as:

- **Surveys and questionnaires**: Use structured surveys to collect quantitative data on user satisfaction and feature usage. Tools like SurveyMonkey and Google Forms can be effective.

- **User interviews**: Conduct in-depth interviews to gain qualitative insights into user experiences and pain points. This method provides context that quantitative data alone cannot capture.

- **Analytics tools**: Leverage tools like Google Analytics, Mixpanel, and Amplitude to track user behavior and engagement metrics. These insights can reveal how users interact with your product and highlight areas for improvement.

- **Customer support interactions**: Analyze interactions with customer support to identify common issues and user concerns. This can offer valuable insights into areas that require attention.

- **Social media and community forums**: Monitor social media platforms and community forums for user feedback and discussions about your product. Engaging with users in these spaces can provide direct and unfiltered insights.

Pivoting and adjusting goals

Sometimes, feedback and market response may indicate the need for a meaningful change in direction, known as a **pivot**. Recognizing when to pivot and how to execute it effectively is critical for startup success. Indicators for pivoting are:

- **Low user engagement**: If user engagement remains low despite efforts to iterate and improve, it might indicate a misalignment with market needs.

- **Negative feedback trends**: Consistent negative feedback or recurring issues that cannot be resolved through minor adjustments may necessitate a pivot.

- **Market shifts**: Significant changes in market conditions, such as new regulations or emerging technologies, may require a strategic shift.

Let us check out the steps to pivot:

1. **Assess the situation**: Thoroughly analyze feedback, data, and market trends to understand the root causes of underperformance.

2. **Reevaluate goals**: Based on your findings, redefine your MVP goals and objectives to better align with market demands.

3. **Develop a new strategy**: Outline a clear plan for the pivot, including the changes to be made and the expected outcomes.

4. **Communicate with stakeholders**: Ensure all team members and stakeholders understand the reasons for the pivot and their roles in the new strategy.

5. **Implement and monitor**: Execute the pivot and closely monitor the impact of changes. Continue to gather feedback and be prepared for further adjustments.

Instagram was originally launched as a check-in app called *Burbn*. Feedback from the users indicated a preference for photo-sharing features. The founders pivoted to focus on photo-sharing, leading to Instagram's massive success.

Slack was initially developed as an internal communication tool for a gaming company. Slack pivoted based on feedback and recognition of broader market needs. It became a widely adopted team collaboration platform.

PayPal started off as a cryptography company. PayPal focuses on digital payments based on market response and user feedback, eventually becoming a leader in online payments.

Adapting goals and objectives based on feedback is not just about responding to criticism or requests; it is about proactively seeking opportunities for improvement and being willing to make bold changes when necessary. This approach ensures that your MVP remains relevant, competitive, and aligned with user needs and market demands.

Common pitfalls

Navigating the development of an MVP is fraught with challenges. Understanding common pitfalls and how to avoid them is crucial for ensuring your startup's success. By recognizing and addressing these issues early, you can streamline your MVP development process and increase the likelihood of achieving a product-market fit.

Overambitious goals

The journey of building an MVP is quite exciting and enthusiastic. In the early stages, it is quite possible for startups to set overambitious goals. Aiming high is not bad at all, but unrealistic goals can lead to issues listed as follows:

- **Resource drain**: Stretching resources too thin can result in burnout and reduced efficiency.

- **Quality compromise**: Trying to achieve too much, too quickly, can compromise the quality of your product.

- **Team morale**: Consistently missing ambitious targets can demoralize your team and create a culture of disappointment.

Ambition with practicality needs to be balanced. As a product leader or a founder, the following is what you need to do:

- **Set SMART goals**: Ensure that the goals are Specific, Measurable, Achievable, Relevant, and Time-bound. This framework keeps your objectives grounded.

- **Break down goals into objectives**: Divide large goals into smaller, manageable milestones. This allows for gradual progress and frequent reassessment.

- **Frequent and regular reviews**: Frequently review your goals to ensure they remain feasible. Calibrate the goals as necessary based on progress and feedback.

- **Focus on core features**: Prioritize features that deliver the most value. Avoid the temptation to include every possible feature in the MVP.

- **Competitive products**: Do not let competitive products distract you from your focus.

Ignoring customer feedback

Customer feedback is invaluable in shaping an MVP that truly meets market needs. Ignoring this feedback can lead to problems, such as developing features that users do not find valuable or necessary, resulting in misaligned features. Additionally, failing to address user pain points can cause user dissatisfaction, making the product less appealing to the target audience. Overlooking feedback can also result in missed opportunities, where critical insights that could significantly improve the product are neglected. To effectively integrate customer feedback into your goals and objectives, keep the following in mind:

- **Active listening**: Engage with your users regularly through surveys, interviews, and feedback forms.

- **Feedback loops**: Establish mechanisms for collecting, analyzing, and implementing feedback continuously.

- **Prioritize feedback**: Not all feedback is equally important. Prioritize based on the number of users affected and the impact on user experience.

- **Close the loop**: Inform users how their feedback has been incorporated. This builds trust and encourages ongoing participation.

Misalignment with market needs

One of the critical pitfalls in MVP development is setting goals that do not align with the market's actual needs. This misalignment can result in product rejection, as users may not see value in a product that does not solve their core problems. It can also lead to wasted resources, as investing time and money in features that do not address market demands can be costly.

Furthermore, failing to align with market needs can create a competitive disadvantage, giving competitors an edge. You must ensure continuous alignment with market needs using the following techniques:

- **Market research**: Conduct ongoing market research to stay updated on industry trends and customer preferences.

- **User testing**: Regularly assess your MVP with real users to gather direct feedback on its relevance and utility.

- **Competitive analysis**: Monitor competitors to understand what is working in the market and identify gaps your product can fill.

- **Iterative development**: Use an iterative approach to development, where you continuously refine your product based on market feedback.

By being aware of these common pitfalls and implementing strategies to avoid them, startups can enhance their chances of developing a successful MVP. Balancing ambition with realism, prioritizing customer feedback, and ensuring market alignment are essential steps in the MVP journey.

Conclusion

In this chapter, we have taken a deep dive into the essential practice of defining clear goals and objectives for your MVP. Starting with the importance of setting well-defined goals, we have explored how these goals provide direction, focus, and measurable benchmarks for success. We then moved on to the SMART goals framework, illustrating how to craft goals that are Specific, Measurable, Achievable, Relevant, and Time-bound.

We also discussed the importance of success criteria and metrics, differentiating between short-term and long-term success, and emphasizing the significance of customer-centric metrics. We introduced techniques for translating high-level goals into specific objectives, and methods for prioritizing these objectives to ensure they are both impactful and feasible.

In the next chapter, we will bridge the theory of MVP development with practical strategies for turning concepts into reality. We will explore MVP design patterns in depth and illustrate them with industry case studies.

Points to remember

- **The importance of clear, actionable goals**: Setting clear goals provides a roadmap for your MVP, ensuring that every effort is aligned with your startup's vision and market needs.

- **SMART goals framework**: Specific, Measurable, Achievable, Relevant, and Time-bound goals help in creating a focused and effective MVP strategy.

- **Success criteria and metrics**: Establishing success criteria and selecting the right metrics is crucial for evaluating your MVP's performance and guiding iterative development.

- **Customer-centric focus**: Keeping customer satisfaction and engagement at the forefront ensures that your MVP addresses real market needs.

- **Adaptability**: The ability to pivot and adjust goals based on feedback and market response is key to achieving long-term success.

Join our Discord space

Join our Discord workspace for latest updates, offers, tech happenings around the world, new releases, and sessions with the authors:

https://discord.bpbonline.com

CHAPTER 4
MVP Development Stages

Introduction

In the last chapter, we laid the groundwork by outlining the strategic goals and measurable objectives required for steering the **minimum viable product** (**MVP**) toward success. Now, it is time to look at the practical, step-by-step process of developing your MVP, from an initial concept to a market-ready product. The path to a successful MVP is rarely linear. It involves iterative cycles of ideation, prototyping, testing, and refining. This chapter will guide you through these stages, offering insights and best practices to ensure that your MVP is not only viable but also poised for market impact. By the end of this chapter, you will have a comprehensive understanding of the MVP development stages, armed with practical knowledge and actionable strategies to bring your product vision to life.

Structure

In this chapter, we will cover the following topics:

- Key concepts
- Product vision and MVP features
- MVP prototyping
- Technical readiness of MVP

- MVP planning

- Development and iterations

- Testing and quality assurance

- Preparing for launch

Objectives

By the end of this chapter, you will be able to understand the MVP development process, learn the journey from ideation to a market-ready product, including stages such as prototyping, testing, and refinement. We will also understand how to apply development principles, learn how iterative cycles of building, measuring, and learning help create a robust and user-aligned MVP. Moreover, we will develop an actionable MVP roadmap and learn how to structure a development plan that aligns with business goals, user needs, and market demands. We will mitigate common pitfalls, recognize potential challenges in MVP development, and apply strategies to navigate them effectively.

Key concepts

To transform an MVP from idea to reality, it is essential to understand and implement several key concepts:

- **Ideation**: This stage involves generating and refining ideas through brainstorming sessions, innovation workshops, and involving cross-functional teams. It is crucial to assess the feasibility and market potential of these ideas before proceeding.

- **Prototyping**: Prototyping involves creating both low-fidelity and high-fidelity prototypes to visualize the product and gather early user feedback. It helps in refining the product concept and making necessary adjustments before development.

- **Core feature identification**: Identifying and focusing on core features that address the primary problem of the target users is essential. This stage involves defining user journeys, writing user stories, and prioritizing features using techniques like the MoSCoW method and impact-effort matrix.

- **Prioritization**: Effective prioritization ensures that the most critical features are developed first. Startups must balance innovation with practicality, using techniques like the impact-effort matrix to decide which features to include in the MVP.

- **Iteration**: Iteration is a continuous process of refining the product based on user feedback and testing. Agile methodologies like Scrum and Kanban support this iterative approach, enabling startups to make incremental improvements.

- **Testing**: Testing and **quality assurance (QA)** are vital for delivering a reliable MVP. This stage involves automated and manual testing techniques, bug tracking, and usability testing to ensure the product meets the desired quality standards.

Product vision and MVP features

In the last chapter, we learned creating a successful MVP begins with the crucial stages of ideation and conceptualization, where innovative ideas are generated, validated for market potential, and shaped into a compelling product vision aligned with business goals and customer needs. Equally important is defining the core features of your MVP and identifying key functionalities that provide maximum value to users while keeping development manageable and focused. This unified approach ensures that startups can effectively determine, articulate, and prioritize features, leveraging practical techniques and tools for a streamlined and impactful MVP development process.

Drafting the product vision

A product vision is a clear and concise statement that encapsulates what the product aims to achieve and the value it will deliver to customers while aligning with the company's strategic goals and objectives. It serves as the purpose statement, ensuring that all efforts are aligned with the overarching goals of the product and the company.

This statement should be inspiring and provide direction for the team. You must identify and articulate the core values that your product stands for. These values should resonate with your target audience and differentiate your product in the market.

Here is a template that can help you create a comprehensive product vision:

Section	Details
Vision statement	Revolutionize personal productivity by providing an intuitive and seamless task management tool that empowers users to achieve their goals effortlessly.
Target audience	Busy professionals, students, and entrepreneurs who struggle with managing their tasks and time effectively.
Customer needs	Users need a simple, user-friendly interface that helps them organize their tasks, set priorities, and track progress without feeling overwhelmed.
Core values	Simplicity, efficiency, empowerment, innovation.
Unique selling proposition	Our tool offers a unique combination of AI-driven task suggestions and seamless integration with popular productivity apps, making it easier for users to stay on top of their tasks.
Business goals alignment	Aligns with our goal to become the leading productivity software provider, increasing our market share and boosting user retention and satisfaction.

Key features	AI task suggestions, calendar integration, customizable task views, and real-time collaboration features.
Success metrics	User satisfaction score of 90%+, monthly active users' growth by 20% and an increase in user retention rate by 25% within the first year.

Table 4.1: Product vision draft template

Approaching essential features

Identifying and prioritizing essential MVP features is a critical task that ensures your product meets user needs while remaining manageable for development. Let us check how to approach this effectively:

- **Follow your customers**: Conducting user research by engaging with potential users through surveys, interviews, and observational studies helps uncover their pain points and needs. Developing detailed user personas that represent different segments of your target audience can guide feature prioritization by providing a clear picture of who your users are and what they require.

- **Define core value proposition**: Articulate the key benefit the MVP will deliver to users. This focus on the primary value helps to ensure that features directly contribute to this value. Additionally, align these core features with your startup's overall vision and strategic objectives to maintain coherence between the product and business goals.

- **Prioritize features**: The MoSCoW method, which categorizes features into Must-have, should-have, could-have, and will not-have, helps to focus on the key must-have features necessary for the MVP to function. Another useful tool is the impact-effort matrix, which evaluates features based on their potential impact on user satisfaction and the effort required to implement them. By prioritizing high-impact, low-effort features, you can maximize value with minimal resource expenditure.

- **Must-have versus nice-to-have features**: Must-have features are critical functionalities without which the product cannot solve the primary problem it is designed to address. Nice-to-have features enhance the user experience but are not essential for the initial launch. For example, for a new social media app, basic posting and commenting functionalities are must-haves. If users cannot share content or interact, the app fails its core purpose. However, advanced photo editing tools might be nice-to-have features.

Example scenario

For a fintech startup developing a budgeting app, the must-have features might include expense tracking, budget setting, and spending categorization. Nice-to-have features could be integrations with investment platforms or a chatbot for financial advice. Refer to the following table for feature prioritization using the must-have vs nice-to-have method:

Feature	Description	Must-have/ Nice-to-have	Reason for categorization
Expense tracking	Users can track their daily expenses	Must-have	Core functionality for budgeting
Budget setting	Users can set monthly budgets	Must-have	Essential for managing finances
Spending categorization	Categorize spending into categories	Must-have	Help users understand spending habits
Investment integrations	Link to investment accounts	Nice-to-have	Enhances value but not core
Financial advice chatbot	Provides tips and advice	Nice-to-have	Improves user experience

Table 4.2: *Sample feature prioritization using the must-have vs nice-to-have method*

User journeys, user stories, and use cases

Creating a successful MVP involves mapping out detailed user journeys, writing effective user stories, and developing comprehensive use cases. Each of these elements provides valuable insights into user behavior, helping you to design a product that meets their needs and expectations. Let us briefly understand these terms:

- **Persona definition**: Create detailed personas of your target users, including demographics, goals, challenges, and behaviors. Start by giving a name to the persona, closely resembling the demographic profile. Use tools like *Xtensio* to create and share personas with your team. For instance, a persona for a fitness app might be *Emily, 28, busy professional who works out after work and seeks quick, efficient workout plans.*

- **Persona (user) journeys**: Map out the steps these personas take to achieve a specific goal with your product, identifying key touchpoints and potential pain points. Tools like *Miro* or *Lucidchart* can help in visualizing these journeys. For example, for Emily, the user journey might include discovering the app, signing up, selecting a workout plan, completing a workout, and tracking progress.

- **Writing effective user stories**: Use the format *As a [user type], I want to [action] so that [benefit]*. Ensure stories are clear, concise, and prioritized based on user needs. For example, *As a user, I want to create a post so that I can share my thoughts with my followers.* Make sure stories are clear, concise, and prioritized based on user needs.

- **Developing use cases**: Illustrate how users will interact with the product to accomplish specific tasks. Use case diagrams can be created using tools like *Microsoft Visio* or UML tools. For example, for a social media app, a use case might involve a user logging in, creating a post, and viewing comments. Detail each step in the process to ensure thorough understanding and coverage.

Practical tips for startups

When developing an MVP, it is important to remember that not every feature can be directly translated into a user story. Here are some practical tips for startups to effectively navigate this process:

- **Understand the user perspective**: Put yourself in the user's shoes to understand their needs and pain points. Ensure that each user story reflects a feature that provides tangible value to the user. For example, for a productivity app, think about the daily challenges users face in managing their tasks and time. The user story could be *As a user, I want to receive reminders for my tasks so that I do not forget important deadlines.*

- **Break down features into smaller stories**: Large, complex features should be broken down into smaller, more manageable user stories. You may even choose to start with a basic version of the feature and iterate on it. For example, instead of a single story for *Advanced Search Functionality*, create stories like *As a user, I want to filter search results by date,* and *As a user, I want to sort search results by relevance.*

- **Use clear and concise language**: User stories are a fundamental aspect of Agile methodologies. Ensure that user stories are simple, clear, and specific, avoiding technical jargon.

- **Focus on outcomes, not outputs**: Ensure that each user story has clear acceptance criteria and success metrics. Prioritize user stories based on the value they deliver to the user and the business. This helps in focusing on the most impactful features first.

For example, *As a user, I want to receive a confirmation email after registration so that I know my account is created successfully*, with acceptance criteria like *The email should be sent within 5 minutes of registration.*

Use the following template to structure a user story:

Field	Description
User story title	A brief, well-indented title of the user story.
As a [*User Role*]	Clearly define who the user is (e.g., customer, admin, visitor).
I want to [*Action*]	Describe what the user specifically wants to do.
So that [*Value/Benefit*]	Explain why the user wants to perform this action. What value or benefit do they get from it?

Acceptance criteria	1. Given [Context/Initial state]: Describe the starting situation.
	2. When [Action/Event occurs]: Explain the action or event that triggers the story.
	3. Then [Outcome/Result]: Describe the expected outcome or result.
Priority	Indicate the priority level (e.g., high, medium, low).
Story points	Estimate the effort required to complete the story (e.g., using story points or hours).
Notes	Add any additional information or context that may be useful for understanding or implementing the user story.

Table 4.3: User story template

Prioritizing features for a first time MVP

Prioritizing features for an MVP, especially when it is being developed for the first time, can be a challenging task. Here are some practical steps and tips to help you effectively prioritize:

- **Focus on core value proposition**: Identify the core problem your product addresses and the unique value it provides. It might sound simple, but remember, *a problem well defined is a problem half solved*. For instance, if you are developing a new social media app, the primary issue might be the need for a more private and secure way to share moments with close friends.

- **Conduct user journey mapping**: Define user personas to understand different user needs and priorities. Identify the key touchpoints and interactions users will have with your product.

- **Use the MoSCoW method or impact-effort matrix**: Leaders must brainstorm with key stakeholders to categorize features into must-have, should-have, could-have, and will not-have buckets or plot the impact-effort matrix. Anticipate potential conflicts during these discussions. To mitigate this, conduct a thorough value proposition analysis for each feature as pre-work. This preparation will ensure more informed and objective decision-making during the prioritization process.

MVP prototyping

The prototyping stage in the MVP development process provides a tangible representation of your product ideas. It allows you to assess assumptions, gather user feedback, and make necessary adjustments before moving to full-scale development. This section will guide you through the different types of prototypes, tools for creating them, and best practices for testing and iterating based on feedback.

Note: **For startups, prototyping is crucial. It bridges the gap between conceptual ideas and real-world applications, offering a low-risk, high-reward approach to product development. Prototypes help startups validate their concepts, attract investors, and align their teams with a clear vision. By investing in prototyping, startups can avoid costly mistakes, adapt quickly to market demands, and increase their chances of success.**

Low-fidelity prototypes

Low-fidelity prototypes are simple and quick to create, providing a basic visual representation of your product. Sketches, wireframes, and mock-ups are ideal for early-stage brainstorming and concept validation.

Sketches are hand-drawn representations that outline the basic structure and flow of the product. These are the quickest and most flexible forms of low-fidelity prototypes. *Wireframes* are digital outlines that focus on the layout and hierarchy of information without detailed design elements. They provide a clearer picture of the product structure. *Mock-ups* are detailed static designs that incorporate branding elements such as colors and typography, but lack interactivity. The following figure shows a rough UI sketch of a mobile wireframe:

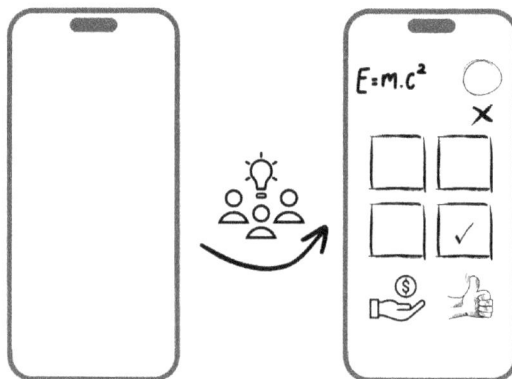

Figure 4.1: Brainstorming sessions help in building low-fidelity prototypes

The tools and templates to build a low-fidelity prototype can be as simple as a pen and paper. Refer to the following:

- **Paper and pen**: The simplest tools for initial sketches and brainstorming sessions.
- **Balsamiq**: A user-friendly tool for creating wireframes that mimic the hand-drawn look.
- **Adobe XD and Figma**: Tools that offer wireframing capabilities with the option to transition to high-fidelity designs.

The following template can be used to track low-fidelity prototype progress:

Step	Description	Completed (Yes/No)
Identify key features	List the essential features to include in the prototype.	
Sketch initial ideas	Create rough sketches of main screens and flows.	
Create wireframes	Develop structured wireframes for detailed layout.	
Design mock-ups	Add visual elements to wireframes for a polished look.	
Review and iterate	Get feedback from team members and make necessary changes.	

Table 4.4: Low-fidelity checklist template

High-fidelity prototypes

High-fidelity prototypes are detailed, interactive models of the product. They provide a realistic user experience and are crucial for thorough usability testing. The realistic nature of high-fidelity prototypes allows users to provide precise feedback on the product's usability and design.

Unlike low-fidelity prototypes, high-fidelity prototypes are created using digital tools and templates as follows:

- **Canva[1]/Figma[2]**: Offers robust prototyping features along with design collaboration tools.

- **Sketch[3]**: Paired with plugins like *InVision*, it provides comprehensive high-fidelity prototyping capabilities.

- **Adobe XD[4]**: A versatile tool that allows for creating detailed and interactive prototypes.

Use the following template to track and manage the progress of your high-fidelity prototype:

Step	Description	Completed (Yes/No)
Define user interactions	Identify key interactions and flows to prototype.	
Create detailed designs	Develop high-fidelity designs for all screens.	
Build interactive prototypes	Use tools to create clickable, interactive prototypes.	
Test with users	Conduct usability testing with real users.	
Gather feedback	Collect detailed feedback on the user experience.	

---

1   Canva - **https://www.canva.com/**
2   Figma - **https://www.figma.com/**
3   Sketch - **https://www.sketch.com/**
4   Adobe XD - **https://adobexdplatform.com/**

Iterate and improve	Make necessary adjustments based on user feedback.	

Table 4.5: High-fidelity checklist template

User testing of prototypes

Testing your prototypes with actual users validates your assumptions and identifies the areas for improvement. The following are the steps to conduct usability tests:

- **Define and align test objectives**: Clearly outline what you want to learn from the usability tests.

- **Recruit participants**: Choose participants who represent your target audience.

- **Create test scenarios**: Develop realistic scenarios for users to complete using the prototype.

- **Brief, observe, and record**: Watch how users interact with the prototype and record their behavior and feedback.

Please refer to the following template that can be used for user testing:

Section	Details
Test Objectives	Define the main goals of the usability test.
Participants	Describe the target user group and how they will be recruited.
Test Scenarios	List the tasks and scenarios users will complete.
Observation Plan	Outline how observations will be conducted and recorded.
Feedback Collection	Describe how feedback will be gathered and analyzed.
Interpretation	1. Collect feedback: Gather qualitative and quantitative feedback from users. 2. Identify patterns: Look for common issues or themes in the feedback. 3. Prioritize issues: Determine which issues are most critical to address based on their impact on the user experience.

Table 4.6: User testing template

Learning from the industry practices

Adopting industry practices can streamline the prototyping process and ensure high-quality outcomes. Collaborate with UX/UI designers, involve cross-functional teams, and stay updated with the latest tools and methodologies. Let us go through some of the parallel practices followed in the industry:

- **Agile methodologies**: Incorporate Agile practices to iterate quickly and efficiently.

- **Cross-functional teams**: Emphasize the role of collaboration between designers, developers, and product managers in creating effective prototypes. Share how collaborative tools like *Figma* allow for real-time collaboration and feedback, enhancing the prototyping process.

- **Continuous feedback loops**: Explain the importance of a continuous feedback loop during the prototyping stage. Provide methods for effectively integrating user feedback into subsequent iterations.

- **Rapid versus thorough prototyping**: Discuss strategies for balancing the need for rapid iteration with maintaining a high-quality prototype. Compare scenarios where a quick-and-dirty prototype might be appropriate versus when a more polished prototype is necessary.

- **Budget-friendly tools and techniques**: Provide tips for startups on how to prototype effectively within a limited budget. Highlight affordable or free prototyping tools and resources.

- **Web versus mobile versus desktop**: Discuss the nuances of prototyping for different platforms and the specific challenges and considerations for each. Explain how a mobile-first approach can influence the prototyping process and user experience design.

- **Future-proofing prototypes**: Provide guidance on creating prototypes that not only address current needs but are also scalable for future growth. Discuss design principles that ensure the prototype can evolve with the product.

- **Data privacy and security**: Address the importance of considering data privacy and security during the prototyping phase, especially when dealing with user data. Share best practices for protecting user data during testing and feedback collection.

- **Interactive and animated prototypes**: Explore advanced techniques like interactive and animated prototypes to provide a more realistic user experience. Describe how tools like *Principle* or *Adobe XD* can be used to create dynamic prototypes.

- **Success metrics for prototypes**: Define metrics and KPIs to measure the success and effectiveness of prototypes. Discuss how usability testing results, user satisfaction scores, and iteration counts can serve as indicators of a successful prototype.

Rapid prototyping

Rapid prototyping allows startups and product teams to create quick proof of concepts, gather feedback, and iterate on designs before committing to full-scale development. By leveraging rapid prototyping, startups can test their assumptions, validate ideas, and reduce the risk of building a product that does not meet market needs:

- **Speed**: Rapid prototyping accelerates the development process, allowing startups to move from concept to prototype in a matter of days or weeks.

- **Cost-effectiveness**: By identifying potential issues early in the development cycle, rapid prototyping helps avoid costly changes later.

- **User feedback**: Early prototypes provide a tangible product that stakeholders and potential users can interact with, offering valuable feedback for refinement.

- **Flexibility**: Prototypes can be easily modified based on feedback, ensuring that the final MVP closely aligns with user needs and expectations.

Technical readiness of MVP

In the journey from ideation to an MVP, ensuring the technical readiness of your development team and environment is the key to execution. Let us look at the steps and best practices to prepare your team and set up a robust development environment, manage technical debt, and design for scalability.

Preparing the development team

Before diving into development, every team member must have a clear understanding of the product vision and MVP goals. This alignment ensures that everyone is working towards the same objectives and understands the importance of each feature and task. Draw the team's alignment in the following areas:

- **Product vision and goals**: Conduct kick-off meetings to communicate the vision and goals clearly. Visual aids like roadmaps and user journey maps can be helpful.

- **Documentation**: Share documentation that outlines the product vision, goals, user personas, market analysis, and key features.

- **Technical strategy and planning**: Share the product and tech strategy with the team and the overall execution plan. Equipping your team with the necessary skills and knowledge is crucial for efficient development.

Setting up the development environment

A development environment survives on picking the right technologies, balancing risks, integrating necessary services, and ensuring seamless operations. One must evaluate the specific tech and infra needs of the MVP, including performance, scalability, and maintainability. Choose technologies that align with your product goals and team expertise. Consider factors like community support, futureproofing, and integration capabilities. For example, for a web application, you might choose *React* for the front end, *Node.js* for the back end, and MongoDB for the database.

Here are some commonly used tech stacks and their applications:

- **LAMP stack**: Linux, Apache, MySQL, PHP.

    o **Use cases**: Ideal for building dynamic websites and web applications. It is highly versatile and has a large support community.

    o **Pros**: Open-source, cost-effective, robust security features.

    o **Cons**: Can be less performant compared to newer stacks, limited to PHP for server-side scripting.

- **MERN stack**: MongoDB, Express.js, React, Node.js.

    o **Use cases**: Suitable for building high-performance, single-page applications. It allows for full-stack JavaScript development.

    o **Pros**: Fast development, high-performance, flexible, and scalable.

    o **Cons**: Rapid changes in the ecosystem can make it challenging to keep up to date.

- **Modern age tech stacks**:

    o **JAM stack**: JavaScript, APIs, Markup. This stack is used for building static websites that are fast, secure, and scalable. Popular frameworks include *Gatsby* and Next.js.

    o **MEAN stack**: MongoDB, Express, Angular, and Node. This is a JavaScript-based framework for developing scalable web applications.

    o **MEVN stack**: MongoDB, Express.js, Vue.js, Node.js. Similar to MERN but uses Vue.js for the front end, known for its simplicity and ease of integration.

- **Mobile tech stacks**:

    o **React Native**: Allows for building mobile apps using React. It supports both iOS and Android with a single codebase.

    o **Flutter**: Developed by *Google, Flutter* allows for building natively compiled applications for mobile, web, and desktop from a single codebase.

    o **Swift and Kotlin**: Swift is used for iOS development, while *Kotlin* is for *Android* development. Both are preferred for their performance and integration with native APIs.

- **Web tech stacks**:

o **Front-end**: HTML, CSS, JavaScript, and frameworks like Angular, Vue.js, and React.

o **Back-end**: Node.js, Ruby on Rails, Django, Laravel.

o **Full-stack**: Combinations like **MongoDB, Express.js, Angular, Node.js (MEAN)**, and LAMP.

Refer to the following table to compare MERN, MEAN, and LAMP stacks:

Criteria	MERN	LAMP	MEAN
Team expertise	High	Medium	High
Scalability	High	Medium	High
Community support	High	High	High
Development speed	Fast	Medium	Fast
Maintenance complexity	Medium	Low	Medium

Table 4.7: Common tech stack comparison matrix

Development practices

Let us explore some of the most used development practices by the teams:

- **Version control and CI/CD pipelines**: Implementing version control systems like Git is a software practice for managing and tracking code changes, ensuring collaboration, and maintaining code quality. Setting up **continuous integration and continuous deployment (CI/CD)** pipelines can automate the testing, building, and deployment processes, making the development workflow more efficient. Tools like *Jenkins, CircleCI*, and *GitHub Actions* can significantly streamline this process.

  Note: **For early-stage startups, it is essential to balance best practices with resource management. While version control and CI/CD are beneficial, they can be introduced progressively as the team grows and the project scales. This approach allows startups to maintain agility while gradually adopting standards that will support long-term success.**

- **Integration with third-party services**: Evaluate and choose third-party services that enhance your MVP's functionality. Ensure these services are reliable and well-documented. Plan for seamless integration of third-party services, ensuring they align with your MVP's architecture and objectives. For example, integrating payment gateways like Stripe and social media logins via OAuth.

- **Continuous monitoring and improvement**: Implement monitoring tools to track the performance, errors, and user behavior of your MVP. Early-stage startups must integrate Google Analytics to capture user insights like demographics, usage patterns, clickstream[5], and product performance. Use monitoring data from tools like *New Relic* and *Sentry* to continuously improve your MVP, addressing issues and enhancing features based on real-time feedback.

- **Ensuring data privacy and compliance**: Implement robust data privacy measures to protect user data. Ensure compliance with relevant regulations such as GDPR or CCPA. Regularly review and update your data protection practices, staying compliant with evolving laws. For example, conducting regular data privacy audits and using tools like *Data Privacy Manager* to ensure compliance.

- **Documentation and knowledge sharing**: Develop comprehensive documentation for your MVP, including technical specifications, user guides, and API documentation. Foster a culture of knowledge sharing within your team. Use platforms like *Confluence* or *Notion* to maintain and share project documentation.

Technical debt and scalability

Technical debt refers to the future cost of reworking code and architecture that are convenient in the short-term but are suboptimal for long-term maintenance and scalability. Accumulating technical debt can lead to increased maintenance costs, slower development cycles, and more complex refactoring efforts down the line. While taking on technical debt can be a pragmatic decision to accelerate development and validate the market, managing it effectively is crucial to ensure long-term success and scalability.

While technical debt due to environmental factors can be inevitable, the debt arising from unawareness or deliberate shortcuts can be mitigated through clear documentation, regular refactoring sessions, and consistent QA efforts to identify and address gaps in the product.

Note: **For startups, while initial technical debt might be necessary to achieve quick market entry, a long-term strategy must be in place to address it without compromising scalability.**

MVP planning

MVP planning is not merely about outlining features; it involves a comprehensive approach to understanding market needs, prioritizing core functionalities, and ensuring that the development environment is primed for rapid, yet sustainable, progress.

It is imperative to align the team's efforts with a well-defined plan that encompasses strategic goal setting, resource allocation, and iterative development. This section will cover key aspects such as team hierarchy, make versus buy decisions, the role of low-code tools, and communication and collaboration platforms.

---

5   A clickstream is the sequence of a user's clicks and actions on a website or app.

Team organization

The structure of your MVP team significantly impacts the efficiency and quality of your development process. Here is a breakdown of typical roles and their responsibilities:

- **Product and technology leader**: Guides the technical direction, architecture, and implementation. Ensures technical feasibility and scalability. The industry titles could be *chief technology officer* or *chief product* and *technology officer*.

- **Product manager**: Oversees the product vision, strategy, and roadmap. Ensures the team stays aligned with the goals and objectives.

- **Developers**: Execute the development tasks, write code, and build the product.

- **UX/UI designers**: Focus on the user experience and interface design, ensuring the product is user-friendly and visually appealing.

- **QA engineers**: Test the product to ensure it meets quality standards and functions correctly.

- **Marketing and sales**: Develop strategies for market entry and user acquisition.

Make versus buy decisions

One of the most critical decisions you will face in the MVP journey is whether to build components in-house or to leverage third-party solutions. The *make versus buy* decision can significantly impact your development timeline, costs, and product flexibility. Here are some key considerations:

- **In-house development**: In-house development offers several advantages, including full control over the product, customization to meet specific needs, the opportunity to upskill, and the potential for long-term cost savings. However, it also requires significant time and resources, involves higher initial costs, and may face potential skill gaps. For instance, a startup developing a unique AI algorithm might choose in-house development to maintain proprietary control and ensure the product is tailored precisely to their requirements.

- **Third-party solutions**: Third-party solutions have several advantages and disadvantages that startups must carefully consider. The primary benefits include faster implementation, lower initial costs, and access to expertise and established technologies. These solutions can significantly reduce the time and effort needed to get a system up and running. However, there are also notable drawbacks, such as limited customization options, potential dependency on the vendor, and recurring costs. For instance, a startup in need of a **customer relationship management** (CRM) system might opt for a third-party solution like Salesforce to save on development time and leverage its robust features and reliability despite the trade-offs involved.

Here is a cost-benefit analysis matrix that can help you make make versus buy decisions:

Factor	In-house development (Make)	Third-party solution (Buy)
Initial costs	High (development, hiring, tools)	Low (subscription/licensing fees)
Time to market	Longer (development cycle)	Shorter (ready-made solution)
Customization	High (tailored to needs)	Low to Medium (limited customization)
Long-term costs	Lower (once developed)	Higher (ongoing fees)
Control and flexibility	High (full control)	Low (vendor dependency)

Table 4.8: Make versus buy decision template

Team communication and collaboration platforms

Whether your team is co-located, remote, or hybrid, leveraging robust communication tools and collaborative project management software is key to maintaining clarity, driving innovation, and taking the project forward efficiently. These platforms facilitate real-time interactions, enable documentation sharing, and provide transparency, ensuring everyone stays on the same page throughout the MVP lifecycle.

The following table highlights the leading communication and collaboration tools used across the industry, along with a brief overview of their key features:

Category	Tool	Features	Use case	Example
Communication tools	Slack	Channels, direct messaging, file sharing, integrations with other tools	Real-time communication, quick updates, cross-department collaboration	Creating channels for different aspects of the MVP, such as #design, #development, #marketing, and #feedback
	Microsoft Teams	Chat, video conferencing, file sharing, integration with Microsoft Office	Seamless communication and collaboration for teams using Microsoft Office products	Weekly video calls to review MVP progress and discuss next steps
	Zoom	Video conferencing, screen sharing, breakout rooms, webinar hosting	Face-to-face interactions, detailed project discussions for remote teams	Holding virtual sprint planning and retrospective meetings to maintain rhythm in Agile development process

Collaboration tools	Trello	Boards, lists, cards for task management, integration options	Organizing tasks, tracking progress, ensuring team member responsibilities are clear	Creating a Trello board for the MVP project where cards represent individual tasks like *design UI mock-ups*
	Asana	Task assignments, project timelines, progress tracking, integrations	Comprehensive project management, tracking deadlines, task dependencies, project milestones	Mapping out MVP development timeline, assigning tasks to team members, setting deadlines for timely completion
	Jira	Issue and project tracking, Agile reporting, backlog management, integrations	Agile project management for software development teams	Managing sprint backlog, tracking development tasks, generating progress and bottleneck reports
	Confluence	Document collaboration, knowledge sharing, integration with Jira	Centralized knowledge base for documenting processes, sharing information, collaborating on content	Creating a Confluence space for the MVP project to store all relevant documents, meeting notes, and product specs

Table 4.9: Communication and collaboration tools

Budget planning

Effective budget planning ensures that resources are allocated efficiently, and the project can sustain its momentum from ideation to launch. Here are some key considerations for budgeting during this crucial phase:

- **Prioritize core features and infrastructure**: Focus your budget on developing the core features that define the MVP and the infrastructure to host the MVP. This ensures that you allocate resources to functionalities that provide the most value to your target audience and validate your business hypothesis. Avoid the temptation to overspend on non-essential features.

- **Lean development approach**: Adopt a Lean development approach to minimize waste and maximize value. This involves iterative development cycles, frequent testing, and continuous feedback loops. If possible, allocate a portion of your budget to regular user testing and feedback sessions to ensure you are on the right track.

- **Resource allocation**: Carefully allocate resources across different areas such as development, design, marketing, and operations. Ensure that you have a balanced budget that supports not only the creation of the MVP but also its promotion and support.

- **Contingency fund**: Set aside a contingency fund to address unexpected expenses. This financial cushion can help you manage unforeseen challenges without derailing your project.

- **Cost-benefit analysis**: Conduct a cost-benefit analysis for each major expenditure. Evaluate the potential **return on investment (ROI)** of various features, tools, and services to ensure that every dollar spent contributes meaningfully to the success of your MVP.

- **Utilize cost-effective tools**: Leverage cost-effective tools and platforms, such as open-source software and low-code development platforms, to reduce development costs. Many cloud service providers offer free tiers or credits for startups, which can help manage hosting and infrastructure costs.

- **Monitor and adjust**: Regularly monitor your budget and adjust as necessary based on actual spending and progress. Use budgeting tools and software to track expenses in real-time and make data-driven decisions.

For example, a typical budget for an MVP may look something like this:

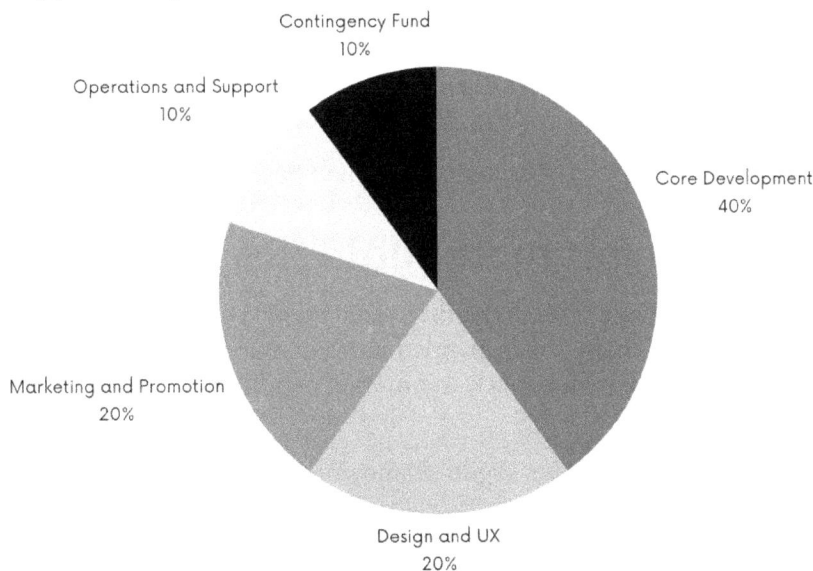

Figure 4.2: *A sample MVP budget allocation*

Remote and hybrid team collaboration

Modern dynamic workplaces are driven by effective communication, engagement, and adaptability. Here are some of the best practices to ensure seamless collaboration and productivity:

- **Regular check-ins**: Schedule regular team meetings to ensure everyone is aligned and any issues are addressed promptly. This practice of daily stand-up meetings, common in Agile methodologies, helps maintain team cohesion and accountability.

- **Clear documentation**: Maintain detailed documentation of all decisions, processes, and progress updates to avoid misunderstandings.

- **Use of collaborative tools**: Leverage integrations between tools (e.g., Slack and Trello, Jira and Confluence) to streamline workflows and reduce manual updates. Employ cloud-based document collaboration tools such as Google Workspace or Microsoft Office 365. These platforms allow multiple team members to work on documents simultaneously, ensuring everyone has access to the latest version.

- **Encourage open communication**: Foster a culture where team members feel comfortable sharing ideas, feedback, and concerns. Leverage tools like Slack, Microsoft Teams, and Zoom for real-time communication. These platforms facilitate quick interactions, video conferencing, and group discussions.

- **Reward and recognize**: Organizations build policies to reward victories, but quite often, they fail to recognize contributions. Regularly acknowledge and celebrate team and individual achievements to boost morale and maintain motivation.

Development and iterations

The development and iteration stages are crucial for transforming your MVP from a concept into a functional product that can be tested and refined based on user feedback.

Agile development methodologies

Agile methodologies provide the flexibility and iterative approach needed for MVP development. They help manage the dynamic nature of startup environments and allow for quick adjustments based on user feedback and market conditions. Let us explore the industry-relevant Agile frameworks:

- **Scrum**: Scrum is a popular Agile framework that emphasizes iterative progress through sprints. It involves specific roles, such as the scrum master, product owner, and development team, and uses artifacts like the product backlog, sprint backlog, and increments to manage work. Here are the steps to execute a sprint:

1. Define the sprint duration (typically two to four weeks).

2. Conduct sprint planning meetings to select backlog items for the sprint.

3. Hold daily stand-ups to discuss progress and impediments.

4. End with a sprint review and retrospective to assess what went well and what can be improved.

- **Kanban**: Kanban is another Agile method that visualizes work using a board with columns representing different stages of the workflow. It focuses on continuous delivery and optimizing the flow of work. The steps to manage workflows are given as follows:

  1. Use a Kanban board to track tasks and their progress.

  2. Limit work-in-progress to ensure team focus and efficiency.

  3. Continuously review and adjust the workflow to improve productivity.

- **Lean**: Lean methodology emphasizes maximizing value by eliminating waste and ensuring efficient processes. It promotes validated learning, Build-Measure-Learn loops, and continuous improvement. The steps to implement Lean principles are as follows:

  1. Focus on delivering value to customers.

  2. Remove unnecessary processes and steps.

  3. Use customer feedback to drive improvements and adjustments.

This sprint planning template is designed to help teams outline tasks, objectives, and timelines for each sprint effectively. Use this template to organize and track the progress of your sprint goals and ensure all team members are aligned:

Section	Details
Sprint information	
Sprint number	Sprint 1
Sprint duration	01/01/2024 - 14/01/2024
Sprint goal	Complete the user login and registration feature
Team members	
Product owner	Priya Sharma
Scrum master	Arjun Mehta
Development team	Ananya, Ravi, Suresh, Kavita
Backlog items	

ID	User story / Task
1	As a user, I want to register an account
2	As a user, I want to log in to my account
3	As a user, I want to reset my password
Task breakdown	
User story / Task	Sub-tasks
Register an account	Design registration form
	Implement form validation
Sprint timeline	
Week / Day	Task
Week 1 / Day 1	Design registration form
Week 1 / Day 2	Implement form validation
Sprint review	
Completed backlog items	[List of completed items]
Incomplete backlog items	[List of incomplete items and reasons]
Retrospective notes	[Key takeaways, improvements for next sprint]

Table 4.10: Sprint planning template

MVP architectural patterns

When developing an MVP, choosing the right architectural pattern is crucial to ensure scalability, maintainability, and rapid development. The architecture you select can significantly influence the success of your MVP by determining how well it can adapt to changes, handle user load, and integrate new features. Let us explore several architectural patterns that are particularly effective for MVPs.

Monolithic architecture

Monolithic architecture is the traditional approach where the entire application is built as a single, cohesive unit. All components are interconnected and managed as one codebase. Let us explore the advantages and challenges of this pattern:

Pros	Cons
Easy to develop and deploy initially, ideal for startups looking to launch quickly	Difficult to scale specific components independently
All components are in one place, simplifying management and debugging	As the application grows, making changes becomes more complex and risk-prone

| Better performance due to less overhead in communication between components | Limited flexibility in using different technologies for different parts of the application |

Table 4.11: *Monolithic architecture benefits*

For instance, a startup launching a simple e-commerce platform might choose a monolithic architecture to rapidly develop and deploy its MVP, focusing on delivering core features like product listings, cart management, and checkout.

Microservices architecture

Microservices architecture breaks down the application into small, independent services that communicate over APIs. Each service is responsible for a specific functionality. Let us explore the advantages and challenges of this pattern:

Pros	Cons
Individual services can be scaled independently based on demand	Requires robust management and coordination tools due to its distributed nature
Allows using different technologies and programming languages for different services	More complex deployment and monitoring processes
Issues in one service do not necessarily impact the entire system	Higher operational complexity

Table 4.12: *Microservices architecture benefits*

For example, a SaaS platform providing various tools for project management can benefit from microservices, where each tool (e.g., task management, time tracking, reporting) is a separate service that can be scaled and updated independently.

Serverless architecture

Serverless architecture relies on third-party services to manage server infrastructure. Developers focus solely on writing code, which runs in stateless containers that are triggered by events. Let us explore the advantages and challenges of this pattern:

Pros	Cons
Pay only for the compute resources used during execution	Initial execution may have a delay due to cold starts
Automatically scales with demand	Dependence on a specific cloud provider's service (vendor lock-in)
No need to manage server infrastructure	Limited control over infrastructure

Table 4.13: *Serverless architecture benefits*

A mobile app startup that requires backend services for user authentication, data storage, and notifications can use serverless architecture to quickly build and scale its MVP without worrying about server management.

Event-driven architecture

Event-driven architecture focuses on the production, detection, consumption, and reaction to events. It is particularly useful for applications that require real-time processing. Let us explore the advantages and challenges of this pattern:

Pros	Cons
Ideal for applications needing immediate responses to events	Requires a robust event management system
Each component can scale independently based on event load	Ensuring data consistency across distributed components can be challenging
Promotes a loosely coupled system where components communicate via events	Higher complexity in design and implementation

Table 4.14: Event-driven architecture benefits

If you are building a financial trading platform where real-time processing of transactions and market data is crucial, you can go for event-driven architecture to handle high volumes of events efficiently.

Layered (N-Tier) architecture

Layered architecture divides the application into layers, each with a specific responsibility, such as presentation, business logic, and data access. Let us explore the advantages and challenges of this pattern:

Pros	Cons
Each layer focuses on a specific aspect, making development and maintenance easier	Additional layers can introduce latency
Layers can be updated independently	Managing dependencies between layers can be challenging
Common functionalities can be reused across different parts of the application	Potential for increased complexity over time

Table 4.15: Layered architecture benefits

An educational platform providing online courses and assessments can use a layered architecture to separate user interfaces, business logic (e.g., course management), and data access (e.g., student records).

Testing and quality assurance

Effective QA processes help identify and rectify bugs, optimize performance, and enhance overall usability. By integrating rigorous testing strategies and continuous quality checks, startups can deliver a polished product that meets market demands and exceeds user expectations.

Need for quality assurance

QA ensures that the MVP delivers a reliable and satisfactory user experience. It involves systematic activities and processes designed to prevent defects and ensure that the product meets the required specifications and standards. A comprehensive testing strategy outlines the approach and methodologies for testing the MVP. It includes various types of testing, tools, and techniques to be used, along with the roles and responsibilities of the QA team.

Automated testing and manual testing

Automated testing involves writing scripts to execute tests automatically, saving time and effort. It is particularly effective for repetitive and regression testing. Here is an example of an automated testing workflow:

- **Write test scripts**: Use tools like Selenium or JUnit to write test cases.

- **Execute tests**: Run automated tests through CI/CD pipelines.

- **Review results**: Analyze test results and identify any failures.

- **Fix issues**: Developers address the issues, and tests are rerun to validate fixes.

On the other hand, manual testing is important for identifying usability issues and unexpected behaviors. There are two techniques for effective manual testing:

- **Exploratory testing**: QA testers actively explore the application to discover defects.

- **Usability testing**: Evaluate the user interface and experience to ensure it is intuitive and user-friendly.

For clarity and quality coverage, three types of tests must be included in the QA plan:

- **Unit tests**: Validate individual components or functions of the software.

- **Integration tests**: Ensure that different modules or services work together as expected.

- **End-to-end tests**: Simulate real user scenarios to test the complete flow of the application.

Bug tracking and management

Efficient bug tracking and management are vital for maintaining the quality and stability of the MVP. It involves recording, prioritizing, and resolving defects systematically:

- **Using tools like Jira, Trello, or Bugzilla**: These tools help in organizing and tracking bugs throughout the development process. They provide features for reporting bugs, assigning tasks, tracking progress, and maintaining communication within the team.

- **Bug bounty drives and war room testing**: Of late, product testing, bug bounty programs, and war rooms have proven to be highly effective techniques for conducting focused initiatives. War rooms are dedicated spaces where cross-functional teams collaborate intensively to tackle critical issues or drive key initiatives quickly and effectively. Encourage external testers and users to find and report bugs in exchange for rewards. Intensive testing sessions where the team works collaboratively to identify and fix critical issues.

Preparing for launch

A well-planned and executed launch strategy ensures that your product reaches the right audience, generates valuable user feedback, and establishes a strong market presence. By carefully considering each element of your launch plan, you can maximize your MVP's impact and set the stage for future success. This stage sets the tone for your product's market entry and can significantly influence its initial reception and long-term success. Here is how to approach this crucial phase.

Pre-launch checklist

Ensuring all features are ready and tested is paramount. This involves rigorous internal testing, bug fixing, and performance optimization. Each of the following features should be functional, and the overall user experience should be seamless:

- **Sign-off from internal stakeholders**: Before launch, it is essential to get approval from key internal stakeholders, including product managers, developers, and marketing teams. This ensures everyone is aligned and confident in the product's readiness.

- **Online versus offline marketing strategy**: Decide on a comprehensive marketing strategy that includes both online and offline elements. Online strategies may involve social media campaigns, email marketing, and SEO efforts. Offline strategies might include attending industry events, print advertising, and direct mail.

- **Finalizing marketing and launch plans**: Develop a detailed launch plan that outlines key activities, timelines, and responsibilities. This plan should cover everything from the launch announcement to post-launch follow-up activities.

Soft launch versus full launch

A soft launch involves releasing the MVP to a limited audience, allowing you to test the water and make necessary adjustments based on initial feedback. A full launch, on the other hand, targets a broader audience and requires more robust marketing efforts. Do not forget to pursue some of the tips listed as follows:

- **Create buzz**: Generate excitement through teaser campaigns, countdowns, and exclusive previews.

- **Leverage influencers**: Partner with industry influencers to amplify your reach and credibility.

- **Engage early adopters**: Offer incentives such as discounts or special access to attract early adopters who can provide valuable feedback and testimonials.

- **Clear messaging**: Ensure your product's value proposition is clear and compelling.

- **Support readiness**: Have a dedicated support team in place to handle any issues or questions that arise post-launch.

- **Track performance**: Use analytics tools to monitor the launch's success and identify areas for improvement.

Post-launch activities

The work does not end with the launch. Post-launch activities are critical for maintaining momentum and ensuring continuous improvement. Let us explore the top three activities immediately after the launch.

- **Feedback collection**: Actively seek feedback from your users through surveys, user reviews, and direct interactions. This feedback is invaluable for identifying strengths and areas for improvement.

- **Monitoring performance and user adoption metrics**: Track **key performance indicators (KPIs)** such as user engagement, retention rates, and conversion rates. These metrics help you understand how well your MVP is performing in the market.

- **Planning for future updates and enhancements**: Based on the feedback and performance data, prioritize and plan for future updates. Continuous improvement should be a core part of your product strategy to keep your users engaged and satisfied.

Importance of flexibility and adaptation

In the dynamic world of startups, the ability to remain flexible and adapt to changing market conditions, customer feedback, and technological advancements is crucial. Your MVP should not be a static entity but a dynamic model that evolves continually. The principles of Agile development, characterized by flexibility, responsiveness, and iterative progress, are not just methodologies but must be ingrained in the startup's culture.

Encouragement for startups

To all the entrepreneurs and startup teams embarking on this journey, remember that your path is unique, and while the challenges may be daunting, they are not insurmountable. Stay focused on your vision, but be willing to adapt your strategies as new learnings and insights emerge. Embrace the iterative nature of MVP development; each phase offers a learning opportunity and a step closer to achieving product-market fit.

Here are a few final tips:

- **Stay user-centric**: Always keep user feedback at the forefront of your development process. It is not just about building what you think they need, but truly understanding and solving their pain points.

- **Keep learning**: The tech landscape is perpetually evolving, and so should you. Continuous learning and adapting are not just for your product but also for your team and yourself.

- **Be patient and persevere**: Success may not come overnight, and your first MVP might not be a breakthrough. What is important is the iterative process and the continuous refinement based on actual user feedback and metrics.

Final call

A successful MVP launch requires attention to several critical details that can significantly impact its reception and performance:

- **Comprehensive testing**: Ensure all features are thoroughly tested in various scenarios. This includes usability testing, performance testing, and security testing to guarantee a smooth user experience.

- **Backup and recovery plans**: Prepare for any technical glitches by having robust backup and recovery plans. This ensures minimal downtime and data loss in case of unexpected issues.

- **Clear communication channels**: Establish clear communication channels for user support. This could be through email, chat support, or a dedicated support portal, ensuring users can easily reach out for help.

- **Legal and compliance checks**: Ensure your product complies with relevant legal and regulatory requirements. This includes data privacy laws, industry-specific regulations, and intellectual property rights.

- **Infrastructure readiness**: Ensure your infrastructure can handle the anticipated user load. Scalability is crucial to prevent crashes and slow performance, especially if the launch generates significant traffic.

Conclusion

Developing an MVP is a strategic process that balances speed, functionality, and user validation. An MVP should never be a static product, but must evolve based on industry trends, feedback, and technological advancements.

This chapter explored the key stages of MVP development, starting with identifying core features that address the primary problem. Prototyping helps visualize the concept, while tech readiness ensures the product is stable and scalable. Proper planning is crucial to aligning resources, timelines, and market positioning, while launch preparation sets the stage for gathering real-world feedback.

Each stage plays a vital role in refining the product before full-scale development. An effective MVP is not just about building a simplified version, but it is about testing assumptions, learning from users, and iterating quickly. By following a structured approach, startups and businesses can minimize risks, optimize resources, and create products that truly meet user needs. With a clear roadmap and a focus on continuous improvement, an MVP becomes a powerful tool for long-term success.

Points to remember

- **Defining core features**: Identifying what is crucial for your MVP and focusing on those elements first.

- **Prototyping**: Transitioning from low-fidelity to high-fidelity prototypes to refine your product's interface and interactions.

- **Technical readiness**: Preparing your development team and setting up your development environment to support robust and scalable MVP development.

- **MVP planning**: Addressing the strategic decisions around team structure, tool choices, and the balance between in-house development and third-party integrations.

- **Development and iteration**: Implementing Agile methodologies to foster rapid development and continuous iteration based on real-world feedback.

- **Preparing for launch**: Outlining the steps for a successful launch, from ensuring all systems are go to engaging with your audience and scaling based on demand.

Join our Discord space

Join our Discord workspace for latest updates, offers, tech happenings around the world, new releases, and sessions with the authors:

https://discord.bpbonline.com

CHAPTER 5
Building Blocks for MVP Development

Introduction

In the last chapter, we walked through the stages of an MVP from ideation to its launch. The journey from an idea to a successful product begins with a well-crafted MVP. The foundation you lay during the development stage is crucial, not only for validating your concept but also for setting the stage for scalability, adaptability, and long-term success.

Structure

In this chapter, we will cover the following topics:

- Key concepts
- Modern MVP landscape
- Forward-thinking leadership
- Product organization
- Tech infrastructure essentials
- Enhancing UX in SaaS product development
- Sales and marketing strategies for MVPs

- Futureproofing your MVP
- Key considerations for startup founders

Objectives

This chapter aims to provide startup founders, product managers, and technology leaders with a comprehensive guide to the essential components required for MVP development in the modern technological landscape. We will cover the technical, strategic, and organizational aspects that form the backbone of a successful MVP, ensuring that your product is not only viable but also poised for future growth and adaptability.

Key concepts

The following is the list of the key concepts covered in this chapter:

- Technology infrastructure essentials
- Tools and platforms for MVP development
- Team organization, hiring strategies, and roles alignment
- Designing a user-friendly interface
- Rollout strategies, feedback loops, sales, and marketing strategies
- Futureproofing the MVP
- Key considerations for entrepreneurs and startup founders

Modern MVP landscape

Traditionally, MVP development involves simple prototypes or basic versions of products designed to test fundamental assumptions with minimal features. This approach primarily relied on manual processes, limited use of data insights, and was often faced with significant scalability issues.

The product landscape has shifted since then. Customer expectations have evolved from being a passive user to being an active participant. At the same time, the product leaders are also watchful of factors like launch strategy, **user experience** (**UX**), tech robustness, and retention. This transition enables startups to create user-centric products. Whether it is a full-blown product or an MVP, customers look for the following elements:

- **Functionality**: *Does the MVP deliver on its objectives?* Even in its minimal form, the product must solve a specific problem for the customers.
- **Usability**: *Is the product easy to use and accessible?* A well-designed user interface and intuitive UX are critical for initial adoption.

- **Reliability**: Customers expect the MVP to be free of bugs and capable of handling expected usage loads.

- **Scalability**: Any new feature or enhancements in the product help gain the confidence of the customers.

- **Innovation**: *Is the product doing something new or doing something old in a new way?* Customers are drawn to MVPs that push the boundaries of what is possible, especially when leveraging new technologies like AI.·

Forward-thinking leadership

Remember, your MVP is not a makeshift solution. Neither is it meant to fully measure the depth of a problem. It requires a balance between technology and UX, while maintaining competitiveness and innovation. Forward-thinking leadership and product mindset play a role in driving success in this exercise. Let us explore the top five leadership elements that make this possible.

Product mindset

A product mindset emphasizes identifying core user needs, enabling prioritization of essential features that offer maximum value with minimal resources. This mindset encourages iterative development, where early user feedback shapes and refines the product. By keeping the end goal clear but adaptable, a product mindset helps bring a concept to life efficiently, setting a solid foundation for future growth.

Embracing change

Leaders who embrace change and stay abreast of technological advancements can better navigate the complexities of product development. They foster a culture of innovation, encouraging their teams to experiment with new tools and methodologies. This proactive approach ensures the organization can quickly adapt to evolving market conditions.

Data-driven decision making

Leverage data analytics to make informed decisions, optimize product features, and improve UXs. According to *McKinsey*[1], data-driven organizations are 23 times more likely to acquire customers and 19 times more likely to be profitable. This underscores the importance of integrating data analytics into the MVP development process.

---

1   Growth, Marketing & Sales Insights - **https://www.mckinsey.com/capabilities/growth-marketing-and-sales/our-insights**

Scalability, flexibility, and adaptability

MVPs must be designed for scale and flexibility for the long run. This involves architectural principles, technology stack, cloud scalability, and engineering precision. Forward-thinking prioritizes continuous learning and adaptation, staying informed about the latest industry trends and best practices. This mindset allows them to refine their strategies, improve their products, and maintain a competitive edge.

Product organization

In a relatively high-hustle environment of startups, swift product entry is much more than just an advantage. With limited resources and Lean teams, startups must navigate challenges by building a team of both specialists and generalists, each with clearly defined roles. Team growth depends upon a strategic approach to hiring and strong alignment between business objectives and team functions. This synergy ensures that every member contributes effectively, driving the startup towards its goals with agility and purpose.

Team organization at startups

Startups typically operate with Lean teams, which means each member often wears multiple hats and contributes across various functions. However, as you move from ideation to MVP development, it is essential to structure your team around core competencies that align with the MVP's needs. Let us take a look at the key roles in a product development team:

- **Chief (CXO)**: The head of technology, or a CTO in early-stage startups, is responsible for the technology stack, architecture, and overall technical direction. They ensure that the development process aligns with best practices and that the product is scalable and secure.

- **Product manager**: This role brings cross-functional teams together. The **product manager** (**PM**) is responsible for defining the product vision, prioritizing features, and ensuring that the product aligns with market needs and business goals.

- **Engineering**: Engineers and developers are the core executioners in the team, translating the product vision into a functional MVP. In startups, the division between frontend and backend roles might blur, with developers handling both ends as needed.

- **UI/UX designer**: In the MVP stage at startups, it is essential for product leaders to take ownership of UI/UX design. While it might seem logical to rely on a dedicated designer, the back-and-forth iterations can consume a significant amount of valuable time. As a product entrepreneur, you are uniquely positioned to understand and judge the customer's experience. This direct involvement ensures that the design aligns closely with the product vision and resonates with your target audience, ultimately saving time and leading to a more effective MVP.

- **Quality assurance (QA) specialist**: While a dedicated QA adds a good mix to the team, in the initial stage, the product leader or managers can take up the add-on responsibility to test the product for critical flows.

- **Growth hacker/marketing lead**: Nowadays, startups often outsource growth hacking and marketing activities. However, as a product leader or entrepreneur, it is crucial to personally validate the outreach strategy, including both **above the line** (ATL) and **below the line** (BTL) campaigns, to ensure they align with your product's goals and vision. ATL campaigns focus on mass marketing to build broad brand awareness through channels like TV, radio, and print media. BTL campaigns are highly targeted, aiming to drive specific customer actions or engagement through channels like email marketing, events, in-store promotions, and direct outreach. Together, they balance reach with precision in a well-rounded marketing strategy.

For early-stage startups, the above team structure may be too ambitious. It is recommended to begin with essential roles and expand as the company grows. The following table shows what roles are must-haves at the early stage of a startup:

Role	Must have/ Good to have	Key responsibilities	Skills required
PM	Good to have	Define product vision, prioritize features	Strategic thinking, communication, market knowledge
Chief/CTO	Must have	Technical direction, product mindset, and technology translator	Leadership, technical expertise, decision-making
Engineering	Must have	Quality coding	Coding skills, problem-solving
UX/UI designer	Good to have	Customer-centricity, UX, empathy	Design tools, user research, creativity
QA specialist	Good to have	Test case definition, rigorous testing	Attention to detail, testing frameworks
Growth hacker/ Marketing lead	Good to have	Drive user acquisition, early marketing efforts	Marketing, analytics, creativity

Table 5.1: Product team roles and responsibilities at startups

Hiring strategies for startups

Hiring the right people for the right roles at the right time is crucial. In startups, especially in the early stages, the luxury of extensive hiring may not be available. Your hiring strategy should align with your MVP development goals, focusing on bringing in individuals who are not only skilled but also a cultural fit and aligned with the startup's mission. Here are a few practical hiring tips for startups in the early stages:

- **Hire generalists early**: In the early stages, hiring generalists who can adapt to multiple roles is better than bringing in specialists. This gives flexibility to navigate the uncertainties and changing priorities of startup life.

- **Culture fit**: Given the small size of startup teams, cultural fit is equally important as technical skills. Look for individuals who come with an entrepreneurial mindset, are adaptable, and are aligned with the company's vision.

- **Leverage contract and freelance talent**: For roles that require specific expertise, consider bringing in interns or freelancers. This approach allows you to access high-level skills without long-term commitment, which can be particularly useful during the early phase.

CB Insights[2] (via Wikipedia's *Startup company* page) highlights that 23% of startups fail due to personnel or staffing problems. This statistic underscores the importance of building a team that is not only skilled but also aligned with the startup's goals.

Roles alignment and Agile practices

Once the team is on board, the next step is to ensure that roles are aligned with the product strategy and objectives. Talent management can be daunting as a founder pursuing certain objectives, so it is essential to focus on building the right mindset first. At startups, alignment is the key to ensuring that every team member is working towards the connected goals.

Roles with goals

As a founder, the positions you hire should neither have redundancy nor overlap. Alignment and clarity are needed for an individual to perform the responsibilities of their role. For product organization, here are the three points that will drive clarity and engagement:

- **Clear communication**: Daily connects, planning sessions, and retrospectives are the essentials to keep the team aligned. Tools like Slack and JIRA can facilitate communication and track progress. For early-stage startups, the product leader (or the CXO), must take control of communication and alignment.

- **Agile methodologies**: Implementing Agile practices like Scrum or Kanban can help keep the team focused on delivering value incrementally. This iterative approach allows for quick adjustments based on feedback, which is vital in the MVP development process.

- **Objective and Key Results (OKRs)**: Use OKRs to align the team around specific, measurable objectives. For example, a key result for a startup developing an MVP might be to achieve a certain number of active users within the first month of launch.

---

2   The Top 20 Reasons Startups Fail - **https://s3-us-west-2.amazonaws.com/cbi-content/research-reports/The-20-Reasons-Startups-Fail.pdf**

The following table includes key objectives and role alignment through the OKRs:

Objective	Key result	Role responsible
Launch MVP by Q2	Complete development of core features by Q1	Leadership and engineering
Achieving 1,000 active users in first month	Run targeted marketing campaign	Growth and marketing
Ensure MVP is user-friendly	Conduct three rounds of usability testing	Leadership and designers

Table 5.2: Sample OKR structure with the role mapping

In the high-stakes world of startups, a well-organized team with the right blend of skills and alignment is critical to the success of your MVP. By adopting practical hiring strategies, ensuring role alignment, and leveraging Agile methodologies, startups can enhance their ability to bring a successful MVP to market. The insights, templates, and examples provided in this section are designed to help startup founders and leaders build and manage teams that are not only capable but also aligned with the rapid, iterative nature of MVP development.

Tech infrastructure essentials

When building an MVP, the infrastructure you choose can significantly impact the product's development speed, scalability, and overall UX. This section explores the essentials of setting up tech infrastructure for an MVP, focusing on cloud infrastructure, startup approaches, dev tools selection, and UX.

Cloud infrastructure: Backbone of modern MVPs

In today's digital native industry, cloud infrastructure is largely a no-brainer for startups developing an MVP. It offers flexibility, scalability, and cost-effectiveness, which are crucial for early-stage ventures. Let us understand these advantages in detail:

- **Scalability**: Cloud platforms like AWS, Google Cloud, and Azure allow startups to scale their resources up or down based on demand. This elasticity ensures that your MVP can handle varying levels of user traffic without the need for significant upfront investment in hardware.

- **Cost-effectiveness**: The pay-as-you-go model of cloud services means you only pay for what you use. For startups, this is vital, as it keeps costs low while providing access to world-class infrastructure.

- **Security and compliance**: Major cloud providers invest heavily in security measures and compliance certifications, ensuring that your MVP meets industry standards for data protection and privacy.

Startup approach: Lean and Agile

Startups must adopt a Lean and Agile approach to infrastructure setup. This means starting small and iterating based on feedback rather than overcommitting to a complex infrastructure from day one.

Begin with a minimal viable infrastructure that supports your MVP's core features. As you gather user feedback and your user base grows, gradually scale and optimize your infrastructure.

Implementing **continuous integration and continuous deployment** (**CI/CD**) from the start can streamline the development process. Tools like Jenkins, CircleCI, and GitHub Actions allow for automated testing, integration, and deployment, which helps in maintaining a rapid development cycle. It is advisable to implement CI/CD automation as an activity parallel to the development and product-market fit efforts.

The following table gives a high-level view of a Lean infrastructure for early-stage startups:

Step	Action	Tool/Platform	Outcome
Initial setup	Deploy basic cloud infrastructure	AWS, Azure	Basic environment for MVP deployment
Automation	Implement CI/CD pipeline	Jenkins, CircleCI	Automated testing, integration, and deployment
Monitoring	Set up monitoring and alerts	Datadog, New Relic	Proactive issue detection and resolution
Scaling	Enable auto-scaling for cloud resources	AWS Auto Scaling, Kubernetes	Efficient handling of traffic spikes

Table 5.3: Sample Lean infrastructure at early-stage startups

Productivity tools

Selecting the right development tools is essential for boosting productivity and ensuring a smooth development process. Let us explore the tools needed to improve the dev productivity:

- **Version control**: Git, hosted on platforms like GitHub or GitLab, is a must for managing code changes, collaboration, and versioning.

- **Integrated development environments (IDEs)**: Tools like Visual Studio Code, IntelliJ IDEA, or PyCharm provide powerful code editing, debugging, and testing capabilities that streamline the development process.

- **Collaboration tools**: Slack for communication, Jira for task management, and Confluence for documentation help maintain a clear and organized workflow.

As per *Stackoverflow*[3], more than 87% of developers across the globe use Git for version control, highlighting its importance in modern development practices.

Development platforms and frameworks

Low-code and no-code platforms have become increasingly popular, allowing startups to build and test MVPs without deep technical expertise. These platforms are ideal for quickly validating ideas before investing in full-scale development. Although there are hundreds of such tools available for consumption, we will list down a few examples for reference:

- **Bubble**: Allows for building web applications with a drag-and-drop interface.

- **Airtable**: Combines the power of a database with a user-friendly interface to create workflows and simple applications.

- **Framer**: Design web landing pages with AI.

- Process automation platforms like *Automation Anywhere*.

  As per *Gartner*[4], the **low-code application platform** (**LCAP**) market is projected to reach $16.5 billion by 2027, growing at a 16.3% CAGR, offering strong opportunities for both established players and new entrants.

- **Tech stacks**: When deeper customization and control are required, traditional tech stacks offer the flexibility needed for complex MVPs.

- **LAMP stack**: (Linux, Apache, MySQL, PHP) A reliable and time-tested stack for building web applications. Ideal for startups that need a robust, scalable backend.

- **MERN stack**: (MongoDB, Express.js, React, Node.js) Popular among startups focused on developing single-page applications with a modern, dynamic user interface.

- **Modern stack**: Incorporating cloud-native technologies like *Kubernetes* for orchestration, *Docker* for containerization, and *Terraform* for infrastructure as code, provides startups with a scalable and flexible environment.

User experience and ensuring seamless interactions

One of the most critical aspects of MVP success is delivering a seamless and intuitive UX to customers. This sets your offering apart from off-the-shelf solutions provided by potential competitors. It is not just about look and feel; the experience should ensure ease of use, easy maintenance, and include subtle engagement nudges for customers. Let us check some of the key considerations for a great UX:

---

3   2022 Developer Survey - **https://survey.stackoverflow.co/2022/#section-version-control-version-control-systems**

4   Risk and Opportunity Index: Low-Code Application Platforms - **https://www.gartner.com/en/documents/5459763**

- **User research and insights**: This is a foundational step focusing on understanding user needs, behaviours, and pain points. Effective user research informs better design decisions, resulting in products that are both user-friendly and valuable.

- **Customer-centricity**: Empathize with users by incorporating their feedback early in the design process. For first-time developments, market research helps with feedback on existing products and the pain points. Tools like *Figma* or *Sketch* can be used for prototyping and testing UI designs before full-scale development.

- **Performance optimization**: Ensure your cloud infrastructure is optimized for low latency and high availability. Use **content delivery networks** (**CDNs**) like Cloudflare or AWS CloudFront to deliver content quickly to users around the globe.

- **Analytics and feedback loops**: Integrate tools like Google Analytics, Mixpanel, or Hotjar to gather insights into user behavior and feedback, enabling continuous UX improvement.

The tech infrastructure you choose for your MVP sets the foundation for your product's success. By adopting a Lean, scalable approach, leveraging cloud infrastructure, selecting the right development tools, and prioritizing UX, startups can create a robust and adaptable MVP. The modern tech landscape, with its emphasis on cloud computing, automation, and user-centric design, offers unprecedented opportunities for innovation and growth. However, it is essential to remain Agile, continually iterating and optimizing your infrastructure as your product evolves.

Enhancing UX in SaaS product development

Designing a **user interface** (**UI**) is not only about aesthetics, but also about creating a seamless UX that drives engagement, reduces friction, and ultimately leads to higher retention rates. As startups focus on building their MVPs, the emphasis on UI/UX design becomes crucial for delivering a product that resonates with users. This section explores practical strategies and best practices for designing a user-friendly interface that enhances UX in SaaS products.

Prioritizing simplicity and clarity

One of the key principles in UI/UX design for SaaS products is simplicity. A cLean, intuitive interface allows users to accomplish tasks with minimal effort and confusion. In the MVP stage, where resources are limited and the need for rapid development is paramount, simplicity should be a guiding principle. Let us go through three practical and fundamental inputs on UX simplicity:

- **Cognitive load**: Avoid loading the users with too many options or complex workflows. Each screen or interaction should focus on a single and clear objective.

- **Visual hierarchy**: Guide users' attention to the most important elements first. Use contrasting colors, fonts, and sizes to create a clear visual hierarchy.

- **Consistency**: Ensure that your design elements (buttons, icons, colors) are consistent throughout the product. This consistency helps users get accustomed to the product, predict how the product will behave, reducing the learning curve.

Consider the design approach of *Stripe*, a SaaS company that provides payment processing solutions. Stripe's interface is minimalistic yet powerful, with a clear focus on functionality. Their dashboard is designed to highlight key metrics and actions, making it easy for users to navigate and perform critical tasks without unnecessary clutter.

Responsive design for multi-platform access

Users are no longer categorized by the devices they own and use. Rather, the products must adopt a platform-agnostic design to provide a consistent experience. Be it desktops, tablets, or smartphones, ensuring that your MVP's interface is responsive and provides a consistent experience across all platforms is critical. Let us check the practical tips pertaining to the responsive design:

- **Adopt a mobile-first approach**: Design the interface with mobile users in mind first. This ensures that the most essential features are easily accessible on smaller screens. A mobile-first approach ensures that design prioritizes the users who access content via smartphones, leading to faster and more responsive experiences across all devices.

- **Test across devices**: Conduct testing on various devices and screen sizes to identify and fix issues related to responsiveness.

- **Optimize for touch interaction**: For mobile and tablet users, ensure that buttons and interactive elements are large enough to be tapped easily.

Productivity tools like Slack or Jira provide a responsive design. Whether accessed on a desktop or a smartphone, their interface adapts seamlessly, thereby providing a consistent experience regardless of the device.

Enhancing onboarding experience

The onboarding process is the first touchpoint of a user with your product that can significantly impact user adoption and retention rates. It is essential to guide users through the product's features and functionalities in a way that makes them feel intuitive and helpful. Let us go through the best practices that enhance the customer onboarding experience:

- **Interactive tutorials**: For SaaS products like ERPs, guided tours or interactive walkthroughs can help users understand key capabilities of the product.

- **Progress indicators**: If the onboarding requires multi-step processes, show the users how far they have come in the onboarding, making the experience feel less daunting. For example, for logo design products, capturing preferences is essential to achieve uniqueness.

- **Personalization**: Tailor the onboarding experience based on user roles or preferences to make it more relevant.

Social media tools like Loom offer an onboarding experience with a series of interactive tutorials that walk new users through creating their first design. This approach helps users quickly grasp the platform's capabilities, leading to faster adoption.

User feedback for continuous improvement

User feedback is a goldmine for refining the UI/UX of your SaaS product. Continuously gathering and analyzing feedback allows you to identify pain points and areas for improvement. Here are some tips on how to gather user feedback:

- **In-app surveys**: Use in-app surveys to gather real-time feedback from users while they interact with your product.

- **User testing**: Regularly conduct user testing sessions to observe how users interact with your interface and identify usability issues.

- **Iterative design process**: Implement an iterative design process where feedback is continuously incorporated into the UI/UX design.

Let us understand the feedback on the bookkeeping process through the following table:

Feedback source	Issue identified	Suggested improvement	Priority level
In-app survey	Navigation is confusing	Simplify menu structure	High
User testing	Buttons too small on mobile	Increase button size	Medium
Customer support	Difficult onboarding process	Add more tooltips and help options	High

Table 5.4: Sample bookkeeping template to capture user feedback

Measuring UI/UX success: Metrics and KPIs

To ensure that your efforts in designing a user-friendly interface are effective, it is crucial to track relevant metrics and KPIs that reflect user satisfaction and engagement. Let us understand what metrics to measure for UI/UX success:

- **User engagement**: Track metrics like **daily active users (DAU)** and **monthly active users (MAU)** to gauge how often users return to your product.

- **Conversions and drop off**: Measure the percentage of users who successfully complete key tasks within the product. Analyze the flow of a step where users drop out of the product.

- **Churn rate**: Monitor the rate at which users stop using your product to identify potential UX issues.

Designing a user-friendly interface is a critical component of MVP development, especially for SaaS products. By focusing on simplicity, ensuring responsiveness, enhancing onboarding experiences, leveraging user feedback, and tracking key metrics, startups can create a product that not only meets user needs but also delights them. The insights, examples, and templates provided in this section are intended to guide startups in building a SaaS MVP that stands out in today's competitive digital landscape.

Sales and marketing strategies for MVPs

The success of your project depends on how well it is built, the plan to launch it, and how you create interest to drive demand. The transition from development to market launch requires planning, feedback loops, and robust sales and marketing strategies. This section will delve into these critical components, providing insights into soft launches versus full-scale rollouts, creating buzz, and ensuring a successful launch.

Soft launch versus full-scale rollout

Soft launch: A soft launch involves releasing your MVP to a smaller, controlled audience before making it available to the broader market. Startups love soft launches as they give them progressive feedback, which can be worked upon in parallel before taking the product to a larger audience. Not only does it allow you to test the waters and gain real users, but it also gives customers time to understand what you are building. Let us understand the advantages of a soft launch:

- **Risk mitigation**: By launching to a smaller audience, you can identify and address any critical issues before a full-scale launch, minimizing the risk of a poor first impression.

- **Feedback gathering**: A soft launch provides an opportunity to gather valuable feedback from early adopters, which can be used to improve the product.

- **Cost-effective**: It allows you to test your marketing and sales strategies on a smaller scale, optimizing them before scaling up.

Full-scale rollout: A full-scale rollout involves launching your MVP to the entire target market simultaneously. This approach requires confidence in your product's stability and the readiness of your sales and marketing strategies. Thanks to open feedback on social media, full-scale rollouts are generally not recommended these days. The following are the points that may benefit the product with a full-scale launch:

- **Market penetration**: A full-scale rollout allows you to capture a larger market share quickly, which can be crucial in competitive industries.

- **Brand impact**: A well-executed full-scale launch can create significant brand awareness and establish your MVP as a major player in the market.

- **Revenue generation**: With a broader audience, the potential for higher revenue generation increases, making this a preferred strategy for well-prepared products.

Before opting for a full-scale rollout, ensure that your MVP is stable and addresses the key needs of your target audience. Analyzing market conditions is also crucial to determine the right time for a launch; for example, if competitors are preparing for similar launches, a soft launch may provide a competitive advantage. Additionally, consider resource allocation, as a full-scale rollout demands substantial marketing, customer support, and logistics. Make sure your startup is adequately equipped to handle the demands of a large-scale launch.

Here is a short and effective rollout strategy decision matrix:

Criterion	Soft launch considerations	Full-scale rollout considerations
Market readiness	Test market response	Capture large market share quickly
Product stability	Identify and fix issues	Confidence in product robustness
Budget	Lower initial costs	Higher upfront investment
Feedback loop	Early feedback for iteration	Broad feedback with higher stakes
Brand impact	Gradual build-up	Immediate, strong brand presence

Table 5.5: Decision matrix to determine the need for a full-scale rollout

Creating buzz and ensuring a successful launch

Treat your MVP as a product. Whether you are planning a soft launch or a full-scale rollout, a well-crafted sales and marketing strategy can make the difference between a successful launch and a missed opportunity.

B2C product launch planning

A B2C product launch needs the speed to reach a large consumer audience in no time. The outreach strategy must have a strong emphasis on offering, brand messaging, and UX. A successful B2C launch often leverages mass appeal and the ability to scale quickly. The following are strategies that you must look at while planning a B2C product launch:

- **Teaser campaigns**: Build anticipation with teaser campaigns that highlight the benefits and unique features of your MVP. Use social media, email marketing, and PR to generate excitement.

- **Influencer partnerships**: Collaborate with industry influencers to reach a broader audience and build credibility. Influencers can provide authentic endorsements that resonate with your target market.

- **Brand messaging**: Share your long-term vision, values, and mission through innovative methods, something that customers can connect to and relate with.

- **Beta programs**: Invite a select group of users to participate in a beta program. This not only generates buzz but also provides valuable feedback before the full launch.

- **Design your marketing engine**: The marketing engine operates with various levers, including ATL, BTL, TTL campaigns, targeted ads, affiliate marketing, and both online and offline channels. However, a product marketing engine must run with clearly defined objectives. For example, if the goal is visibility, brand building through PR and interviews might be the primary channels. Conversely, if the goal is to drive app installations or maximize foot traffic, different strategies will be required.

B2B product launch planning

A B2B product launch strategy requires a relationship-driven approach. It involves identifying key business decision-makers, building trust, and offering solutions to specific industry pain points. B2B launches often rely on direct sales, industry events, case studies, and long-term partnerships to generate leads. The focus is on demonstrating product value, ROI, and providing in-depth support for complex, tailored needs. The following two points are important in the B2B world:

- **Get the first customer**: B2B products are often driven by pain points that you or your network have experienced or communicated. Ideally, your first customer should be from within your network, as they can sign up to validate the flow and provide initial feedback.

- **Beta launch**: Leverage social media channels or email groups to invite beta sign-ups, offering credits or limited-time free usage in exchange. This beta group will support testing, provide feedback, and drive early conversions.

Other relevant launch techniques that are applicable for both B2C and B2B product lines could be:

- **Launch events**: Host a virtual or physical launch event to showcase your MVP. Use this platform to demonstrate key features, share your product vision, and engage with potential customers.

- **Content marketing**: Create content that educates your target audience about the problem your MVP solves and how it adds value. This can include blog posts, videos, webinars, and case studies.

- **Referral programs**: Implement a referral program that rewards users for bringing in new customers. This can help improve your reach quickly and cost-effectively.

Here is a quick go-to template to build a launch strategy:

Activity	Description	Timeline	Responsible
Teaser campaign	Social media posts, email teasers	2 months prior	Marketing
Influencer outreach	Identify and contact relevant influencers	1.5 months prior	PR/Marketing
Beta program	Select and onboard beta users	1 month prior	Product/Support
Content creation	Develop launch content (blogs, videos, etc.)	1 month prior	Content team
Launch event	Plan and execute the launch event	Launch day	Marketing/PR

Table 5.6: MVP launch strategy template

Post-launch activities

After your MVP is launched, the focus should shift to sustaining momentum, collecting feedback, and planning future updates. This phase is critical for maintaining user interest and ensuring long-term success.

Here is what you must do as the first step after product launch:

- **User reviews**: Encourage users to leave reviews and ratings, which provide social proof and valuable feedback.

- **Net promoter score (NPS)**: Implement NPS surveys to gauge user satisfaction and identify promoters who can become brand advocates.

Next comes the monitoring and planning for the future:

- **Adoption rate**: Track how quickly new users are adopting your MVP. A slow adoption rate may indicate a need for further product refinement or enhanced marketing efforts.

- **Churn rate**: Monitor the churn rate to identify potential issues that cause users to abandon your product. Use this data to inform updates and improvements.

- **Roadmap development**: Based on feedback and performance metrics, develop a roadmap for future updates. Prioritize enhancements that will deliver the most value to your users.

- **Continuous communication**: Keep your users informed about upcoming features and updates. Regular communication helps maintain engagement and sets expectations for the evolution of your product.

The journey from MVP development to a successful launch is a complex and multifaceted process that requires strategic planning, continuous feedback loops, and robust sales and marketing efforts. By understanding the nuances of soft launches versus full-scale rollouts, establishing effective feedback mechanisms, and executing well-crafted marketing strategies, startups can maximize the impact of their MVP and set the stage for sustained growth and success in the market.

Futureproofing your MVP

In today's rapidly evolving tech landscape, creating an MVP that can withstand technological advancements and market shifts is crucial for long-term success. Startups must build their MVPs with a forward-thinking mindset, ensuring that their products remain relevant and adaptable as new technologies emerge and market conditions change. This section will explore strategies for futureproofing your MVP and fostering a culture of continuous improvement and innovation within your team.

Preparing for technological advancements

As technology evolves, so do the users' expectations. To ensure your MVP remains competitive, it is essential to anticipate technological trends and incorporate flexibility into your product's architecture. From the early development cycles, the following considerations help MVP architecture scale and be adaptive during later stages:

- **API first approach**: Ensure the MVP is API-friendly so it can seamlessly connect with emerging tools, platforms, and external services.

- **Cloud-native approach**: Leverage cloud computing for scalability, security, and ease of adopting new technologies like AI, Blockchain, or IoT.

- **Data-driven adaptation**: Use analytics to track trends and guide future upgrades.

- **AI and automation readiness**: Build with the potential to incorporate AI, automation, and predictive tools.

- **Low-code and rapid development**: Utilize frameworks that support fast adaptation with minimal development effort.

- **Security and compliance**: Ensure adherence to regulations for smooth integration of new technologies.

Modular architecture for scalability

Building your MVP with a modular architecture allows you to add or replace components as needed without overhauling the entire system. For example, a SaaS platform built with microservices can easily integrate new features or services as technology advances.

Consider how **Amazon Web Services** (**AWS**) evolved its platform by continuously integrating new services and features without disrupting existing offerings. This modular approach enabled them to stay ahead of the competition.

Leverage AI and machine learning judiciously

Assess the suitability of AI use cases in the product. Your product may not necessarily need AI capabilities until it scales to a level where automated intelligence becomes a key driver.

Artificial intelligence (**AI**) and **machine learning** (**ML**) are transforming industries. Embedding AI capabilities into your MVP can future-proof your product by enhancing UXs through personalization, automation, and predictive analytics.

Cloud-native development

Cloud-native development enables your MVP to scale quickly and efficiently. By utilizing cloud platforms like AWS, Azure, or Google Cloud, startups can take advantage of the latest technological advancements without the overhead of managing physical infrastructure.

Focus on cloud services that offer scalability, security, and compliance, ensuring your MVP can grow alongside your user base. The following table gives a tentative plan of technology expansion and optimization on the public cloud. This is based on certain assumptions like product-market fit, user adoption, and growth trajectory.

Timeframe	Technology focus	Action items	Expected outcome
0-6 Months	Modular architecture	Implement microservices	Flexibility for future features
6-12 Months	AI and ML integration	Integrate AI for user personalization	Enhanced UX
12-18 Months	Cloud optimization	Migrate to cloud-native infrastructure	Scalability and cost-efficiency

Table 5.7: *Cloud expansion and optimization plan*

Strategies for continuous improvement and iteration

Continuous improvement is a necessity for startups aiming to stay relevant in a competitive market. By fostering a culture of continuous iteration and innovation, you can ensure your MVP evolves alongside your customers' needs and industry trends.

For early-stage startups, continuous improvement is the default approach. It begins with experimentation based on assumptions, followed by refinement through user feedback. A rigid, one-time launch can quickly become obsolete, making iteration and adaptability essential for long-term success.

Early user feedback, data-driven insights, and Agile practices can help startups refine their products, enhance UX, and build a strong market fit. Continuous improvement allows founders to identify inefficiencies, test new ideas with minimal risk, and scale their solutions based on real-world usage.

Implementing Agile methodologies

Agile development allows for iterative progress, where teams can continuously adapt and improve the MVP based on user feedback and market demands. This approach fosters rapid iteration and keeps the product aligned with customer expectations.

For instance, *Spotify* uses a unique blend of Agile methodologies to maintain continuous delivery and iteration. Their *product squads* work autonomously, allowing for rapid experimentation and innovation.

Regular retrospectives and feedback loops

Regular retrospectives are critical for evaluating what worked well, identifying challenges, and refining processes for future iterations. By conducting post-launch reviews, teams can systematically apply lessons learned, fostering a culture of continuous improvement. Additionally, establishing strong feedback loops with customers through surveys, NPS, and in-app analytics ensures ongoing insight collection. These real-time inputs help startups make data-driven decisions, prioritize feature enhancements, and address pain points effectively, ultimately leading to a more refined and user-centric product.

Fostering a culture of innovation

For early-stage startups, experimentation is not just a growth strategy; it is the key to survival. In a competitive market, replicating existing solutions may have a short-term life, but true success comes from solving customer problems in an impactful way.

Startups that embrace experimentation can uncover breakthrough innovations that set them apart from copycat products, which merely mimic competitors without adding real value. By fostering a culture where calculated risks are encouraged, teams can test bold ideas, refine their approach based on user feedback, and build a product that resonates with the users.

Organizing internal hackathons and innovation sprints further accelerates this process, allowing startups to explore new technologies and creative solutions that could shape their product roadmap and establish a lasting market presence.

The following table shows a sprint plan with the success criteria for each sprint:

Iteration cycle	Improvement focus	Actions	Metrics for success
Sprint 1	**User interface (UI)**	Gather user feedback, update UI elements	Increase in user satisfaction
Sprint 2	Feature enhancement	Add requested features, refine existing	Reduced churn rate
Sprint 3	Performance optimization	Optimize load times, reduce latency	Improved app performance metrics

Table 5.8: Sample sprint plan structure with success criteria

Setting the stage for future success

To ensure long-term success, startups must not only focus on the present but also prepare for the future. This involves setting up a foundation that allows for scalability, flexibility, and continuous innovation:

- **Design for scalability**: Ensure your tech stack and architecture are designed to handle increased load as your MVP grows. This includes scalable databases, cloud services, and load-balancing techniques. For example, Zoom was able to scale rapidly during the COVID-19 pandemic because of its robust, scalable infrastructure, which could handle the sudden surge in users.

- **Break down silos**: Foster collaboration across different teams—development, marketing, sales, and customer support, to ensure all aspects of the MVP are aligned with the business goals and customer needs. For example, *Atlassian* promotes cross-functional collaboration through tools like *Jira* and *Confluence*, which facilitate communication and project management across teams.

- **Invest in learning**: Encourage continuous learning within your team by providing access to courses, conferences, and industry events. Staying informed about the latest trends and technologies is key to maintaining a competitive edge. Be ready to pivot or adapt your product based on market feedback or shifts in technology. The ability to adapt quickly is a hallmark of successful startups.

The following table shows a 12 to 18-month plan for the product teams to grow their skills and establish cross-functional collaboration:

Timeframe	Focus area	Actions	Expected outcome
0 - 6 months	Scalability	Implement scalable cloud infrastructure	Support for increased user load
6 - 12 months	Cross-functional collaboration	Establish regular cross-team workshops	Improved product alignment
12 - 18 months	Continuous learning	Provide team access to industry certifications	Enhanced team skills and knowledge

Table 5.9: Sample plan to nurture skills within the product teams

In the digital, cloud, and AI age, futureproofing your MVP requires a strategic approach that incorporates flexibility, scalability, and continuous innovation. By adopting the right technologies, fostering a culture of iteration and improvement, and preparing your team for future challenges, you can build an MVP that not only meets current market demands but also thrives in the face of technological advancements and market shifts.

Key considerations for startup founders

In the process of MVP development, entrepreneurs and startup founders must consider several critical aspects *beyond* just technology and product design. Financial planning, legal compliance, customer engagement, and scaling strategies are all essential components that contribute to the success of an MVP. This section will delve into these areas, providing practical guidance, insights, and examples to help startups navigate these challenges effectively.

Financial planning and budgeting

Effective financial planning is crucial for ensuring that your startup can sustain itself through the MVP development stage and beyond. A well-structured budget allows you to allocate resources wisely, prioritize spending, and avoid financial pitfalls that could jeopardize your project.

For early-stage startups, financial control and tracking are non-negotiable. Various areas, such as marketing, outreach, and customer service, often reveal potential fund leakage points. Without thoughtful planning and proper tracking, capital can deplete quickly. Smart financial planning and budgeting ensure that funds are allocated efficiently, risks are managed proactively, and the startup stays on the path to profitability.

Key components of financial planning

In this section, we will cover two essential components of financial planning in a startup setup, *budgeting* and *forecasting*:

- **Budgeting the MVP development**: Startups should strategically allocate funds across key areas such as development, marketing, testing, and operational costs while ensuring a contingency fund is in place for capital flow and unexpected expenses. A balanced budget helps maintain financial stability and supports sustainable growth. For example, a SaaS startup might distribute its budget with 40% allocated to development, 20% to marketing, 20% to customer acquisition, and the remaining 20% for operations and contingencies, ensuring flexibility to adapt to unforeseen challenges.

- **Financial forecasting**: Utilizing financial forecasting tools helps in projecting revenues, expenses, and cash flow, helping startups understand their fund utilization and make informed funding decisions. Use platforms like *QuickBooks* or *Wave* to create forecasts based on various growth scenarios.

The following table shows a budget allocation plan across various categories or departments. You can tweak or calibrate the allocation based on different stages of the product journey.

Budget category	Allocated funds	Percentage of total budget	Notes
Development	$50,000	40%	Includes salaries, tools, etc.
Marketing and customer acquisition	$25,000	20%	Digital marketing, PPC, etc.
Testing and QA	$15,000	12%	Automated/manual testing
Operations	$20,000	16%	Hosting, tools, admin costs
Contingency	$15,000	12%	Unforeseen expenses

Table 5.10: *Sample budget allocation at a startup*

Financial tools and techniques for startups

Startups should leverage financial tools that are tailored to their needs, offering simplicity and scalability as the business grows. Let us take a look at some of these tools:

- **Accounting software**: *QuickBooks, Xero,* and *FreshBooks* are popular for managing finances, tracking expenses, and generating reports.

- **Financial modelling**: Tools like *LivePlan* and *Finmark* can help in building detailed financial models, especially useful for startups seeking investment.

- **Expense management**: Tools like *Expensify* and *Brex* help in managing business expenses and optimizing cash flow.

Many successful startups use a combination of these tools to streamline their financial operations and maintain a clear view of their financial health. For example, Buffer, a social media management tool, used Xero for accounting and financial management during its early stages.

Legal and compliance issues

Navigating legal and compliance issues is crucial to avoid potential pitfalls that could derail your startup's progress:

- Choose the right legal structure (e.g., LLC, C-Corp) based on your business model and growth plans. Airbnb initially incorporated as an LLC but later switched to a C-Corp as it expanded and sought venture capital.

- Protect your startup's IP by filing for trademarks, patents, and copyrights as necessary.

- Ensure compliance with industry-specific regulations, data privacy laws (e.g., GDPR), and tax obligations. Fintech startups must adhere to stringent regulations like **Know Your Customer** (**KYC**) and **anti-money laundering** (**AML**).

Customer engagement, brand, and community building

Building a strong community around your MVP can drive user adoption, provide valuable feedback, and create brand advocates.

Here are some strategies to achieve this:

- **Early access programs**: Offer early access to your MVP to a select group of users in exchange for feedback.

- **Community platforms**: Use platforms like *Discord, Slack, or Facebook Groups* to engage with your early users, gather insights, and foster a sense of community.

- **Content marketing**: Share valuable content related to your product's niche to build trust and authority.

Scaling and growth strategies

Once your MVP gains traction, scaling effectively is key to sustaining growth and maintaining a competitive edge.

Here are some strategies to achieve this:

- **Product-led growth**: Focus on delivering exceptional UXs that drive organic growth through word-of-mouth and user referrals.

- **Partnerships and alliances**: Collaborate with complementary businesses to expand your reach and capabilities.

- **Data-driven scaling**: Use analytics to understand user behavior, optimize your product, and identify new growth opportunities.

Startups must approach MVP development with a comprehensive strategy that includes robust financial planning, legal and compliance readiness, and strong customer engagement. By leveraging the right tools and strategies, founders can navigate the complexities of early-stage development and position their startups for sustained growth and success. As you move forward in your MVP journey, remember that the foundations you build now will set the stage for your future success.

Conclusion

In this chapter, we have explored the key components necessary to build a scalable, adaptable, and future-ready MVP. From picking up the right technology infrastructure and development tools to nurturing a team and designing a user-friendly interface, each aspect plays a role in shaping a successful product.

We also covered rollout strategies, feedback loops, and effective marketing approaches to ensure a strong launch. Additionally, we discussed financial planning, compliance, and future-proofing strategies to help entrepreneurs navigate the complexities of MVP development. By integrating these foundational elements, startups can build an MVP that meets current market needs and is positioned for long-term growth.

Points to remember

- **Choose the right tech stack**: Select a scalable and maintainable technology stack that aligns with your team's expertise.

- **Prioritize UX**: Design intuitive interfaces to enhance engagement and retention.

- **Leverage Agile development**: Use prototyping tools, CI/CD pipelines, and feedback loops for rapid iterations.

- **Plan the rollout**: Implement soft launches, targeted marketing, and data-driven refinements.

- **Ensure financial and legal preparedness**: Maintain a Lean budget, secure funding wisely, and adhere to regulatory compliance.

CHAPTER 6
MVP Execution

Introduction

In the previous chapter, we established the foundational principles of MVP development, starting with a clear problem statement, prioritizing features, and building Lean. This chapter builds on that foundation by zooming in on the execution.

MVP design patterns are the essential strategies that guide how an MVP is structured and brought to reality. These patterns serve as blueprints for building a functional product efficiently while keeping the user's needs at the forefront. Whether it is simulating a service manually or combining existing tools to test functionality, design patterns help startups focus their efforts where it matters most, i.e., delivering value and learning quickly.

This chapter explores the practical techniques and frameworks for designing and executing MVPs. By breaking down well-established patterns and illustrating their applications, it equips you with tools to minimize risk, maximize learning, and accelerate time-to-market. Additionally, the chapter addresses how startups at different stages, early-stage or growth, can adapt these patterns to their unique circumstances.

Structure

In this chapter, we will cover the following topics:

- MVP design patterns
- Types of design patterns
- MVP design patterns for early-stage startups
- MVP design patterns for growth startups
- Key considerations for early and growth stages

Objectives

This chapter introduces key MVP design patterns and how to apply them effectively. We will explore popular patterns, learn when to use each based on your startup stage, and understand how to adapt and evolve them as your product grows.

By the end of this chapter, we will explore what design patterns are, why they are essential for successful MVP execution, and the role these patterns play in structuring your product development process. We will delve into examples of popular MVP design patterns such as concierge MVPs, Wizard of Oz MVPs, and piecemeal MVPs. Additionally, we will examine industry case studies where these patterns were effectively applied. We will identify which patterns are most suitable for early-stage startups facing limited resources and high uncertainty. We will discover how growth-stage startups can scale and refine their MVP strategies to broaden their market reach. We will understand how to choose the right pattern based on your hypothesis, resources, and user needs, and gain insights into transitioning from one pattern to another as your product evolves.

Whether you are launching a new product for the first time or expanding an existing offering, this chapter provides practical guidance for every step of the process. With real-world examples, actionable insights, and industry best practices, it aims to empower you to make informed decisions that keep your MVP on track.

Let us learn about various MVP design patterns that help you turn the product vision into reality with efficiency and confidence.

MVP design patterns

MVP design patterns simplify product creation and help focus your efforts on delivering core value while minimizing waste. Let us examine what MVP design patterns are, why they matter, and when to recognize their use.

MVP design patterns are structured approaches for developing a product that satisfies its minimum viable criteria. Think of them as blueprints for innovation; they guide you in building something functional and meaningful without getting bogged down in unnecessary complexities.

The following are the key characteristics of MVP design patterns:

- **Focused on validation**: They aim to test critical assumptions with the least effort.

- **Iterative by nature**: Patterns are adaptable and evolve based on feedback.

- **Resource conscious**: They prioritize efficiency in time, money, and effort.

Think of the MVP design patterns as the starter recipes. Whether you are making a pizza dough or sourdough bread, they help you get started without needing every tool or ingredient in a fully stocked bakery.

The following figure highlights how MVP design patterns benefit startups:

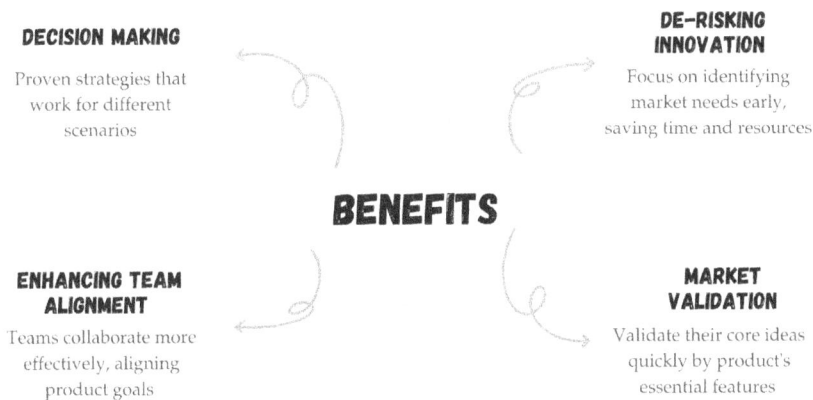

DECISION MAKING

Proven strategies that work for different scenarios

DE-RISKING INNOVATION

Focus on identifying market needs early, saving time and resources

BENEFITS

ENHANCING TEAM ALIGNMENT

Teams collaborate more effectively, aligning product goals

MARKET VALIDATION

Validate their core ideas quickly by product's essential features

Figure 6.1: How MVP design patterns benefit startups

When to use

Knowing when to apply MVP design patterns is vital to their success. Here are scenarios where they come in handy:

- **Early product development**: When you have an idea but lack clarity about your target audience or their needs, the design patterns provide focus. A concierge MVP manually delivers a service to understand user pain points deeply. A prototype MVP uses mock-ups to gather usability feedback before building anything substantial.

- **Entering a new market**: When expanding to relatively newer customer segments or regions, patterns can help validate demand with minimal investment.

- **Localized webpage (landing page MVP)**: A localized webpage can help you test and gauge the market interest. Similarly, a piecemeal pattern can be used to combine existing tools to provide a quick solution tailored to the new market. Startups try this to gauge early interest by profiling their services, podcasts, blogs, or sign-up forms.

- **Limited resources or time constraints**: Startups often operate with tight budgets and deadlines. MVP design patterns maximize impact without overburdening resources. The Wizard of Oz MVP pattern helps simulate automation to give users a real experience while you work behind the scenes.

- **Scaling existing products**: As a product gains traction, MVP patterns can help test and refine new features or extensions. The social media app Instagram launched its app with just photo editing and filters, a *Single-Feature MVP*. Only after user feedback did they expand into messaging and video sharing.

As a quick reference, the following table shows the fitment of MVP patterns to the scenarios:

Scenario	Recommended pattern	Purpose
Exploring market demand	Landing page MVP	Validate interest with minimal effort.
Testing usability or workflow	Prototype MVP	Gather feedback on user experience.
Simulating functionality	Wizard of Oz MVP	Test complex ideas without full builds.
Personalized insights	Concierge MVP	Engage users directly for deep insights.
Rapid iteration on features	Single-Feature MVP	Focus on refining one critical function.

Table 6.1: MVP pattern selection based on scenario

Types of design patterns

Let us get into the details of the MVP design patterns. Each pattern offers distinct advantages, challenges, and real-world applications, enabling startups and businesses to find the right fit for their specific context.

Concierge MVP

The concierge MVP is akin to providing a highly personalized service where the creator performs tasks manually to simulate an automated system. Imagine you are testing a meal subscription service. Instead of building a full-fledged platform, you directly curate meal plans and deliver them yourself based on user preferences.

This pattern allows you to gain rich, qualitative insights by observing your customers closely. It emphasizes understanding their needs deeply before investing in automation. Zappos, an online retailer, famously tested its idea by manually purchasing shoes from local stores to fulfill the online demand. This hands-on approach not only validated the need but also provided invaluable customer insights.

This approach can be labor-intensive and does not scale easily. Its strength lies in the depth of customer interaction, making it an excellent choice for early-stage startups looking to validate niche ideas.

Case study one

Consumers often face difficulties finding the right products quickly, leading to a frustrating shopping experience. Retailers need a way to offer personalized assistance to enhance customer satisfaction and increase conversion rates.

Key takeaways are as follows:

- This MVP will be manually operated to test user demand and gather insights before automation.

- A human assistant provides tailored product suggestions based on user input. The assistant helps users with placing orders, applying discounts, and selecting delivery options.

- Create scripts and guidelines for the concierges to follow during customer interactions. Continuously collect and analyze feedback from users to improve the service.

- Calculate the cost per interaction and assess the financial viability of scaling the service. Based on the insights, plan for automating parts of the service (e.g., chatbot integration).

- Develop a plan for scaling the service to more users, possibly transitioning to a hybrid model combining human and automated assistance.

Wizard of Oz MVP

The Wizard of Oz MVP involves creating a façade of functionality while the underlying processes are handled manually. Think of it as the product equivalent of the famous line from the Wizard of Oz, *pay no attention to the man behind the curtain.*

Dropbox leveraged this pattern in its early days with a video demo showcasing a seamless cloud storage solution. Behind the scenes, there was no fully functional product, but the demo was enough to test demand and gather feedback from potential users.

This approach is ideal for testing complex concepts without the need for full-scale development. The main challenge lies in transparency; users should not feel deceived when they discover the product's actual capabilities. For startups aiming to validate ambitious ideas with limited resources, the Wizard of Oz pattern strikes a compelling balance between realism and feasibility.

Case study two

A startup is developing an AI-powered personal shopping assistant but lacks the resources to build a fully functional AI system for the MVP phase. They need to validate the idea, gather user feedback, and test market demand with minimal investment in technology development. Key takeaways are as follows:

- Instead of building the AI, use human operators behind the scenes to perform tasks that the AI would eventually handle. Users interact with what appears to be an AI system, but the responses are generated manually by the team.

- By simulating the AI, the startup can observe how users interact with the system, what features they value, and what improvements are needed, all without the high upfront cost of AI development.

- Test the viability of the product concept by seeing if users find value in the AI-powered shopping assistant and determine if the product meets their needs and expectations.

- Use feedback from users to iteratively refine the experience, ensuring the final product aligns closely with user needs before investing in building the actual AI technology.

- Avoid expensive and time-consuming AI development at the early stages, reducing financial risk and allowing for more Agile adjustments based on user input.

Piecemeal MVP

The piecemeal MVP combines existing tools and technologies to create a functioning product without building everything from scratch. Instead of reinventing the wheel, you piece together readily available solutions. For instance, you might use *Typeform* for surveys, *Stripe* for payments, and Google Sheets for data management to simulate a solution to a frequently faced problem.

In its early days, *Airbnb* adopted this approach to list properties and attract its first customers. This allowed them to focus on understanding market demand and user preferences without incurring significant development costs.

The piecemeal MVP is cost-effective and quick to implement, but it may face limitations in customization and scalability. Its strength lies in its ability to get you to market quickly while validating your core value proposition.

Case study three

A startup aims to launch an online platform for selling organic produce directly from farmers to consumers. With limited resources, the founders are considering a piecemeal MVP approach to validate the business idea. Instead of building a full-fledged platform from scratch, they plan to leverage existing tools and services to create a functional prototype quickly and at a lower cost. Let us explore how a startup can use a piecemeal MVP approach to validate its business model while minimizing development time and costs.

Key takeaways are as follows:

- Use platforms like *Shopify* or *WordPress* to set up the initial online store.

- Utilize third-party logistics and payment gateways like *Razorpay* or Stripe to handle payments.

- Initially, handle processes like order management, customer service, and inventory updates manually or through basic tools like Google Sheets, allowing focus on core business validation.

- Prioritize the essential features needed to test the core value proposition, such as listing products, order checkout, and deliveries, and defer complex features like automated inventory management.

- Launch quickly with the piecemeal solution and collect user feedback to understand their needs and refine the product accordingly, ensuring resources are allocated based on real user demands.

- Leverage social media and content marketing for initial outreach instead of investing in large-scale advertising to build awareness and attract early adopters within budget constraints.

Single-Feature MVP

The Single-Feature MVP focuses on delivering one critical feature that addresses a specific user need. This approach minimizes complexity while providing users with a clear and compelling value proposition. Instagram is a prime example of this pattern. When it was launched, its sole focus was on enabling users to take, edit, and share photos with filters.

By concentrating on a single feature, startups can refine the user experience and messaging around their core offering. This approach is particularly effective in competitive markets where differentiation is essential. The challenge, however, lies in ensuring that this single feature is sufficiently valuable to attract and retain users.

Case study four

A startup aims to develop a task management app but wants to test the market with a Single-Feature MVP focusing solely on task creation and reminders. The goal is to validate the core functionality before expanding to other features like collaboration, tagging, or analytics.

Key points are as follows:

- Focus on the essential functionality that addresses the primary user need. In this case, task creation and reminders.

- Ensure the feature is intuitive and provides a seamless user experience. Gather user feedback early to refine the functionality.

- Limit the scope to accelerate development and deployment, allowing for rapid testing and iteration.

- Design the architecture to easily integrate additional features in the future without major refactoring.

- Implement basic analytics to track user interaction with the single feature, providing insights for future development. Allocate resources efficiently, focusing on the core feature while minimizing costs and effort on non-essential elements.

- Establish a robust feedback mechanism to collect user opinions, which will guide further development and feature expansion.

Landing page MVP

A landing page MVP involves creating a simple website or online presence to gauge user interest and collect feedback. It is a lightweight way to validate demand and test messaging before building the actual product. For example, Buffer used a landing page to explain its value proposition and gauge interest. Visitors who clicked on the **Sign Up** button were informed that the product was not ready yet, and their email addresses were collected for follow-up.

This pattern allows you to test multiple variations of your value proposition using A/B testing tools like *Optimizely* or *Google Optimize*. The landing page MVP is cost-effective and data-driven, but it is limited in gathering insights about product usability.

Case study five

You are tasked with designing an MVP landing page for a new retail-tech startup that aims to streamline online shopping experiences. The landing page must effectively communicate the value proposition, capture leads, and be simple enough to develop quickly while leaving room for future enhancements. Key points accelerated are as follows:

- Communicate the core value of the retail store with concise headlines and subheadings. Use a cLean layout with a visual hierarchy to guide users to key information and **call-to-action** (**CTA**).

- Keep the design simple to ensure quick development and fast loading. Ensure the page is mobile-friendly by using responsive design principles.

- Highlight CTAs like *Sign Up* or *Learn More* to make them visually prominent and easily accessible.

- Include a short lead capture form to gather essential user information. Display testimonials or early adopter logos to build trust and credibility.

Prototype MVP

A prototype MVP focuses on creating a low-fidelity, interactive version of the product to test usability and gather feedback. This approach is especially useful for testing workflows, design elements, and user interaction before committing to full-scale development.

Figma exemplifies this approach. Before launching its collaborative design tool, it created prototypes to showcase how users could work together on designs in real time. This allowed the team to refine the concept based on actual user feedback before developing the platform further.

Prototypes can range from simple wireframes to more interactive models created using tools like *Figma, Adobe XD,* or *InVision.* However, while they are excellent for testing user experience, prototypes might not reveal challenges related to backend functionality or scalability.

Case study six

A startup aims to launch an innovative mobile app for meal planning that integrates AI to suggest personalized recipes based on user preferences and available ingredients. They need to create a prototype MVP to validate their concept, but have limited time and budget.

Key takeaways are as follows:

- Identify the essential features that solve the primary user problem. For the app, this could be allowing users to input available ingredients and generating personalized recipe suggestions.

- Use no-code/low-code platforms, wireframes, or clickable prototypes to quickly create and iterate on the MVP without heavy technical investment.

- Launch the prototype to a small, targeted audience (e.g., environmentally conscious users) and collect qualitative and quantitative feedback through surveys and usage data.

- Define KPIs such as user engagement, sign-up rates, or task completion times to evaluate the MVP's performance and determine whether to pivot, persevere, or scale.

- Use the prototype to convey the broader vision of the app to early adopters and stakeholders, ensuring that their input aligns with the long-term product goals.

Choosing the right MVP pattern

Each MVP design pattern serves a specific purpose, aligning with different stages of product development and varying business goals. The concierge MVP and Wizard of Oz patterns are ideal for deep qualitative insights during early validation. Piecemeal and Single-Feature patterns help build and test functional solutions rapidly. Landing pages and prototype MVPs are excellent for market demand testing and user experience validation.

Selecting the right pattern depends on your resources, the nature of your hypothesis, and your intended audience. By leveraging these patterns thoughtfully, startups can navigate uncertainty with clarity and purpose, accelerating their journey from idea to impact.

MVP design patterns for early-stage startups

Early-stage startups operate in a unique environment of high uncertainty and limited resources. The challenge is to balance speed with learning, all while creating something that resonates with users. MVP design patterns, when adapted effectively, can be the perfect ally in this high-stakes journey. This section explores the unique challenges faced by early-stage startups, the most suitable MVP patterns, and actionable strategies to overcome barriers.

Common challenges

Early-stage startups are the embodiment of the *unknown*. Here is a breakdown of the key challenges startups must encounter:

- **Limited resources**: A CB Insights report [1] cites that 38% of startups fail due to running out of money. Startups often operate with small teams, minimal funding, and little time. Every dollar and minute spent must contribute directly to learning or growth.

- **High uncertainty**: Founders rarely have a complete understanding of their target market or product fit. Hypotheses around the problem, audience, and solutions are often untested. Startups are vulnerable to pursuing ideas based on intuition rather than data, leading to potential misalignment with user needs.

- **Building credibility**: As newcomers, startups need to earn users' trust. Unlike established brands, they cannot rely on reputation or an existing customer base to drive adoption.

- **Pressure for speed**: In competitive industries, being first or fastest to market can be critical. Delays in testing or development may result in missed opportunities or the loss of relevance.

Recommended MVP patterns

Startups in their early stages benefit from MVP patterns that maximize learning with minimal investment. These patterns ensure a strong foundation without overextending resources.

Here are some recommended MVP patterns for early-stage startups:

- **Concierge MVP**: A manual version of the product or service allows startups to engage with early users, gather qualitative insights, and validate demand without investing in

---

1   The Top 12 reasons startups fail - **https://www.cbinsights.com/research/report/startup-failure-rea-sons-top/**

infrastructure. Testing new service ideas like a personal shopping assistant or fitness coaching app.

- **Wizard of Oz MVP**: Allows teams to **test core assumptions** without investing heavily in building a fully automated system. With a mocked-up backend, startups can focus on what matters most, validating whether users truly want the solution.

- **Landing page MVP**: A simple webpage that explains the product concept and collects user interest through sign-ups, click-throughs, or waitlists.

  It also helps in building an early user base or community before the product is even launched. Ultimately, it is a smart way to de-risk product development and attract potential investors or partners with real user data.

- **Single-Feature MVP**: Focusing development on one core feature that addresses the most critical user need.

  It keeps complexity low while demonstrating the product's primary value. Instagram initially focused solely on photo-sharing with filters. Launching in competitive markets where differentiation hinges on one standout feature.

Best practices

Spotify's pitch was initially framed as *Netflix for Music*. Early-stage startups can create a clear path from concept to validation using MVP design patterns. The focus remains on learning quickly, spending wisely, and iterating confidently, turning nascent ideas into products with genuine market impact.

Here are a few handy techniques that can help startups optimize time and effort in the initial phase:

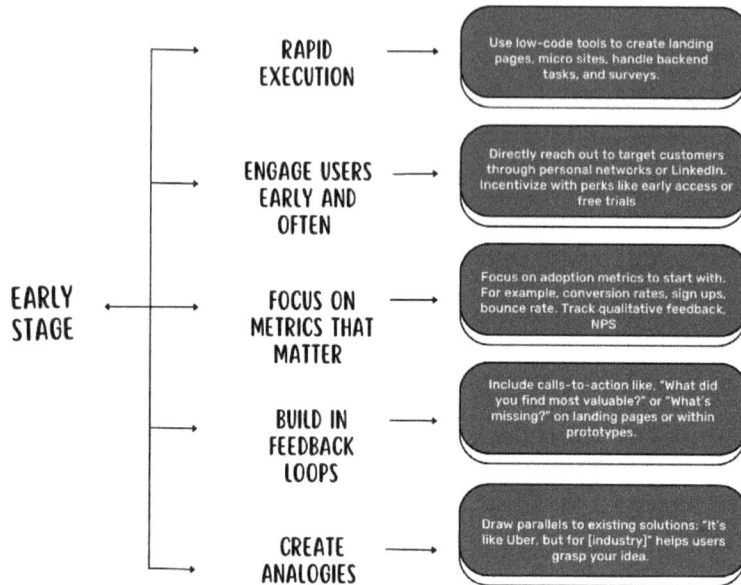

Figure 6.2: Optimization techniques for early-stage startups

MVP design patterns for growth startups

As a startup transitions from its early-stage hustle to a growth-focused business, its product strategy must evolve. Growth startups face unique challenges in scaling operations, reaching broader audiences, and maintaining product quality while iterating quickly. Let us explore these challenges, recommended MVP design patterns, and practical scenarios to successfully scale an MVP.

The challenges are as follows:

- **Balancing innovation with scalability**: In the early stages, startups can afford to experiment freely, but growth-stage companies must balance creative innovation with the operational realities of scaling. The reason is the experience and expectation levels already established by the initial group of users. The MVP must transition from being a scrappy proof-of-concept to a stable and reliable product that can handle increased demand.

- **Expanding market reach**: Growth startups must cater to diverse customer segments, each with varying needs and expectations. What would have worked for early adopters may not resonate with the main majority of users. Crossing the chasm between early adopters and the majority market is a critical growth stage.

- **Managing team and technical complexity**: Growth brings larger teams and more complex technology stacks. Coordinating cross-functional teams while maintaining a unified vision becomes a logistical challenge, requiring clear communication, robust processes, and strong leadership. As the organization scales, ensuring alignment between innovation, execution, and user expectations becomes critical to sustaining momentum and avoiding silos that can derail progress.

- **Delivering at scale without losing agility**: As startups scale, the pace of iteration often slows down. This shift occurs due to several factors, including the increased complexity of dependencies across teams and systems, the accumulation of technical debt that requires attention, and a growing sense of risk aversion driven by the need to maintain stability for a larger, more diverse user base. With more stakeholders involved, the customers, investors, and partners, every change carries higher stakes, demanding thorough testing and careful execution to avoid disruptions. Balancing agility with reliability becomes the key challenge for scaling organizations.

Let us explore the design patterns relevant for the growth of startups:

- **Piecemeal MVP**: A piecemeal MVP leverages existing tools and platforms to introduce scalable functionality quickly. Growth startups can use this pattern to test new features or markets without overcommitting resources.

  For example, a SaaS company integrates third-party analytics tools like Google Analytics or Mixpanel to gather user behavior data while focusing on building its core product.

- **Single-Feature MVPs**: Focusing on a single impactful feature allows growth startups to explore new use cases or verticals while minimizing development risks. Slack initially targeted small teams with simple messaging and file-sharing capabilities before expanding into enterprise-level collaboration tools.

- **Prototype MVP with A/B testing**: This pattern uses multiple prototypes to test variations of a feature with different user groups. A/B testing ensures data-driven decisions when expanding the MVP.

- **Incremental MVP expansion**: Instead of adding full-fledged features, incremental expansion focuses on building small, interconnected modules. This minimizes risks and provides opportunities for continuous feedback.

  For instance, a fintech app may first release budgeting tools, then incrementally add investment tracking, savings plans, and loan calculators.

Case studies

In this section, we will study early-stage and growth startups that have successfully leveraged MVP design patterns to validate demand, refine their concepts, and eventually transition their MVPs into fully scaled products. By analyzing real-world examples, we will illustrate the key principles and tactics that made these MVP strategies effective.

Early-stage startups typically operate in a world of uncertainty. Their goal is to validate core assumptions quickly and with minimal investment, time, and effort. MVPs at this stage are often used to measure demand, understand user preferences, and gather insights that guide future product development.

Here, we will look at examples of how early-stage startups leveraged MVP design patterns to validate demand and drive their transition into fully developed products.

Buffer

Buffer, a social media scheduling tool, started with the hypothesis that businesses would be willing to pay for a simple solution to automate their social media posts. The founders needed to validate this hypothesis before committing to full-scale development.

Landing page MVP: Buffer began by creating a simple landing page (**http://bufferapp.com**) that explained the concept of their service. The landing page included a CTA that encouraged visitors to sign up for a free trial. The page displayed a description of Buffer's features, such as scheduling social media posts and analytics, but none of the functionality existed at that point.

Take a look at *Joel Gascoigne's* first message on the *Y Combinator* discussion thread titled *Buffer - My November Sprint App*:

Hi everyone,

I'm delighted to share my latest little venture just in the nick of time for the November Startup Sprint which I've really enjoyed.

Been working away on the MVP for most of the last month, so it is awesome to be able to keep working on it having got the "launch" out of the way. I've been lucky to have some great friends trying it out for weeks now and helping me shape it, so this does not feel like a huge event, just another step in iterating to keep improving the product.

Please check it out and let me know your feedback, you are always awesome - http://bufferapp. com

Execution

Buffer did not build the full product first. Instead, they spent time crafting a compelling narrative that resonated with their target audience. The key here was not just to collect email sign-ups but to measure actual demand. They tracked how many users clicked on the **Sign Up** button and how many provided their email addresses, gauging interest in the product.

Let us assess the outcomes:

- **Traffic conversion**: After launching the landing page, Buffer saw an impressive conversion rate of 50%, which means half of the visitors clicked the CTA to sign-up for more information or access a beta version.

- **Key learnings**: The sign-up rate confirmed that there was a genuine demand for Buffer's product, but it also revealed a key insight - users preferred social media tools with simple, intuitive interfaces and clear analytics.

The product journey: With the early validation of the demand, *Joel Gascoigne* used the landing page's success as a foundation to start building the product. They focused on developing the core features of the app based on feedback from early sign-ups. As development continued, the Buffer team remained in close communication with the sign-ups to ensure that they were meeting user expectations.

Dropbox

Dropbox's founders, *Drew Houston* and *Arash Ferdowsi*, had a clear vision of a seamless cloud storage solution. However, they needed to validate whether people were actually willing to use and pay for it. The main question was whether the market was ready for cloud storage and file-sharing at the scale they were envisioning.

Wizard of Oz MVP: Instead of building a fully functioning product right away, Dropbox used the Wizard of Oz approach. They created a basic prototype that appeared fully functional to users, but in the background, the founders were manually fulfilling requests. Essentially, Dropbox used this illusion to test the product's appeal without needing to develop a complex infrastructure from the start.

Execution

Dropbox released a demo video showing how easy it was to drag and drop files into a cloud folder that syncs across multiple devices. The video was designed to showcase the product's simplicity and its promise of easy, secure cloud storage. In the backend, the founders manually handled the file storage and synchronization. The outcomes were as follows:

- **Video impact**: The video was a massive success, garnering over 70,000 sign-ups within the first 24 hours of its release.

- **Key learnings:** This demo confirmed the demand for a product like Dropbox but also provided valuable insights on how users interacted with cloud storage. The founders learned that users were particularly concerned about file security and ease of access across devices.

The product journey: With overwhelming interest from users, Dropbox transitioned into the development of a fully automated product. They focused on building out the backend infrastructure to handle user files securely while scaling the app. The core features remained the same, but now they were able to deliver on the promises made in the MVP.

As startups mature and grow, they face new challenges. While early-stage startups validate demand, growth-stage startups work to refine the product, improve usability, and expand to a larger market. MVPs at this stage are used to scale features, expand the user base, and transition from a single product to a more complete solution. Let us look at two examples of how growth startups used MVP patterns to refine their products and measure demand on a scale.

Airbnb

Airbnb's founders, *Brian Chesky* and *Joe Gebbia*, needed to test whether users would be willing to rent out their homes to strangers. The challenge was to understand whether there was demand for such a service and how to structure a platform for this business model.

Concierge MVP: In the early stages, Airbnb operated as a concierge MVP, meaning they manually arranged everything that users would later do themselves through the platform. The founders manually took photos of the apartments, handled listings, and communicated with users directly.

Execution

Airbnb's first listings were for a small, shared space during a design conference in San Francisco. They manually organized and facilitated the booking process. They did not have a scalable platform; instead, they acted as the *concierge* service to ensure everything went smoothly for users.

The results were:

- **Key learnings**: Airbnb's early users appreciated the human touch, and it gave the founders insights into how guests and hosts interacted with the service. This manual process helped refine their understanding of user needs, such as safety concerns, payment processes, and the importance of a reliable listing system.

- **Early growth**: After validating demand and ironing out key processes, the founders were able to scale quickly. The concept of renting personal space caught on rapidly as Airbnb expanded to other cities.

The product journey: With the core idea validated through the concierge model, Airbnb was able to build out a scalable platform. They automated the booking process, developed a rating and review system for trust, and expanded the platform to allow hosts to upload their own listings. As their user base grew, they iterated quickly, adding new features and improving the user experience.

Spotify

Spotify's founders needed to determine if people were willing to pay for a subscription-based music streaming service that offered an alternative to free, ad-supported options. They also had to refine the product based on user preferences and demand for features like playlists, recommendations, and mobile access.

Piecemeal MVP: Spotify began by integrating existing music services and technologies to create a seamless user experience without building all the infrastructure from scratch. They used a piecemeal MVP, stitching together various tools to provide a simple music streaming solution.

Execution

Spotify's initial MVP used existing content from music labels and existing streaming technology to deliver a basic service. Users could search for songs, create playlists, and share music with others. Instead of building every feature internally, Spotify used a combination of external APIs and platforms to assemble the initial version of the service. The details are:

- **Market fit**: The piecemeal MVP allowed Spotify to launch quickly and collect data on how users interacted with the service. The result was an enthusiastic response from users who wanted more control over their music experiences and features like mobile streaming.

- **Key learnings**: This MVP validated the product concept while giving Spotify valuable user feedback on essential features like mobile access, personalized recommendations, and offline play.

The product journey: After proving that users were ready for a more complete music streaming experience, Spotify transitioned to building its own backend infrastructure. They integrated a more robust recommendation engine, improved music catalog management, and refined the app's mobile capabilities. Spotify expanded quickly, ultimately leading to its position as a global leader in music streaming.

Key considerations for early and growth stages

The journey from an early-stage startup to a growth-stage company is both exciting and challenging. It marks a shift from testing assumptions and validating core product concepts to refining operations and scaling for market expansion. For founders and leaders, understanding how to manage this transition is crucial to achieving sustainable success. In this section, we will explore how startups can make this shift effectively, scaling their team, resources, and focusing on user centricity.

Transitioning from early to growth stage

The transition from early to growth stage is often referred to as *crossing the chasm*, a term popularized by *Geoffrey Moore* in his book *Crossing the Chasm*. The chasm represents the gap between early adopters (those who are willing to try a product despite imperfections) and the early majority (mainstream customers who require more reliability and refinement). Successfully navigating this chasm requires understanding the differences between early-stage and growth-stage operations and adjusting strategies accordingly.

Early stage

In the early stage, the focus is on discovering what works. This phase is defined by:

- **Experimentation**: Validating product-market fit through MVPs and small-scale launches.

- **Customer feedback**: Gathering qualitative insights from early adopters.

- **Minimal resources**: Operating with a Lean budget and team, often relying on the founder's efforts to do everything.

For example, Airbnb in its early days hosted a website that allowed hosts to rent their apartments, but the product was still being built, with founders manually responding to customers and booking stays. They used this manual process (a Wizard of Oz MVP) to validate demand without building the complete product.

Growth stage

Once product-market fit is confirmed, the startup enters the growth stage. At this point, the focus shifts to scaling the product and operations. Characteristics of this stage include:

- **Focus on efficiency**: Building scalable processes and infrastructure.

- **User acquisition:** Expanding the customer base through marketing, sales, and partnerships.

- **Team expansion**: Bringing in specialists to improve product development and operations.

A great example of growth-stage success is Spotify, which transitioned from a simple MVP offering a free music streaming service to an advanced platform that integrates data-driven personalization and global licensing. The focus here is on enhancing the product, improving customer experience, and scaling infrastructure to support millions of users. The following table shows the focus area of startups at different stages:

Factor	Early-stage focus	Growth-stage focus
Product Development	Lean, MVP-based, iterative development	Full-featured product with refinements and enhancements
Customer Base	Small, engaged, early adopters	Larger, more diverse user base with varied needs
Resources	Limited budget, often bootstrapped or seed-funded	Increased funding, allowing for hiring, infrastructure, and marketing spend

| Team Structure | Small, multi-disciplinary team | Larger, more specialized teams (engineering, sales, marketing) |
| Marketing | Organic growth through word-of-mouth and referrals | Targeted marketing campaigns and partnerships |

Table 6.2: MVP pattern selection based on scenario

Understanding these differences helps set expectations and guides the decisions that need to be made during the transition. The goal is to grow the business without losing the agility that made the startup successful in the first place.

Scaling the team and resources

As startups grow, one of the most critical challenges is scaling the team and resources to meet the increasing demands of the business. Early-stage teams are usually small, with founders wearing many hats, but as the company enters the growth stage, specialization becomes necessary. Below, we break down key considerations for scaling the team and resources.

Hire for the future, not the past

In the early days, a startup team is often a mix of generalists who are comfortable handling multiple roles. However, as the business grows, the need for specialists becomes more pronounced. Scaling the team requires careful planning:

- **Hire for scalability**: As needs change, hire individuals with experience in scaling businesses. For instance, engineers with experience in building scalable infrastructure or marketers who understand how to execute customer acquisition strategies on a scale.

- **Build complementary skills**: Early teams may be driven by the founder's vision, but as the startup grows, you need people who bring new perspectives and expertise, such as data analysts, growth marketers, and product managers.

Consider Dropbox, which initially grew through a referral-based system with a small, focused team. As the company grew, Dropbox brought on specialists to scale its technology infrastructure, user support, and marketing efforts, expanding its team from a few people to thousands over time.

Balance efficiency and quality

As the team grows, maintaining the balance between speed (necessary for growth) and quality (important for retention) becomes challenging. Growth-stage startups need to:

- **Implement efficient processes**: Streamline development cycles using Agile methodologies. For example, adopting CI/CD pipelines (continuous integration and continuous delivery) can help automate testing and deployment, allowing faster iterations while ensuring code quality.

- **Foster cross-functional collaboration**: Teams across departments (product, engineering, marketing, etc.) need to work closely together to address user needs and meet business goals.

A great tool for fostering efficiency is using project management platforms like *Asana* or *Trello*, which can help align cross-functional teams on goals and timelines.

Financial resources and capital allocation

In the early stages, many startups operated with limited funds, often bootstrapped or financed through angel investments. However, once the startup reaches the growth stage, it may attract **venture capital** (**VC**) funding. Here is how to manage this growth:

- **Allocate capital for growth**: Focus on spending resources where they will have the most significant impact. For instance, investing in marketing and customer acquisition strategies to rapidly expand the user base, or upgrading server infrastructure to handle increased traffic.

- **Track ROI on scaling efforts**: As resources increase, the complexity of managing them grows. Tracking the **return on investment** (**ROI**) from each department or initiative becomes crucial to avoid overspending.

Role of user centricity in scaling

No matter the stage of a startup, maintaining a user-centric approach is vital for long-term success. As startups move into the growth stage, staying close to the customer helps ensure that the product continues to meet user needs, even as the business scales.

Listening to the users

A user-centric approach means continuously gathering feedback and integrating it into product development:

- **User research**: Conduct regular user interviews, surveys, and usability tests to understand how your product is being used. Tools like *Hotjar* can provide heatmaps and user recordings to analyze behavior.

- **Data-driven decisions**: Use analytics platforms like Google Analytics, Mixpanel, or Amplitude to track user interactions and derive actionable insights.

Create scalable customer support

As your user base grows, providing scalable, personalized customer support becomes crucial. Startups often begin with one-on-one support through emails or phone calls, but as they grow, they need to build systems that allow for efficient support at scale:

- **Self-service options**: Build a comprehensive knowledge base or help center where users can find solutions to common issues.

- **Chatbots and AI**: Implement AI-powered chatbots for handling common queries and automating responses.

For example, *Zendesk* has been widely used by growing companies to scale customer support while maintaining a high level of user satisfaction.

Retain user-centricity amidst growth

As the company scales, it is easy to become distracted by internal processes or the urgency of expanding the business. However, keeping the focus on the customer is crucial:

- **Personalized user experience**: Use personalization to tailor the experience for users at scale. Spotify's personalized playlists or Amazon's product recommendations are prime examples of using data to create a more personalized experience.

- **Customer advocacy**: Turn loyal customers into advocates through referral programs, testimonials, and social proof. This creates a network of brand ambassadors who can help attract new users.

Navigating the transition from an early-stage startup to a growth-stage company is a dynamic challenge. It requires startups to adapt their strategies, scale their resources wisely, and maintain a focus on the user experience. By understanding the key differences between these stages, scaling the team and resources strategically, and ensuring user centricity is at the core of every decision, startups can position themselves for sustainable growth and success.

By focusing on these principles, startups can continue to build on their early-stage momentum and scale effectively, turning their initial product ideas into market-leading innovations.

Conclusion

As we draw our exploration of MVP design patterns to a close, it is essential to understand that the concept of the MVP itself is not static. Rather, it is a living process, a fluid, adaptive approach that grows alongside the product and its market. Just as a startup evolves from an idea to a fully established business, the MVP journey demands continuous refinement based on feedback, data, and shifting user needs. In this section, we reflect on the key takeaways, the learning outcomes from this chapter, and how MVP design patterns evolve through different stages of a startup's lifecycle.

The fundamental principle behind an MVP is to validate assumptions early by delivering the smallest version of the product that provides value to users. However, once an MVP is launched and validated, it is not a final product; it is simply the beginning of an ongoing journey. The product, and the way it evolves, will shift depending on factors like user feedback, market demands, competition, and internal resources.

Consider the example of Airbnb, which started as a simple landing page MVP (targeting attendees of a local conference) to validate the need for short-term rental services, and has evolved into a full-scale global platform offering a wide range of services. As Airbnb's understanding of its users grew, so did the product's features, user base, and market segments. It is a perfect example of how MVP design patterns are flexible, requiring iterative improvements and constant realignment with business objectives and user needs.

In the next chapter, we will explore testing strategies for the MVP phase and learn how to integrate testing into your product development process to ensure a smooth transition from MVP to a full-scale product.

Points to remember

- **Understanding MVP design patterns**: By now, you should understand the core MVP design patterns, concierge, Wizard of Oz, piecemeal, Single-Feature, landing page, and prototype, and how each serves a unique purpose. Recognizing which design pattern to implement based on your startup's stage, resources, and goals is crucial to creating a valuable MVP without unnecessary waste.

- **Iterative validation is key**: The MVP is not a one-off launch; it is part of an ongoing process. The key to success is validating, iterating, and improving continuously. Collect insights from each iteration, focus on real user needs, and use data-driven decisions to refine your product.

- **Flexibility over perfection**: An MVP is not a polished, perfect product; it is a way to test assumptions and validate the market. Embrace imperfection and avoid the temptation to overbuild at an early stage. Perfect products are rare; successful products emerge through iteration and adaptation.

- **Tailoring MVP design patterns to your startup's needs**: Early-stage startups are focused on validating core assumptions with minimal resources. In contrast, growth-stage startups are concerned with scaling and refining their product based on a broader user base. Understanding this dynamic and adapting your MVP design pattern accordingly will ensure that you stay efficient and focused on the right objectives.

CHAPTER 7
MVP Testing Strategies

Introduction

In the previous chapter, we explored MVP design patterns, delving into how startups can build Lean and effective prototypes to validate their ideas. In this chapter, we move on to the next step, i.e., testing those MVPs. We will explore why testing is the cornerstone of successful product development and how startups can use strategic testing to unlock actionable insights, optimize their processes, and bring products closer to market fit.

The purpose of this chapter is to guide you through the art and science of MVP testing. Whether you are building a simple landing page or a concierge MVP, testing helps you refine your solution and minimize the risks of scaling too early or too fast. You will not only validate your assumptions but also build a solid foundation for iteration and growth.

Structure

In this chapter, we will cover the following topics:

- Defining testing objectives
- Picking the right metrics
- Testing techniques and approaches

- Common pitfalls in MVP testing

- Case studies

- Future of MVP testing

Objectives

In this chapter, we will learn how to test your MVP effectively, while gathering insights, making data-driven decisions, and setting up a framework that supports continuous improvement and scale. By the end of this chapter, we will be able to design a structured approach to MVP testing that aligns with your startup's unique needs. Select and implement the right testing methods for gathering actionable user insights. Analyze data with confidence, distinguishing meaningful trends from noise. Develop a repeatable framework for iterating on and improving your MVP based on user feedback. Integrate testing into your overall product development strategy, ensuring a smoother transition from MVP to full-scale product.

MVP testing is not just a phase; it is a continuous rigor for quality. As we dig deeper into this chapter, we will learn how to integrate testing into your innovation process, enabling you to develop products that resonate and succeed.

Defining testing objectives

Building a **minimum viable product** (**MVP**) is as much about purpose as it is about execution. Without clear objectives, your MVP risks becoming a collection of arbitrary features instead of a strategic tool for learning and growth. Defining precise testing objectives sets the foundation for every decision you will make, ensuring that your efforts lead to actionable insights and meaningful progress.

Translating the MVP's purpose

Success in MVP testing is not about perfection, but it is about learning. Your MVP's purpose should translate directly into measurable goals. It should factor in if you are validating market demand, testing usability, or even gauging willingness to pay.

For instance, if your product idea is a platform for freelance writers to connect with publishers, a clear goal might be:

- **Acquire 100 sign-ups from freelance writers in the first month**: This goal reflects whether the product resonates with the target audience.

- **Avoid vague ambitions like gain traction or create buzz**: Instead, ensure your objectives are:

    o **Specific**: Pinpoint the exact question you are answering.

- o **Measurable**: Use metrics that provide clarity.

- o **Achievable**: Stay within the scope of an MVP.

- o **Relevant**: Tie goals to core business outcomes.

- o **Time-bound**: Set deadlines to maintain focus.

Identifying key hypotheses

Every MVP is built on assumptions. Testing is the process of verifying which ones are true. Start by framing your assumptions as hypotheses. For example:

- **Hypothesis 1**: *Freelance writers struggle to find publishers willing to pay fair rates.*

- **Hypothesis 2**: *A curated platform can reduce its search time by 50%.*

- **Hypothesis 3**: *Publishers will benefit from demand content services.*

The goal is to design your MVP to test these hypotheses. If the results validate your assumptions, you are on the right track. If not, you have identified a gap to address, an equally valuable outcome.

Aligning objectives with the team

Your MVP goals must resonate with your team's vision and capabilities. Misalignment here can lead to confusion, half-hearted efforts, and wasted resources.

To align your team:

- **Collaborate early**: Involve team members in defining objectives. Let engineers, designers, and marketers share their perspectives.

- **Be transparent**: Clearly explain the *why* behind each objective. For example, *We are focusing on the writer side first because we need to supply before publishers join.*

- **Empower ownership**: Assign responsibility for different aspects of testing. When everyone knows their role, execution becomes seamless.

When objectives feel like a shared mission rather than a top-down directive, the team's energy and focus become a force multiplier.

Aligning objectives with stakeholders

Startups rarely operate in isolation. Founders, investors, and advisors often hold significant influence, and their alignment is critical to your MVP's success. Misaligned expectations can derail your efforts, so bringing stakeholders on board is essential.

To align stakeholders, you have to keep the following in mind:

- **Speak their language**: While your team might focus on user engagement metrics, stakeholders might care more about market validation or potential ROI. Tailor your objectives to address their priorities.

- **Showcase the bigger picture**: Explain how testing objectives fit into the startup's broader vision. For instance, *This MVP will validate the core demand, helping us secure a larger round of funding.*

- **Seek feedback**: Involve stakeholders in discussions to make them feel invested. For example, asking them questions like *Does this approach align with your understanding of the market opportunity?*

- **Commit to communication**: Regularly update stakeholders on progress. Transparency builds trust and keeps them engaged in the process.

Outcome

When you take the time to define testing objectives, align them with your team, and secure stakeholder buy-in, you create a unified direction for your MVP. Your testing becomes purposeful, your team stays motivated, and your stakeholders remain supportive.

In startups, clarity is a competitive advantage. Well-defined testing objectives ensure your MVP is not just a product; it is a strategic experiment designed to bring your vision to life.

Picking the right metrics

Metrics play a key role in product testing as they serve as the key indicators of success, progress, and growth. However, like any other indicator, they must be calibrated correctly. The wrong metrics or worse, too many, can distract, mislead, or even derail your efforts. In this section, we will explore how to identify and use meaningful metrics that drive actionable insights, align with your goals, and keep your product team focused on what truly matters.

Actionable metrics versus vanity metrics

Vanity metrics reflect the touch-and-feel elements of the product, such as page views, app downloads, or social media likes. While they might look impressive in a presentation, they often lack real substance when it comes to decision-making. These metrics tell you what is happening but not why, or more importantly, what to do next.

In contrast, *actionable metrics* drive clarity and decisions. These include activation rates, customer retention, and **average revenue per user** (ARPU). Actionable metrics are directly tied to your product's goals and offer insights you can act upon to improve performance.

Before collecting data, ask, *What action would I take based on this metric?* If you cannot answer, it is probably vanity. The following table lists a few vanity and actionable metrics for various functions in an organization:

Functions	Vanity metrics	Actionable metrics
Marketing	• Website traffic • Social media followers • Impressions on a post	• Conversion rates • **Cost per lead** (**CPL**) from campaigns • Engagement rate
Sales	• Number of calls made, or emails sent • Total leads in the pipeline • Revenue generation	• Lead-to-customer conversion rate • ARPU • Sales cycle length (time to close a deal)
Product management	• Total app downloads • Number of registered users • Pageviews per session	• Active daily or monthly users • Retention rate • Feature usage percentage
Customer support	• Number of tickets closed • Total customer interactions	• **First response time** (**FRT**) • **Customer satisfaction score** (**CSAT**) • **Net promoter score** (**NPS**)
E-Commerce	• Total page views on product listings • Number of products added to the cart	• Cart abandonment rate • Repeat purchase rate • **Customer lifetime value** (**CLV**)

Table 7.1: *Vanity and actionable metrics by organizational functions*

Key performance indicators

Key performance indicators (**KPIs**) are the few critical metrics that measure your MVP's progress against its core objectives. Unlike general data points, KPIs are intentionally chosen based on what success looks like for your product. For example:

- **For a subscription-based MVP**: **Customer acquisition cost** (**CAC**) and **monthly recurring revenue** (**MRR**).

- **For a marketplace MVP**: The number of active buyers and sellers, and transaction volume.

Demystifying OKRs versus KPIs

The startup world often debates between **objectives and key results** (**OKRs**) and KPIs. While they are complementary, they serve distinct purposes, listed as follows:

- KPIs are static and measure ongoing performance. Think of them as the health metrics of your MVP.

- OKRs are dynamic and aspirational. They set specific, time-bound goals that push your product toward growth and innovation.

- For instance:

  - **KPI**: Maintain a 20% monthly user retention rate.

  - **OKR**: Increase the monthly retention rate from 20% to 30% in Q1.

The key is to use KPIs to monitor the status quo and OKRs to stretch for improvement.

The north star metric

The **north star metric** (**NSM**) is the ultimate guiding light for your MVP. It captures the core value your product delivers to users and is directly linked to long-term growth. This metric should encapsulate the essence of why your product exists.

Examples of strong NSMs are as follows:

- **For a social media app**: Time spent in meaningful interactions.

- **For an e-commerce platform**: Number of purchases per active user.

- **For a SaaS product**: Number of active subscriptions.

To identify your NSM, ask the following key questions:

- What is the core value your product/service delivers to customers?

- What activity directly reflects how customers derive value from your product?

- Which metric best aligns with long-term business growth?

- Is this metric trackable, and can it guide team decisions?

- Does this metric capture the success of your most loyal users?

Designing a product metric framework

Designing a product metric framework involves more than just picking numbers to track, but it is about creating a system that aligns data with strategy. Here is a step-by-step approach:

1. **Define your product goals**: Break your goals into measurable outcomes. For instance, if your goal is user growth, metrics like sign-up rates and referrals will be key.

2. **Establish a metric hierarchy**: Organize metrics into layers:

    - **Strategic**: NSM, OKRs.

    - **Operational**: KPIs for day-to-day tracking.

    - **Diagnostic**: Supporting metrics that explain anomalies in KPIs.

3. **Prioritize metrics**: Avoid metric overload by focusing on the most impactful ones. Use frameworks like **reach, impact, confidence, effort (RICE)** to prioritize.

4. **Create feedback loops**: Ensure your framework integrates with tools for real-time feedback (e.g., dashboards, reports) and allows iterative improvements.

5. **Review and iterate**: Revisit your metrics regularly to ensure they remain relevant as your MVP evolves.

By understanding and applying these principles, you can transform raw data into strategic insights that drive your MVP forward. Metrics are not just numbers; they are the architect of your startup's growth story. Stay focused on what truly matters, and let the right metrics guide you to success.

The following KPI template is designed to help startups track their MVP's performance against core objectives. It is simple, structured, and actionable, aligning with industry best practices.

Objective	KPI name	KPI description	Measurement formula	Target value
Problem validation	Conversion rate	Percentage of users who signed up after landing page visit.	*(Sign-ups ÷ Total Visitors) × 100*	20%
Market fit	Customer retention rate	Percentage of users returning after first use.	*(Returning Users ÷ Total Users) × 100*	50%
Usability testing	Task completion time	Average time users take to complete a key task.	*Total Time ÷ No. of Users*	< 2 minutes
Monetization	ARPU	Average revenue generated per user.	*Total Revenue ÷ Total Users*	$10/user

Table 7.2: KPI template

For reference, follow these instructions to measure the progress of the MVP effectively and align KPIs with their core business objectives:

- Define the overarching goals of your MVP. These goals must align with the problem your startup is solving.

- List specific, measurable, and actionable KPIs for each objective.

- Break down how each KPI will be tracked and measured.

- Track your MVP's progress and evaluate performance regularly.

- Ensure KPIs evolve with the MVP's growth stage.

- Track what you learn and how you adapt to improve MVP performance.

Testing techniques and approaches

At startups, time and resources are often scarce. Yet, validating your MVP effectively can mean the difference between a breakthrough idea and a costly misstep. By leveraging innovative and targeted testing techniques, you can uncover valuable insights, mitigate risks, and set up your product for long-term success. Here are six powerful approaches that can transform your MVP testing strategy:

- **Smoke tests**: Think of smoke tests as the spark that ignites curiosity. This method involves presenting a core element of your product to gauge market interest, often without even having the product ready. An engaging ad, a signup form, or a simple call-to-action can serve as a smoke test.

  For example, a startup considering a subscription box for plant lovers might run a Meta ad offering *curated monthly plant kits*. If users click the ad or sign up, it is a clear signal of demand.

  Smoke tests require minimal effort and resources, making them an ideal starting point. They help answer the crucial question: *Is this something people actually want?*

- **Landing page experiments**: Landing pages are like digital storefronts for your MVP. With a cLean design and clear messaging, they allow you to present your value proposition and measure user interest. Let us check how it works:

  o Create a landing page that explains the product or service.

  o Include a strong headline, concise benefits, and a single call-to-action (e.g., *Sign Up Now* or *Learn More*).

  o Use analytics to track clicks, signups, or time spent on the page.

  This approach not only validates your idea but also helps you build an initial user base or email list for future communication.

- **Prototypes and clickable demos**: Sometimes, users need to see to believe. Prototypes and clickable demos bring your MVP to life, even if only as a rough outline. Tools like *Figma, InVision,* or *Adobe XD* allow you to create interactive mock-ups that users can explore. Let us check how it works:

    o   Users can visualize and engage with your product, providing richer feedback.

    o   Stakeholders and investors gain a clearer understanding of your vision.

Prototypes do not need to be perfect; they just need to be functional enough to test user flows and gauge interest.

- **A/B testing**: One of the most prominently used, A/B testing is the secret sauce of optimization. By comparing two versions of a feature, design, or message, you can determine what resonates best with your users.

  If your MVP is an app, you might test two versions of a homepage, one with a minimalist design and another with detailed descriptions. The version that leads to higher engagement or conversions becomes your baseline for further development.

  Keep note of testing one variable at a time (e.g., the call-to-action button) to ensure clear and actionable results.

- **Wizard of Oz testing**: In Wizard of Oz testing, users interact with what they believe to be a fully functional product, but behind the scenes, the processes, sometimes product actions, are manually executed.

  For example, a food delivery startup might allow users to place orders via an app, but instead of automation, the orders are manually coordinated with local restaurants and delivery drivers.

  This method is excellent for testing whether users will embrace your solution without committing to full-scale development. It is resource-light but insight-rich.

- **Concierge MVPs**: Concierge MVPs take Wizard of Oz testing a step further by offering a highly personalized, manual service to a small group of users. Here, you act as the product, directly delivering the solution to understand your customers' needs deeply.

  This approach fosters intimate customer relationships and yields invaluable qualitative insights, though it is less scalable in the short term.

Choosing the right technique for an MVP

Each of these techniques serves a unique purpose and fits different contexts. Start with the simplest methods, like smoke tests or landing pages, to validate demand. Then, as your confidence grows, move toward more intricate approaches like A/B testing or Wizard of Oz experiments.

The goal is not just to test your MVP but to gather meaningful insights that guide your next move. By strategically applying these techniques, you will be well-equipped to refine your product and deliver something your users truly need.

Common pitfalls in MVP testing

Testing an MVP is not just about ticking boxes, but it is about navigating a delicate balance between ambition, practicality, and learning. Many startups falter not because they lack ideas but because they stumble into avoidable traps during the testing phase. Here, we look into three common pitfalls that can derail your MVP testing efforts and how to steer clear of them:

- **Overengineering**: Remember (and keep reminding yourself), the *M* in MVP stands for *minimum*, but it is tempting to think that more features mean better validation. This mindset often leads to overengineering, that in-turn, leads to packing the MVP with unnecessary bells and whistles in a bid to impress users.

  Overengineering dilutes focus and drains resources, leaving less room for experimentation and iteration. Instead of validating your core hypothesis, you might end up testing a bloated version of your product, making it harder to pinpoint what is working and what is not.

  To fix this, strip your MVP down to its essence. Ask yourself, *What is the single, most critical problem this MVP is solving?* Build only what is necessary to test that hypothesis. Note that your goal is learning, not perfection. Dropbox did not launch as a fully functional app; it started with a simple explainer video to validate demand.

- **Ignoring negative feedback**: Negative feedback is hard to hear. It challenges your assumptions, your effort, and sometimes, your vision. The instinct to dismiss criticism as *users not understanding the product* can be strong, but this is a dangerous mindset.

  Negative feedback is one of your most valuable tools. Ignoring it means missing opportunities to refine your product. Worse, it creates an echo chamber where only the positives are amplified, leaving blind spots in your strategy.

  What should you do? Shift your perspective. Treat every critique as a clue to what your product is lacking. For instance, if users struggle with a feature, it is not their fault; it is a design flaw. Embrace the discomfort of failure, dissect it, and use it as a blueprint for improvement. Remember, *Instagram* started as *Burbn*, a complex app that failed to gain traction until its founders stripped it down to focus on photo-sharing, based on user feedback.

- **Misinterpreting data**: Numbers never lie. Data is only as good as your interpretation, and it is easy to fall prey to confirmation bias, the tendency to see what you want to see.

  When you interpret data to fit your assumptions, you risk reinforcing flawed ideas. For example, if you are convinced your MVP is a hit, you might cherry-pick metrics that support this belief while ignoring red flags, such as low retention rates or poor engagement.

How to fix this? Approach data with curiosity, not certainty. Focus on actionable metrics that reflect user behavior, not vanity metrics that look good but offer little insight (e.g., sign-ups without engagement). Consider seeking third-party input to avoid blind spots and challenge your assumptions. Airbnb famously tested its early MVP by analyzing guest feedback and identifying a need for better-quality listings, an insight that drove its eventual success.

MVP testing is as much about uncovering flaws as it is about validating ideas. Overengineering, ignoring criticism, and misreading data are all pitfalls that stem from the same root, fear of failure. However, here is the paradox: failure, when embraced strategically, is your most reliable teacher. By staying Lean, listening to all feedback, and analyzing data objectively, you will not only avoid these pitfalls but also build a stronger, smarter path toward product-market fit.

Case studies

Testing an MVP is more than just validating an idea; it is about setting the stage for long-term success by gathering insights and iterating effectively. In this section, we will learn how modern startups have creatively approached MVP testing, including a standout example from India's vibrant startup ecosystem.

CRED

Founded in 2018 by *Kunal Shah*, *CRED* is a platform that rewards users for paying their credit card bills on time. Before becoming a household name among India's urban elite, CRED began with a straightforward MVP aimed at testing one core hypothesis, that the users would engage with a rewards-based credit card bill payment system. Let us learn their testing approach:

- **Exclusive target audience**: CRED focused its MVP on India's top-tier credit card users with high spending potential. This narrow targeting helped the team test its hypothesis without diluting efforts.

- **Gamified engagement**: The MVP offered simple rewards for timely bill payments, testing whether gamification would drive behavior.

- **Data-driven iterations**: The initial version tracked user engagement metrics like bill payment frequency and rewards redemption rates to identify what users valued most.

The MVP validated CRED's value proposition, leading to rapid iteration and the addition of new features like credit score tracking and investment options. CRED became a unicorn within three years, demonstrating the power of a focused MVP and strategic testing.

Blinkit

Blinkit (formerly *Grofers*), the *Zomato*-owned hyperlocal delivery in India, pivoted multiple times before finding its niche. When the company decided to explore the concept of 10-minute grocery delivery, they created a scrappy MVP to validate user demand. Let us find out how they approached testing:

- **Manual operations**: Blinkit initially ran operations manually in a limited number of neighborhoods, using staff to fulfill orders quickly. This *concierge MVP* minimized technical and operational investment.

- **Geo-focused experimentation**: The MVP targeted areas with high population density to test demand and feasibility for ultra-fast delivery.

- **Behavioral analytics**: Metrics such as average order size, delivery time, and repeat customer rate were tracked to refine the model.

The MVP proved that customers valued speed over variety for grocery essentials. With this insight, Blinkit scaled its operations, optimizing inventory and logistics for rapid delivery.

Jar

Founded in 2021, Jar helps users save and invest in digital gold effortlessly. The startup's goal was to address a common pain point for young Indians - the lack of disciplined savings habits. Let us see how they tested their MVP:

- **WhatsApp MVP**: Before building an app, Jar tested its concept using WhatsApp. Users could set up recurring savings by responding to messages, allowing the team to gauge interest without investing heavily in app development.

- **Behavioral hooks**: The MVP focused on small daily savings, experimenting with user-friendly nudges like notifications and gamified streaks.

- **Feedback integration**: Early adopters provided feedback on simplicity, trust, and usability, which guided the product's design.

The WhatsApp MVP confirmed Jar's hypothesis that small, daily contributions appealed to first-time savers. This feedback led to a polished app that now has millions of users.

Zepto

Founded in 2021 by two young entrepreneurs, *Zepto* quickly became a leader in India's ultra-fast grocery delivery space. With minimal infrastructure, the company launched its MVP to test whether users valued speed over price or variety. Let us examine their testing approach:

- **Pop-up dark stores**: Instead of fully stocking warehouses, Zepto set up small *dark stores* in high-demand areas to test delivery efficiency.

- **Operational MVP**: Zepto used a Lean delivery fleet to measure fulfillment times and customer satisfaction.

- **Iterative metrics**: Metrics like customer churn rate, average delivery time, and order frequency helped shape its service model.

Zepto's MVP proved that demand for ultra-fast delivery existed, leading to rapid scaling and significant funding rounds within months of its launch.

Key learnings from modern MVP testing

These case studies in the last section show how modern-day startups can creatively test their MVPs, proving that innovation lies as much in execution as in the idea itself. With a fine-tuned MVP, startups can build not just products, but entire ecosystems of value for their users. Let us summarize the key learnings:

- **Focused testing yields clearer insights**: Startups like CRED and Jar demonstrate the importance of targeting a specific audience and hypothesis.

- **Low-tech solutions are powerful**: Both Jar's WhatsApp MVP and Blinkit's manual operations highlight the value of starting simple.

- **Data-driven iteration wins**: By tracking metrics that matter, these startups pivoted and iterated effectively, ensuring product-market fit.

- **User experience is key**: Gamification, behavioral nudges, and ultra-fast services resonate strongly when the MVP aligns with customer priorities.

Future of MVP testing

As we stand on the precipice of a new era in product development, the way we approach MVP testing is undergoing a profound transformation. While the core principles of MVP testing remain steadfast, validating assumptions, gathering feedback, and iterating swiftly, the tools and trends driving this process are evolving at lightning speed. In this section, we will explore three of the most exciting developments shaping the future of MVP testing, AI and automation, real-time feedback tools, and gamified testing. These trends promise to not only streamline the process but also offer new avenues for startups to innovate faster, with more precision, and with deeper user engagement.

AI and automation in testing

Artificial Intelligence is revolutionizing MVP testing by automating repetitive tasks, reducing human error, and delivering deeper insights with minimal manual intervention. The future of MVP testing is in automation. AI tools can now analyze user behavior, detect patterns, and even predict which features will likely drive engagement or conversion. A sample flow of AI automation testing is provided in the following figure:

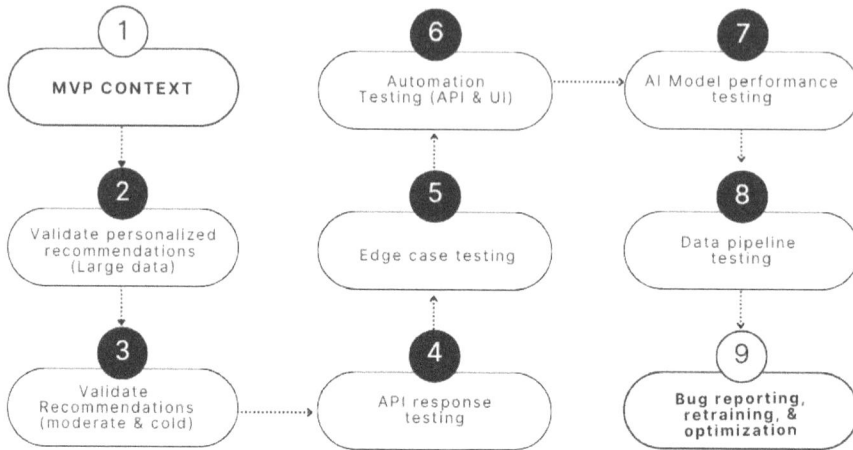

Figure 7.1: A sample flow of AI automation testing

AI-powered automation can enhance both predictive analytics and automated A/B testing in the MVP testing phase. Here is how it can transform the testing strategy, providing quicker insights and better decision-making:

- **Predictive analytics**: Imagine using AI to not only analyze current data but also predict future trends based on user actions. With machine learning algorithms, startups can identify patterns in early user interactions, enabling them to prioritize changes or pivots with a higher degree of confidence. By doing this, startups can focus on what is working and iterate faster, rather than spending time testing every feature or approach.

- **Automated A/B testing**: Traditionally, A/B testing requires manual setup and tracking, but AI-powered platforms can now automate this process, optimizing variations in real-time and providing detailed insights on what drives user engagement. This eliminates the guesswork, ensuring that each test is run with maximum efficiency, all while scaling with minimal effort.

With AI and automation, MVP testing moves from a manual, error-prone process to a streamlined, data-driven activity, freeing up teams to focus on what matters most, i.e., creating an exceptional user experience.

Real-time feedback tools

Gone are the days when MVP testing could only be done in isolated cycles. The next generation of feedback tools allows startups to gather insights in real-time, enabling immediate responses to user behavior and preferences. Here is how it works:

- **Instant feedback mechanisms**: Modern tools like in-app surveys, heatmaps, and live chat feedback loops allow users to express their thoughts while they are actively engaging with the product. Whether it is a quick poll or an interactive questionnaire, these tools offer valuable insights into how real users interact with your MVP, often within minutes of the interaction.

- **Continuous testing and iteration**: The concept of *one-and-done* testing is becoming obsolete. With real-time tools, testing is a continuous process. Teams can launch features, collect feedback, tweak the product, and test again, all in a fraction of the time it once took. This iterative process ensures that startups are always evolving based on fresh data, reducing the lag between ideation, testing, and market entry.

By embracing real-time feedback, startups gain an unprecedented level of agility, allowing them to adapt to user preferences and demands almost as quickly as they evolve. This approach ensures products are always in tune with their target audience, making the testing phase a dynamic and continuous conversation.

Gamified testing

User engagement is no longer just about how well your product works; it is about how it makes users feel. As startups look for ways to drive more meaningful feedback, gamified testing is quickly becoming a powerful strategy to boost user participation and make the testing process more enjoyable and rewarding. Here is how they help:

- **Incentivized participation**: By introducing elements of game design, like rewards, leaderboards, and progress tracking, startups can motivate users to actively engage in testing activities. Whether it is a badge for completing a task or a point system for providing valuable feedback, gamification fosters a sense of accomplishment and encourages users to return for additional feedback cycles.

- **Creating a fun experience**: Beyond incentives, gamification can make the testing process itself enjoyable. For example, interactive tutorials or challenges that require users to explore specific features of an MVP can result in deeper engagement and more detailed feedback. Users may feel like they are not just passive testers, but active participants in shaping a product they care about.

- **Increasing retention**: Gamified elements do not just increase participation during the MVP phase; they can extend beyond testing. Once users are accustomed to the idea of earning rewards or making progress within an app, they are more likely to continue using the product after the MVP phase concludes. This creates a built-in community of engaged users who feel personally invested in the product's success.

The following figure illustrates how simple gamified nudges can keep users engaged and invested in the product journey:

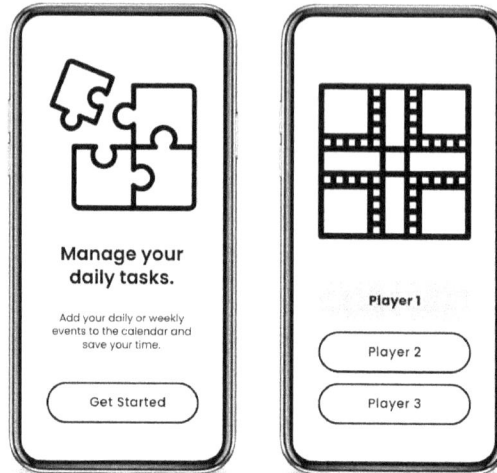

Gamification turns products into
experiences and users into loyal players

Figure 7.2: *Gamified MVP testing not only gathers insights but also creates lasting user loyalty*

Conclusion

As we conclude this chapter on MVP testing strategies, let us take a moment to reflect on the journey we have just embarked upon and the powerful tools we have uncovered to refine your startup's product development process.

We began by emphasizing the importance of strategic testing in the MVP phase. Testing is not just about validating your ideas; it is about gaining actionable insights that guide your next steps and prevent costly missteps. We explored how to set clear objectives, select the right metrics, and utilize a range of testing techniques such as smoke tests, landing pages, and A/B testing. We also highlighted the significance of iterative cycles, moving from feedback to improvement, not just for product refinement, but also for aligning your team around data-driven decision-making.

In the next chapter, we shift focus from building to scaling. We will cover practical strategies for founders and product leaders to turn a validated MVP into a scalable, successful business.

Points to remember

- **Testing objectives**: Establishing clear goals to measure success and failure, ensuring you stay focused on what truly matters.

- **Testing technique**: Understanding the value of various MVP testing approaches and how to apply them in real-world scenarios.

- **Metrics**: Choosing the right KPIs that not only validate your product but also inform future iterations.

- **User feedback**: Gathering insights that are not just numbers but actionable behaviors, pain points, and desires that shape your product's future.

- **Iteration**: Using feedback loops as a constant engine for improvement, ensuring your MVP evolves into something that truly serves your audience.

The goal of MVP testing is not to prove your idea right, it is to prove it wrong early, when the stakes are low, so you can build the right product for the right audience. Think of each test as a data point, not an endpoint, and embrace the process of continual discovery.

Join our Discord space

Join our Discord workspace for latest updates, offers, tech happenings around the world, new releases, and sessions with the authors:

https://discord.bpbonline.com

CHAPTER 8

Scaling MVP to Success

Introduction

Scaling an MVP from a Lean prototype to an industry product that customers love is one of the most rewarding phases of a product organization. This stage represents the evolution of the product, processes, and team to meet the demands of a growing market while staying aligned with your core mission. While building and testing an MVP is critical to proving the viability of your idea, scaling it requires an executional rigor and strategy.

In the previous chapter, we explored MVP testing strategies. Armed with insights from those tests, the next step is to focus on growth, refining the product, reaching a broader audience, and establishing a foundation for long-term market success.

This chapter will act as your playbook for navigating this critical phase. Whether you are a founder aiming to capture your first significant market share or a product manager refining a growth strategy, this chapter will equip you with the tools and tactics to turn an MVP into a sustainable business.

Structure

In this chapter, we will cover the following topics:

- Navigating the growth stage
- Refining the MVP

- MVP to full-scale product development

- Strengthening product-market fit

- Marketing and distribution

- Establishing operational excellence

- Navigating challenges

- Case studies

Objectives

In this chapter, we will learn how to take your MVP beyond validation and into growth. We will cover the challenges of scaling, refining product features, building operational strength, marketing effectively, and securing the resources needed to compete and thrive in a crowded market. By the end of this chapter, you will understand the key challenges of scaling an MVP, learn how to refine your product features, discover strategies for marketing and distribution, build operational excellence, gain insights into securing funding and resources, and prepare for competition and market saturation.

Navigating the growth stage

Launching an MVP is the start of an ever-evolving product journey. The real test is whether the target users actually want it, keep using it, and are willing to pay for it. If the product does not drive value by solving a real problem or does not excite users, it will not last long.

The harsh truth is that only 1% of startups make it big, while 90% fail. This could be because some build products nobody needs, some cannot handle competition, and others run into pricing issues, legal hurdles, or flawed business models. Even a great idea can fail if it is not positioned well in the market.

Most new products do not turn a profit right away, and even those that do often run on razor-thin margins. If growth stalls, startups can fall into the *death valley curve*. It is a tough phase where sales drop, money runs low, and marketing stops delivering results. The only way to move forward is by constantly improving the product, planning finances wisely, and making sure the business has a clear path to scale.

Figure 8.1 shows a phase named the *Valley of Death*. In the entrepreneurial context, it was originally introduced by *Stephen Markham* in 2002. It refers to the phase between the launch of a business or an MVP and the stage until it becomes a scalable, sustainable, and profitable model. During this period, startups typically struggle to generate enough revenue to cover costs. Without revenue, attracting investment becomes an uphill battle.

Most startups do not survive the *Valley of Death*, and even those that do rarely adhere to their original concept. Their business models evolve, shaped by customer feedback, resource constraints, and market dynamics.

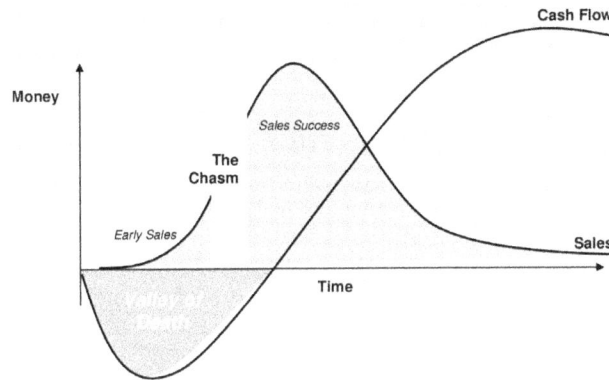

Figure 8.1: Valley of Death with tech chasm overlay[1]

Pivot or scale

Not all MVPs take off as expected. Sometimes, sales fall short, user adoption stagnates, or early projections miss the mark. This could indicate a flawed assumption, weak product-market fit, or even the wrong success metrics.

However, failure at this stage does not have to mean the end. Many great products today started as something entirely different before they pivoted into success. For example, *Twitter* started as *Odeo*, a podcasting platform. When *Apple's iTunes* entered the space, Odeo pivoted. An internal hackathon sparked the idea of a microblogging tool, which became Twitter in 2006. The shift turned a failing startup into a global social media giant. It was indeed a bold pivot that paid off.

Pivoting can be tough. Many founders fall into loss aversion, a psychological bias where the fear of losing outweighs the excitement of potential gains. *Kodak* is a primary example. At its peak, Kodak dominated the film and camera market; however, it hesitated to adapt to digital photography, even though a Kodak engineer invented the world's first digital camera in 1975. Instead of pivoting, the company chose to focus on its existing film business for as long as possible. As a result, Kodak faded into irrelevance while digital photography took over.

The lesson here is clear. Marginal improvements will not save a struggling MVP. If the core product is not working, the best move is to listen to users, identify what works, and be willing to pivot into high-impact opportunities.

Refining the MVP

By now, you have launched your MVP and are experiencing initial user traction. However, the catch is that what got you to this point might not be enough to scale. The early adopters have

---

1 Source – Wayne State University (**https://digitalcommons.wayne.edu/cgi/viewcontent. cgi?article=1615&context=oa_dissertations**)

provided you with valuable feedback, and now it is time to use it to fine-tune your product. Refining the MVP is all about identifying what works, what does not, and what needs to evolve.

Here are some important actions to help you refine your MVP effectively:

- **Capturing user feedback**: User feedback is the lifeblood of refinement, but keep a check, as not all feedback is equal. To gather meaningful insights, you must focus on product usage data, app store reviews, support tickets and complaints, **net promoter scores** (**NPS**), and direct user interviews. The key is to pick up the patterns. If multiple users highlight the same frustration, such as a missing feature, it is a clear signal worth investigating.

- **Prioritize what matters**: You cannot (and should not) act on every piece of feedback. Prioritize improvements that align with your product's mission and drive user retention.

  - Use the RICE or MoSCoW frameworks

  - Double down on what users already love about your product.

- **Iterate quickly and test**: Refinement is not a one-and-done process; it is a cycle. Focus on rolling out small changes and measuring the impact. Use A/B testing to validate the updates to a subset of users before scaling. Make sure your top metrics, like user engagement, retention, and churn, are continuously monitored.

- **Let go of what is not working**: Remember, you are building a product that customers love, not for yourself. Inevitably, you will find yourself in a situation where you have to let go of a feature in the product, which you feel was awesome. Be ruthless if something is not driving value or aligning with user needs.

  A focused and simple product carries a high potential to scale better and quicker.

Refining your MVP is about listening to your users, acting on feedback, and staying true to your product's mission. Do not aim for perfection; aim for progress. Remember, every iteration is a step closer to building a product your users cannot live without.

MVP to full-scale product development

MVPs are often built using an Agile or Lean methodology, prioritizing speed over structure. However, as the product scales, a more mature **software development life cycle** (**SDLC**) is required to ensure stability, maintainability, and long-term success.

Scaling an MVP into a full-fledged product development cycle requires you to lift the *engineering, infrastructure,* and *operational* tiers of the product. The transition involves refining system architecture, design, hardening the codebase, optimizing databases, and refining user experience while ensuring security and reliability.

Refining system architecture

MVPs built on monolithic architecture are great for rapid development, but they become a bottleneck at scale. This may lead to performance degradation, slow deployments, and a tedious task to debug and enhance. The transition to a modular and scalable architecture is crucial before it becomes a technical debt.

Adopting a **service-oriented architecture** (**SOA**) or microservices approach early allows different components of the system to scale independently, improving fault isolation, deployment flexibility, and overall system resilience. This shift ensures that as the product enters its growth phase, it remains Agile, maintainable, and capable of handling increasing workloads efficiently. The earlier this transition happens, the easier it becomes to scale without hitting critical infrastructure roadblocks. Key steps for this transition include:

- Decouple functionalities like user authentication, order processing, and analytics into independent services.

- Using API gateways like *Kong*, *Apigee*, or *AWS API Gateway* to manage service communication efficiently.

- Implementing inter-service communication using RESTful APIs or event-driven architectures with *Kafka* or *RabbitMQ*.

Codebase hardening and refactoring

It is crucial to refactor the product codebase for modularity, efficiency, and maintainability. Moving towards SOA architecture or microservices helps separate concerns, making the system more scalable and resilient. Optimizing inefficient queries, reducing redundant API calls, and implementing unit, integration, and performance tests can prevent system regressions as the workload grows.

Another essential step is version control and CI/CD integration to ensure automated deployments and reduce downtime during releases. Many early-stage products use direct database queries within controllers; at scale, these should be refactored using **object-relational mapping** (**ORM**) with caching strategies to enhance performance.

Database scalability and optimization

The database must be optimized to ensure scalability, availability, and performance. Choosing the right database model is critical; relational databases like *PostgreSQL* and *MySQL* provide strong consistency and vertical scalability, while *NoSQL* solutions such as *MongoDB* and *DynamoDB* offer high throughput and better flexibility for unstructured data. A hybrid approach, where transactions are handled by SQL while large-scale reads are managed through NoSQL, can provide the best of both worlds.

Some areas of optimization that must be looked at during this activity are listed as follows:

- Caching plays a crucial role in database optimization.

- Implementing solutions like *Redis* or *Memcached* can offload frequently accessed queries, significantly improving response times.

- For read-heavy operations, database replication ensures load balancing.

- Sharding helps distribute large datasets across multiple database instances, preventing a single point of failure.

- Indexing must be optimized to speed up search and retrieval operations, ensuring queries remain performant as data volume increases.

Backend and API performance

One essential aspect of scaling APIs is rate limiting and throttling to prevent misuse and ensure fair usage. Tools like *NGINX, Kong*, or *API Gateway* help manage API traffic efficiently, while authentication mechanisms such as JWT-based tokenization provide scalable session management.

Let us learn three tips to optimize backend performance:

- For handling background jobs and computationally intensive tasks, asynchronous processing is necessary.

- Implementing background workers using *Celery* or *Sidekiq* helps offload non-essential tasks, while event-driven architectures using Kafka or RabbitMQ improve system responsiveness and reliability.

- Containerization with Docker and orchestration through Kubernetes ensures efficient scaling of microservices.

Frontend scalability and UX

A product's user interface must not only be functional but also responsive, lightweight, and optimized for high concurrency. Performance improvements can be achieved through code-splitting with Webpack or Rollup, ensuring that only necessary components load on demand. Similarly, lazy loading reduces initial load time, enhancing user experience.

Progressive Web App is a widely adopted approach to enable mobile-responsive, smoother experiences by enabling offline functionality through service workers.

Another critical component of frontend scalability is content delivery. Using a **content delivery network** (**CDN**) like *Cloudflare, AWS CloudFront*, or *Akamai* reduces latency by distributing static assets across global edge servers. This results in faster page loads, improved user experience, and reduced server load.

DevOps, monitoring, and security

From a product play perspective, another key area that needs to be considered is DevOps, security, and monitoring. As your product matures, these good practices ensure reliability, scalability, and resilience.

The following are some of the key pointers to be considered:

- **Infrastructure automation**: Use **infrastructure as code (IaC)** tools like Terraform or AWS CloudFormation to ensure consistent and replicable environments. Containerization with Docker and orchestration using Kubernetes streamlines deployments and scaling.

- **Continuous integration and deployment (CI/CD)**: Implement automated pipelines with *Jenkins*, *GitHub Actions*, or *GitLab* CI/CD to enable faster, error-free releases.

- **Monitoring and observability**: Leverage *Prometheus*, *Grafana*, and *Datadog* for system health tracking. Use **Elasticsearch, Logstash, Kibana Stack** (**ELK Stack**) for centralized logging and debugging.

- **Security and compliance**: Enforce **Open Worldwide Application Security Project** (**OWASP**) best practices, encrypt sensitive data using AES-256 and TLS 1.2+, and implement **role-based access control** (**RBAC**). Regular penetration testing and compliance adherence (GDPR, HIPAA, SOC2) ensure data protection.

Scaling the team

The engineering team must adopt best practices such as **pull request** (**PR**) reviews, static code analysis, and branching strategies (e.g., GitFlow or trunk-based development) to maintain code quality.

Integrating AI-driven chatbots helps automate common support queries, reducing manual workload while enhancing user satisfaction. Additionally, building a self-service knowledge base allows users to troubleshoot issues independently, improving the overall customer experience.

Transitioning from MVP to a full-scale product is about sustainability. A well-envisioned architecture, performance optimization, and security model ensure that the system can scale efficiently. Beyond technology, having the right team structure, operational processes, and customer engagement strategies is equally critical. Startups can successfully evolve their MVP into a market-ready product by focusing on scalable infrastructure, optimized performance, and a user-centric approach.

Strengthening product-market fit

Achieving **product-market fit** (**PMF**) is a continuous process that evolves as you scale. A product that resonates with early adopters may not necessarily appeal to mainstream users, and what works in one market segment might need fine-tuning for another. Strengthening product-market fit is about continuously aligning your product's value proposition with the needs of your customers as you grow.

In this section, we will look at practical steps to deepen PMF and provide actionable templates to help you execute these strategies.

Deepening customer understanding

As your user base grows, so does the diversity of needs and expectations. Strengthening PMF starts with understanding these nuances. Use behavioral data, demographics, and psychographics to create refined user personas. Tools like *Mixpanel* or *Amplitude* can help analyze user behavior.

The following is the template of a sample persona definition:

Persona	Demographics	Pain points	Key motivations	Usage patterns
Tech-savvy millennial	Age: 25 to 35, Urban	Wants convenience, but dislikes clunky UX	Quick access to features	Uses product daily for short bursts

Table 8.1: Sample persona definition along with the key attributes

User interactions hold the key. Schedule customer interviews and surveys on a regular basis. The following are sample questions to help start the conversation:

- What problem does our product solve for you?

- What is one feature you would love to see improved?

- What other tools do you use to solve similar problems?

Refining your value proposition

The value that resonated with early adopters may not be enough to capture the broader market. The mainstream user base typically needs clearer messaging and more seamless experiences.

The following table runs A/B tests on landing pages, email campaigns, and ads to measure the conversion rates across different target audiences:

Version	Headline	Target audience	Conversion rate
A	Simplify team projects	Small business owners	12%
B	Get projects done faster	Freelancers	18%

Table 8.2: A/B testing tracker template

Another way to measure the value proposition is to identify the *tasks* your customers are accomplishing with your product. These tasks help in framing a strong message with clarity, adoption, and testimony.

Monitoring and measuring PMF

We have learned the importance of a metric framework and tracking in earlier chapters. To recap, design the metrics that help you assess and measure the product adoption. Before diving deep into the behaviors and predictions, it is imperative to focus on first-level metrics like NPS and retention. Your north star metrics that you can track are as follows:

- **NPS**: Measures customer satisfaction and loyalty. Ask users, *How likely are you to recommend this product to a friend?*

- **Retention rate**: How many users keep coming back over time. For PMF, set a retention rate of upwards of 40%.

- **Engagement metrics**: Measure usage patterns (daily active users, time spent per session, etc.). Tools like *Segment* or *Heap* can help track these.

- **Cohort analysis**: Observe user behavior over time to see if retention is improving.

The following table lists the north star metrics by categories. As a startup, you can pick a single or a small subset of metrics that can be tied to the vision and mission of the business and can clearly reflect the growth trajectory of the business at any given time.

Category	Metric 1	Metric 2
Revenue	**Annual recurring revenue (ARR)**	**Gross merchandise volume (GMV)**
Customer growth	Paid user base	Conversion rates
Volumetric growth	Transaction volume	Adoption rates
Engagement growth	**Daily active users (DAU)**	**Monthly active users (MAU)**
Impact	**Customer lifetime value (CLV)**	**Customer acquisition costs (CAC)**
User experience	User retention rates	**NPS**

Table 8.3: North start metrics by categories

Marketing and distribution

Once your MVP has shown traction, scaling up means getting your product into the hands of more users. This is not about just throwing money into ads and hoping for the best; it is about finding repeatable, efficient marketing and distribution strategies that bring in the right customers at the right cost. Let us break it down into practical steps to ensure your growth efforts are intentional, sustainable, and scalable.

Choosing the right growth channels

Not all marketing channels are equal. Neither are users the same, nor is the campaign messaging. To scale effectively, you need to understand which channels resonate most with your audience and double down on those.

The following template shows you how to test different growth channels:

Channel	Test budget	Objective	Success metrics	Next steps
Social media ads	$500	Drive initial clicks and signups	CTR, CPA, conversion rate	Scale budget if CPA < $10
Content marketing	$300	Generate inbound traffic	Time-on-site, leads	Continue blog series if CTR > 5%
Email campaigns	$200	Re-engage early adopters	Open Rate, Conversion	Expand if Open Rate > 20%

Table 8.4: Budget and success metrics template for growth channels

Focus on one or two channels that show strong traction instead of trying to do everything at once. For example, Slack grew by focusing on word-of-mouth and targeted content for teams, while Airbnb capitalized on Craigslist for its early distribution.

Mastering growth hacking tactics

Growth hacking means finding creative and data-driven techniques to grow fast. These techniques work marvelously well for startups looking to scale without a heavy burn. Let us explore a few of these tactics:

- **Viral loop**: A viral loop is when your product naturally encourages users to bring in others. It could be a referral program or an incentive-based sharing where users feel rewarded by sharing their experience. Here is what you can try, ideate an incentivization strategy, create a seamless and attractive experience, and track results. You may tweak the incentives based on adoption and traction.

- **Create Fear of Missing Out (FOMO)**: Introduce limited-time, our hour-based offers, or brand or product exclusivity to drive urgency. The first impression, creativity, and narrative are the critical key factors in generating the interest of a user.

Optimizing the sales funnel

Scaling is about converting traffic into paying users and retaining them to build healthy lifetime value. This means obsessing over your sales funnel, from the first interaction to long-term retention.

The following figure shows the stages to optimize the sales funnel:

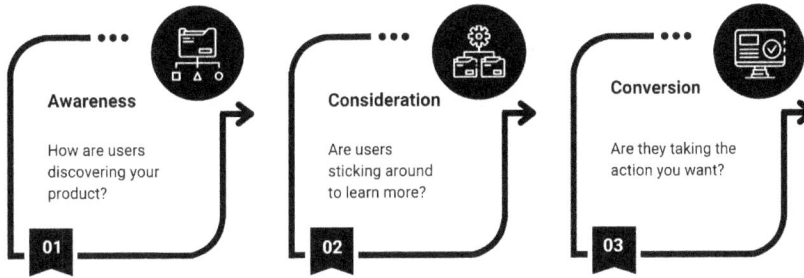

Figure 8.2: High-level stages to optimize the sales funnel

Use the following table to track the metrics at each stage:

Stage	Metric to track	Target goal	Actions to improve
Awareness	Website Traffic	50,000 visitors	Improve SEO; launch ads
Consideration	Email Signups	10% signup rate	Simplify forms; A/B test CTAs
Conversion	Paid Subscriptions	15% trial-to-paid	Optimize checkout; add urgency

Table 8.5: Metric tracker template for various sales funnels

Building partnerships

To have a sharp growth trajectory, industry partnerships are a great option. The content and influencer economy are not just reaching new heights but also contributing significantly to the business growth of consumer-driven products.

Strategic partnerships can help you tap into existing audiences, saving time and money. In addition, the growth engine rides on multiple levers. Here is what startups must look at to make the most out of strategic partnerships:

- **Identify win-win opportunities**: Look for brands or platforms that target a similar audience but do not directly compete with you.
- **Co-marketing campaign**: Collaborate on a shared piece of content, giveaway, or event.
- **Influencer partnerships**: Pick up the influencer whose audience demographics or purchasing behavior resonates with your product offerings. Do not rely on the audience volume alone.

Retargeting and re-engagement

Many of your potential users will not convert the first time they interact with your product. Retargeting is your opportunity to bring them back. Show ads or send emails that highlight specific features, benefits, or success stories that appeal to users who dropped off.

It is not often that we see e-commerce mailers that retarget users with abandoned carts or new offer emails to bring the users back to the platform. Here is an actionable template for a retargeting email:

- **Subject line**: *Still thinking about [Product Name]? Here is why others love it.*

- **Body**: Share a user success story or offer a time-sensitive discount to encourage action.

- **CTA**: *Get Started Now* or *Claim Your Offer*.

Measuring the impact

At scale, every marketing effort should be tied to measurable results. Google Analytics, Mixpanel, or Amplitude help you track the effectiveness of your campaigns. The following figure shows the key metrics to watch:

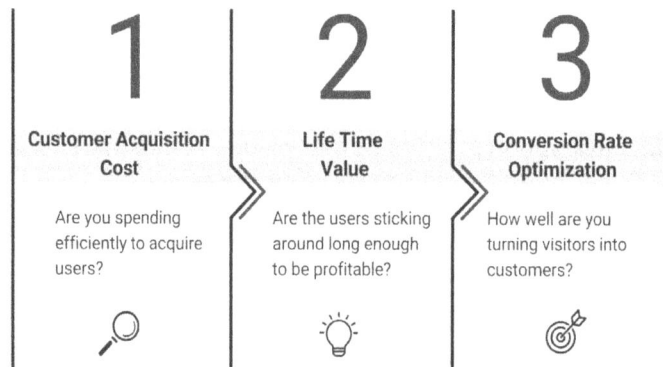

Figure 8.3: Top metrics to record success

Many startups follow the *Rule of 3 - 1* for scaling. Your **life time value** (**LTV**) should be at least three times your **CAC** to ensure healthy growth.

Unless it goes out of control, do not think that marketing is a cost. It is an investment in your future growth. Start small, test constantly, and double down on what works. With the right mix of creative tactics, disciplined funnel optimization, and data-driven decisions, you can take your MVP to the next level and capture a significant market share.

Establishing operational excellence

When you are scaling your MVP, having a robust operation is critical for success. Operational excellence ensures that your team, processes, and tools can handle the increased complexity and volume that come with growth. Without it, even the best product can crumble due to inefficiency, slow decision-making, or poor resource management.

Establishing operational excellence does not mean creating rigid systems that slow you down.

Instead, it is about setting processes that support scalability while maintaining the agility that allowed your MVP to thrive. Let us explore key focus areas for operational excellence.

Team structure and role definitions

As you scale, your team will grow, and so will the complexity of collaboration. You need the right people in the right roles, aligned with clear goals. Start by identifying roles that are critical to your next phase. For example, product managers prioritize user needs, customer success specialists ensure user retention, or even cross-functional teams focused on organization-wide objectives like marketing or sales.

Digitize processes to scale operations

Scaling is not about working harder; it is about working smarter. Digitization, along with automation, reduces manual overhead, increases accuracy, and frees up your team's bandwidth for high-value work. The following are some practical tips:

- Build rapid productivity tools to digitize day-to-day processes.

- Promote data accessibility through data APIs, email alerts, and a data portal.

- Track, monitor, and publish process adherence through unified dashboarding.

Develop playbooks for critical processes

As the team grows, you would not want every process to be reinvented from scratch. Playbooks ensure consistency and efficiency. Start simple and document your most successful processes and share them in a central location for your team.

The following are some sample playbooks:

- **Iterative processes like adding users, stores, or SKU**: Outline the steps and checklist to onboard new users quickly and effectively.

- **Control tower and customer support**: This largely helps in standardizing customer interactions.

- **Incident management**: A clear guide for handling technical downtime or customer complaints.

- **Marketing campaigns**: Templates for launching ads, email campaigns, and social posts.

Navigating challenges

The growth phase is where startups move from survival to thrive mode. It comes with challenges like technical bottlenecks, human resources, managing competition, and stabilizing customer experience. These challenges can feel overwhelming, but with the right mindset and strategies, they are opportunities to build resilience and set the foundation for long-term success.

Let us break down some of the most common challenges and actionable ways to tackle them:

- **Technical bottlenecks**: As your user base grows, the systems that supported your MVP might struggle under the load. Outages, slow performance, or data inconsistencies can quickly alienate users. Identify high-risk areas (e.g., database capacity, server loads) before they become problems. Use tools like *New Relic* or *Datadog* to monitor performance.

  One key proactive activity is conducting IT drills to simulate traffic surges and find infrastructure and process gaps.

- **Scaling team and culture**: Growth demands people. But hiring too quickly or without focus can create chaos. The following are a few tips to build a strong team:

  o **Hire for growth and not to fill up roles**: At the senior level, focus on generalists who can adapt and grow with the company, especially in early growth stages.

  o **Role definitions at junior roles**: Drive clarity for the roles that are focused on execution.

  o **Maintain team growth charter**: Identify core gaps in your team, set hiring priorities for critical roles first, and align hiring goals with company milestones.

- **Battling competition**: The best ideas thrive on execution. Execution excellence differentiates industry leaders from the rest of the crowd. In the growth phase, the growth of competition is inevitable. Here is how startups can stay relevant amidst growing competition and drive value for their customers:

  o **Focus on execution**: Maintain razor-sharp focus on day-to-day execution so that you continue to leverage and build on the existing customer base.

  o **Control customer churn**: Your competitors already have a strategy to poach your customers. Product stickiness is a function of experience, trust, and loyalty. Loyalty programs, referral incentives, and personalized experiences can keep users engaged.

  o **Enjoy the competition**: A healthy competition is a bigger push to keep improving your product and services.

  o **Focus on differentiation**: Double down on your unique value proposition. What makes your product harder to replicate?

  o **Monitor competitors actively**: Use *SimilarWeb* or *App Annie* to track their performance, features, and marketing strategies.

- **Managing costs**: Growth can be expensive. Even if you leave out marketing, the capital involved in scaling servers, hiring, and operations may impact profitability. Even tech unicorns like Uber have had to pull back from growth-at-all-costs strategies to focus on profitability.

As a startup, it is important to adopt a thoughtful approach to picking your growth channels. Assess the options on their demonstrated ROI, scalability, and optimal capital requirements. Double down on channels that have proven ROI. Pause or reevaluate underperforming initiatives. Invest in tools and processes that save time and reduce manual work (e.g., *Zapier* for automation, *Airtable* for tracking).

Scaling is not a straight path; it is filled with pivots, learnings, and sometimes setbacks. The key is to stay proactive, Lean on data, and tackle challenges head-on with a growth mindset. Embrace the obstacles as opportunities to refine your product, processes, and strategy. After all, growth is not just about numbers; it is about building something that lasts.

Achieving market dominance

Market dominance is a state where the product is not an option, but the default choice, or synonymous with solving a problem. This happens by consistently driving value and building trust with customers. Look at Amazon, Uber, or LinkedIn. They did not become leaders overnight. Their journeys were shaped by strategic decisions that made them indispensable in their space. With the right strategies, you can carve out a market position so strong that competitors find it hard to disrupt.

Here is how to aim for market dominance:

- **Build ecosystems, not just products**: Dominant companies create value beyond the core product by building ecosystems that keep users as well as stakeholders engaged and locked in. For example, Apple's ecosystem of devices and services, or how Tesla integrates cars, charging networks, and energy solutions. If your product is a project management tool, consider adding resource allocation, reporting dashboards, or integrations with financial tools.

    The following figure shows a process to map complementary products to grow a product into an ecosystem:

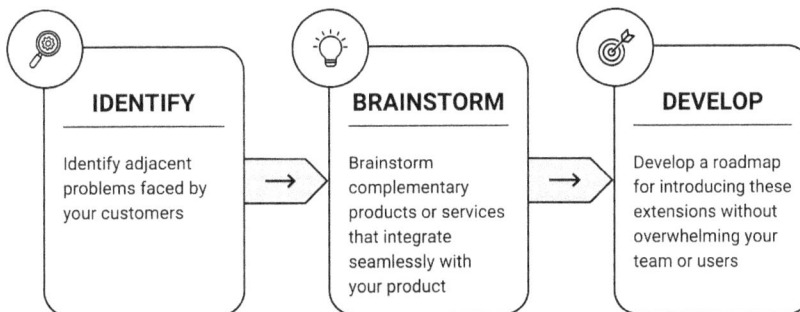

Figure 8.4: Stages to grow product ecosystem with external integrations

- **Leverage network effects**: Products with network effects become more valuable as more people use them. This creates a flywheel that makes it harder for competitors to catch up. Think about LinkedIn; its value lies in the professional connections users can access, which only grows as the network expands. Here is what you must do to create a network effect:

    o Incentivize users to bring others into your product (e.g., referral programs, collaboration features).

    o Encourage user-generated content or interaction that creates a community, like Airbnb's host reviews or Instagram's social sharing.

    o Focus on delivering value for both sides of a marketplace if applicable (e.g., buyers and sellers). Take *Urban Company* in India, for example. It transformed home services, which was a traditionally unorganized sector, by creating a strong supply of professional service providers, generating demand, and ensuring quality and reliability for customers.

- **Grow new markets**: Dominance often requires breaking into new markets, geographic, demographic, or even entirely new industries. For example, *Netflix* started with DVDs-by-mail, then expanded into streaming, and is now a global production powerhouse.

  You can research new markets by analyzing untapped customer segments or geographies. But make sure you test the demand with lightweight experiments, such as running localized marketing campaigns or offering free trials in a new vertical. Post the assessment and validation, the adaptation for the new market in terms of pricing, messaging, or capabilities to cater to local needs should be done on priority.

- **Invest in brand**: You must not forget that the companies that dominate markets do not just sell products, but they offer trust, inspiration, and connection. *Nike* is not just a shoe company; it is a symbol of perseverance. *HubSpot* is not just marketing software; it is a thought leader in inbound marketing.

- **Industry expert**: As an entrepreneur, you must position your company as an expert in your industry through blogs, webinars, and white papers. These activities help you establish an emotional connection with your users through storytelling. Do not forget to highlight customer success stories (with consent) or your mission in action.

- **Stabilize your position**: Staying dominant requires proactive strategies to defend your position. The only way to retain dominance is to continuously innovate and experiment. We have discussed this earlier as well. Complacency kills growth. In the growth phase, you must dedicate time and effort to radical innovation, customer experience, and operational excellence.

  Take note of the following four tips to strengthen your position at the top in your space:

o **Continuously innovate**: Allocate resources to explore the next big thing in your industry.

o **Culture of experimentation**: Do not hesitate to experiment with new experiences with the customers.

o **Monitor competitors** and customer satisfaction metrics to stay ahead of emerging threats.

o **Reinforce switching costs**: Develop features that make it hard for users to leave, like deep integrations or data portability limitations.

Case studies

Let us look at a few examples of how a well-defined MVP can transform into a scalable and profitable business through continuous innovation, user-focused improvements, and strategic expansion.

Zomato

Launched in 2008 as *Foodiebay*, *Zomato* began by providing digitally scanned copies of restaurant menus in Delhi NCR in India, allowing users to browse the menus online.

The convenience of accessing menus online resonated with users, leading to rapid adoption. Within a year, Foodiebay expanded to major Indian cities, building a huge user base.

In 2010, Foodiebay was rebranded as Zomato, a platform where users can post reviews, ratings, and browse restaurant menus. Gauging the market demand, Zomato ventured into food delivery, table reservations, and international markets. By 2021, Zomato had become one of India's leading food tech companies, successfully completing an IPO listing on the stock exchange.

The following table shows the product-led growth trajectory of Zomato since its inception:

Year	Milestone	Stages
2008	MVP launched as Foodiebay, an online restaurant menu listing platform.	MVP launched
2010	Rebranded the MVP as Zomato Expanded restaurant discovery, user reviews, and ratings.	Product transition
2012	International expansion begins, entering UAE, Sri Lanka, and the UK.	Grow new markets
2015	Introduced Zomato Order, entering the food delivery market.	Innovation
2017	Launched Zomato Gold (subscription model) to drive user engagement.	Innovation

2020	Acquired UberEats India, strengthening food delivery dominance.	Network effect
2021	Became one of India's first food tech companies to go public with an IPO.	Market dominance
2023	Expanded into quick commerce (Blinkit acquisition) and deepened supply chain integration.	Building ecosystem

Table 8.6: Zomato growth timeline over the years

Zerodha

Founded in 2010, Zerodha started as a discount brokerage platform, eliminating hefty commissions and offering a flat fee trading model, making stock market investing accessible to retail investors.

The platform gained traction by appealing to first-time investors and traders who sought low-cost trading solutions. Word-of-mouth marketing, strong branding, transparent pricing, and an intuitive user interface helped *Zerodha* rapidly acquire users.

Zerodha scaled its offering by launching *Kite* (a proprietary trading platform), *Coin* (a direct mutual fund investment tool), and *Varsity* (an educational platform). With millions of customers, Zerodha has become India's largest retail brokerage, maintaining profitability without external funding.

The following table shows the product trajectory of Zerodha since its launch in 2010:

Year	Milestone	Stages
2010	MVP launched as Zerodha, introducing discount brokerage with a flat-fee model.	MVP launched
2013	Developed Pi, a desktop-based trading software.	Product development
2015	Launched Kite, a web-based and mobile trading platform.	Product innovation
2017	Introduced Coin, a zero-commission direct mutual funds investment platform.	Product innovation
2018	Became India's largest retail stockbroker, surpassing traditional firms.	Innovation
2019	Bootstrapped company crosses 1 million active clients and remains profitable.	Market dominance
2022	Expanded with Nudge, an AI-driven risk management tool for traders.	Grow new markets
2024	Continues market leadership with over 11 million active traders and diversified product offerings.	Building ecosystem

Table 8.7: Zomato growth timeline over the years

Freshworks

Established in 2010 as *Freshdesk*, the company offered a cloud-based customer support software focusing on ease of use and affordability for small and medium-sized businesses.

Freshdesk's user-friendly interface and competitive pricing attracted a global clientele, leading to rapid adoption among businesses seeking efficient customer support solutions.

Rebranded as Freshworks in 2017, the company expanded its product suite to include IT service management, CRM, and marketing automation tools. Emphasizing integration and scalability, Freshworks has become a significant player in the SaaS industry, serving over 50,000 customers worldwide.

The following is the growth and expansion timeline of Freshworks over the last decade:

Year	Milestone	Stages
2010	MVP launched as Freshdesk, a cloud-based customer support solution.	MVP launched
2012	Gained global traction; hit 10,000 customers across 50+ countries.	Initial traction
2014	Expanded product offerings, adding live chat and call center support.	Product innovation
2017	Rebranded as Freshworks, transitioning from a single-product company to a full SaaS suite.	Branding
2018	Launched Freshsales, an AI-powered CRM solution.	Innovation
2019	Crossed $100 million in ARR.	Market dominance
2021	Became the first Indian SaaS company to list on NASDAQ, with a $13B valuation.	Market dominance
2023	Expanded AI-driven solutions and strengthened global presence.	Grow new markets

Table 8.8: Zomato growth timeline over the years

Conclusion

In this chapter, we explored the essential strategies to maneuver the growth phase of your MVP, which is now a full-blown product. First, we focused on refining your product based on user feedback, ensuring it is ready to meet the needs of a growing audience. We also discussed the importance of strengthening product-market fit by identifying new customer segments and staying competitive through differentiation.

Next, we covered marketing and distribution, including growth tactics to expand your reach and optimize customer acquisition channels. Building scalable operations was another key focus, highlighting how to create processes, tools, and teams that can handle rapid growth without chaos. Finally, we addressed common challenges like managing technical debt, responding to competition, and balancing growth with quality.

In the next chapter, we will explore the most common barriers to growth. We will discuss internal team dynamics, cultural friction, market pressures, and product or tech pitfalls that can trip up even the smartest founders. More importantly, we will understand the mindset shifts needed to navigate and overcome them.

Points to remember

- Refine your product to meet the demands of a growing market.
- Build marketing and distribution strategies that drive sustainable growth.
- Create operational systems and processes that support scale.
- Anticipate and navigate challenges in the growth phase.
- Scaling is about growing intelligently and staying true to the core value of your product.

Join our Discord space

Join our Discord workspace for latest updates, offers, tech happenings around the world, new releases, and sessions with the authors:

https://discord.bpbonline.com

CHAPTER 9

Common Barriers and the Mindset

Introduction

In the previous chapter, we explored the technical and operational steps required to scale an MVP into a full-fledged product. However, before this transition can happen, there is a phase that determines whether the MVP has a future or not. We have discussed these challenges in previous chapters; however, in this chapter, we will take a look at how and where products stall, pivot, or perish.

In the product journey, the real test begins when the product meets reality, i.e., customer feedback, the competitive tactics, cultural differences, and the tussle between vision and adaptation to the market signals. Most startups do not fail because of poor technology or lack of funding, but they fail because they do not capture and capitalize on the market signals.

The founders and teams who truly succeed are the ones who stay curious. They do not see an MVP as just a minimum viable product, but as an evolving experiment. It is their way of figuring out what clicks, what falls flat, and where they need to adapt.

This chapter explores the common barriers, the internal struggles within teams and culture, external pressures from the market, and the product and technological traps that catch even the smartest founders off guard. More importantly, we will uncover the mindset shifts needed to overcome them.

Structure

In this chapter, we will cover the following topics:

- Barriers within the team

- Barriers from the market

- Product and technology barriers

- Mental and emotional barriers

- Mindset of successful MVP teams

- Case studies

Objectives

In this chapter, we uncover the common reasons MVPs fail and explore how successful teams treat the MVP not as a destination, but as a lever for continuous learning. You will also gain insights into the mindset of resilient founders, those who know when to stay the course and when to shift gears.

By the end of this chapter, you will understand why most MVPs fail and how to spot warning signs early. People barriers within the team, management, and stakeholders, along with market barriers including competition, product-market fit, and adoption, are the top takeaways. Other takeaways include MVP as a continuous learning engine, not a final product, and learning how successful founders develop an adaptive mindset, balancing conviction with flexibility.

Barriers within the team

One of the biggest hurdles in the MVP journey comes from within the team itself. The way founders and early development teams think, make decisions, and react to feedback can either accelerate the product's evolution or trap it in a loop of overthinking, conflicts, or overbuilding.

Chasing perfection before launch

Many teams obsess over building the *perfect* MVP, which is largely a contradiction. An MVP is meant to be minimal, yet viable, and proportionately imperfect. Yet, founders often struggle to draw the line between what is essential and what is *nice to have*. This pursuit of perfection not only delays launch but also disconnects the product from real user feedback, which is far more valuable than internal opinions. Agility in incorporating the user feedback can potentially iron out MVP bugs much faster than breaking heads in a closed room.

Emotions with the first idea

Founders often believe their first vision is always the winning idea, ignoring early signs that the market might want something different. This attachment blinds teams from accepting the critical feedback from the users and thereby pivoting or refining the product. Successful MVPs evolve through feedback, not through the intuition of a single mind alone.

The following questionnaire helps builders to elucidate the ego from the product decisions:

- What feature or idea are we most proud of?
- What if customers hate it? How will we respond?
- Did the product explain the feature enough? Is it simple enough to use?
- What is one feature we are willing to kill if the data says so?
- If this product completely fails, what will we have learned?
- On a scale of 1-10, how open are we to pivoting after launch?
- What are the levers of pivot? User feedback, competition, growth, or something else?

Too much to digest

More features do not always make a better product. This is another common trap to impress the market. Instead of focusing on a core problem-solution fit, teams spread themselves thin, trying to solve everything at once. This leads to scope creep, longer development cycles, and more room for bugs, all without clear evidence that users want those features in the first place.

Fear of negative feedback

Some teams hesitate to ship their MVP to real users because they are scared of negative feedback. This fear creates a dangerous cycle where the product lives in internal demo loops but is never exposed to actual market signals. However, negative feedback is a gift. It tells you what is broken and what matters to customers. Avoiding it only delays learning and wastes resources.

The balanced mindset

To overcome these internal barriers, successful teams adopt a learning-first mindset. Launch something simple and viable, and then evolve it with the feedback. Chasing perfection may bring down the speed and dent the agility.

The following figure lists four essentials of a learning-first mindset to overcome internal barriers:

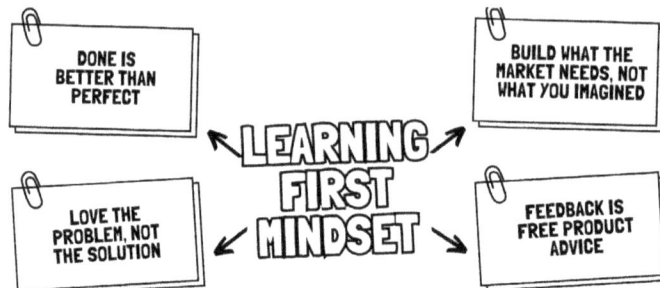

Figure 9.1: Components of a learning-first mindset

Startups that master these internal dynamics treat the MVP as a living experiment, constantly learning, adapting, and moving closer to product-market fit, one small step at a time.

Actionable templates

While negotiating with the internal barriers mentioned above, it is always advisable for the product leaders to adopt a methodological approach to connect the dots and build a holistic view of the problem.

The two templates below will help product leaders and owners to process negative feedback from users and post-MVP launch calibration.

Template 1, processing negative feedback

Negative feedback can crush morale. The following template helps product managers reframe and take action on negative feedback without defensiveness.

To build product resilience, synthesize a particular volume of customer feedback to answer the following questions:

- What exactly did the customer say? Add quoted verbatim to get the exact words used in the feedback.

- What emotion does the feedback trigger in us?

- Is this a preference issue, a usability issue, or a value issue?

- If we act on this feedback, what bigger assumption does it challenge?

- What would have to be true for this feedback to be wrong?

- What is the smallest experiment we can run to test if they are right?

Template 2, the mindset calibration canvas

Product leaders not just build the product but also coach development teams throughout the journey. The following template will help you gauge the team's mindset at different stages of the launch:

- What does success look like in the first 30 days, 90 days, and 6 months? Note that revenue is an output indicator. The focus is to get hold of the intrinsic parameters of success.

- What assumptions are we trying to break?

- What is our tolerance for negative feedback on a scale of 1 to 10?

- How will we reward learning moments, not just wins?

- How to define perfection? What is the pace, if we are chasing it?

- What is our *enough to launch* benchmark?

- What is our plan if customers behave in ways we did not expect?

Barriers from the market

Once the MVP is generally available in the market, the product leaders and founders must closely observe the adoption metrics. Many products and startups stumble because the market does not behave as expected and predicted. Let us explore the top three market barriers that could stumble the product journey:

- **No clear market need**: It is unfortunate, but one of the most brutal truths is that the market might not need your product, at least not in the way you imagined. Startup leaders often assume that if they build it, customers will come, but the reality is not that simple. If the core problem you are solving lacks urgency or a pull factor, the MVP will struggle to gain traction.

  If the early signs indicate this state, founders can take proactive steps as follows:

  1. Engage with early customers to identify gaps in your product offering.

  2. Validate product positioning by emphasizing core values and promoting it on channels where your target audience is most active.

  3. Identify customers who align with your product personas and offer incentives for early feedback.

- **Crowded and noisy markets**: Even if you have identified a real problem, you may not be the only one solving it. Many startups launch into overcrowded spaces, where incumbents, other startups, and substitutes already fight for attention. In such cases, your MVP must stand out quickly. This can be either by being significantly better, cheaper, or faster, or by targeting a more niche or underserved segment.

Product positioning plays a key role in the launch. With minimal effort, the target customer must be prompted to use your product for one of the other problems.

- **Mismatch between price and value perception**: Pricing is an important factor in product adoption. Even if your product solves a realistic problem in a better way, customers may feel the price is not justified in comparison to the alternatives. This becomes even more challenging in price-sensitive markets like India, where perceived value must far exceed the actual price to trigger adoption. Finding the right price-value balance is part of the MVP learning curve.

Early adopter fatigue

Targeting early adopters is smart for an MVP, but these users can also be fickle and impatient. They are constantly bombarded with new products, meaning your MVP needs to deliver value quickly or risk being forgotten. If your onboarding is confusing, your value proposition is unclear, or your product is too buggy, early adopters will churn without giving feedback.

Founders who successfully cross this barrier adopt a market-first mindset.

The following figure shows the essentials of this mindset:

Figure 9.2: Components of market-first mindset

Remember, your job is not to convince the market you are right again and again, but to find where you fit in. The market plays both as a mentor as well as the judge. Startups that listen more than they talk have the best chance of turning their MVP into a product that customers actually want.

Timing as a barrier

Timing may not be the only factor, but it certainly matters. If a product is launched too early without sufficient industry analysis or targeting the problem faced by a handful of users, the market may not be ready, forcing the company to spend excessive resources educating users before adoption takes off.

For example, *Google Glass* (2013) was a promising technology but lacked a compelling use case for mass consumers, ultimately failing to gain traction. On the other hand, launching too late means entering an overcrowded market where competitors have already captured user attention. BlackBerry's reluctance to embrace touchscreen technology allowed iPhone and Android devices to dominate, rendering its products obsolete.

Rather than waiting for the *perfect moment*, startups should embrace fast, iterative releases. A Lean MVP allows startups to test adoption and gather early feedback and adoption patterns. *Slack* was initially launched as an internal tool for a gaming company *Glitch*. When it did not take off, the team pivoted to the internal chat tool they had built, turning a necessity into one of the fastest-growing B2B SaaS products ever. Adapting to technological shifts is crucial. *Zoom* was not the first video conferencing tool, but it scaled rapidly because it is a simple, reliable platform that met the growing need for remote communication during the COVID-19 pandemic.

Product and technology barriers

Sometimes, the biggest obstacles come from the product itself; the way it is designed, built, or positioned. An MVP is not meant to be perfect, but it must be functional enough to demonstrate value to the users. Many startups lose their way by either overengineering the product or cutting corners so much that the core value gets lost. All one needs is a product mindset that balances speed, usability, and scalability. Let us learn some of the common barriers inherent created within the product.

Too complex for the users

MVPs often suffer from *founder's bias*. This is the assumption that customers perceive the product the same way founders do. What feels intuitive to you or your team may be overwhelming or confusing for users encountering it for the first time. This can lead to high drop-off rates during onboarding and weaken the product's ability to hook early adopters.

Founders' bias is a common phenomenon, but replacing the user lens with a layman's helps in assessing the product through an external lens. Before launch, the product must be thoroughly tested for simplicity, usability, and ease of navigation. To assess how intuitive and frictionless your product experience is, tracking user navigation metrics is crucial.

The following table lists the key metrics that reflect usability, simplicity, and efficiency:

Metric	Definition	Why it matters	Benchmark
Time to sign up	Time taken to complete the sign-up process.	A long sign-up process can cause user drop-offs.	< 30 seconds (ideal), < 60 seconds (acceptable)

Clicks to checkout	Number of clicks required to complete a purchase.	More clicks increase friction and cart abandonment.	≤ 5 clicks for optimized checkout
Time to first action (TTFA)	Time taken for a new user to complete their first key action.	Faster TTFA ensures users quickly experience product value.	< 2 minutes post-sign-up
Navigation drop-off rate	Percentage of users who exit before completing a critical journey.	High drop-offs indicate confusing navigation.	< 30% in critical workflows
Task completion rate	Percentage of users who successfully complete an intended action.	A low rate suggests UI issues or unclear steps.	> 80% for smooth workflows
Search-to-action rate	Percentage of users who use search and take an action (e.g., add to cart).	Low rates indicate poor search relevance.	> 80%
Rage clicks and dead clicks	Frequency of repeated clicks on unresponsive elements.	High rates show user frustration or misleading UI.	< 3% of total clicks
Session duration and pages per session	Total time spent and number of pages viewed in one visit.	Short sessions with high exits suggest navigation struggles.	3 - 5 min/session, 2 - 3 pages/session
Error rate and form abandonment rate	Frequency of failed actions and incomplete form submissions.	High errors suggest unclear inputs or validation issues.	Error rate < 2%, Form abandonment < 40%
Support request rate	Percentage of users needing customer support while navigating.	High rates indicate unclear UI or frustrating workflows.	< 2% of users should require support

Table 9.1: Ten user metrics to measure product experience for new users

There are additional UX and user navigation metrics like dwell rate, bounce rate, churn rate, and retention rate that can help refine and optimize product usability.

Unclear value proposition

If the product does not immediately communicate why it matters or what it offers, users will not stick around to figure it out. MVPs that lack a clear and compelling value proposition often get lost in the noise, especially in crowded markets. Users should be able to answer, *What is in it for me?* within the first 30 seconds of interacting with your product.

FrAgile technology foundation

In the race to launch quickly, some teams compromise too much on technical quality. This results in frequent bugs, downtime, or performance issues. While users may choose to ignore minor imperfections in an MVP, they will not tolerate a product that is shaky and unreliable. This is especially critical if your MVP operates in trust-sensitive domains like finance, health, or logistics.

Lack of support and feedback loops

Support and escalation are essential for staying responsive and in control when things go off track. If users cannot get support in real-time, they get frustrated and disassociate themselves immediately. A control tower must act as a bridge between the customer and ground operations.

Successful teams adopt a product mindset to overcome these barriers. The product events must be thoroughly logged to understand the user behaviour, their journey, and hence the usage metrics. The faster you learn, the faster you can turn an MVP into a product that truly fits the market.

The following figure shows the four essentials of a product mindset:

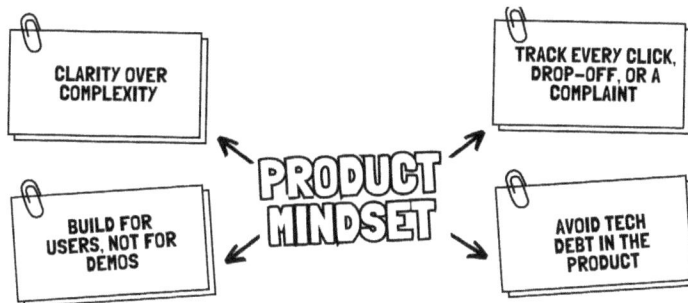

Figure 9.3: Components of a product mindset

Overcoming technological barriers

Overcoming technological barriers at the MVP stage is critical to scaling up the product. Here is how to navigate these challenges effectively:

- **Keep it simple**: Choose a tech stack that allows rapid development and easy maintenance. Avoid over-engineering; start with a monolithic approach before considering microservices. Use widely adopted frameworks with strong community support. Many successful startups, like Instagram, began with simple architectures and scaled later.

- **Build what is necessary**: Focus on core functionality that validates your idea. Do not spend time building complex features when off-the-shelf solutions like Stripe for payments or Auth0 for authentication can do the job. Accept some technical debt, but document quick fixes for future improvements. Airbnb's early version relied on manual processes before automating at scale.

- **Design for scalability**: Your MVP should handle initial traction without excessive infrastructure. Choose a database suited to your data needs and optimize performance only when necessary. Slack and Twitter were initially built for speed, then re-architected when they hit scaling limits. Plan for growth, but do not let it slow you down now.

- **Leverage no-code and automation**: For non-core functionalities like internal dashboards or workflows, use no-code tools like Retool or Zapier. Automate deployments and monitoring with CI/CD pipelines to avoid DevOps overhead. Start with cloud-based managed services rather than setting up complex infrastructure. Many startups use *Webflow*, *Durable*, or *10web* for AI-generated landing pages to move faster.

Mental and emotional barriers

Building an MVP or a product is about how well one thinks and plans the solution to a problem. Your mindset as a founder and team directly influences how fast you learn, how you react to failure, and how you adapt to reality. Many MVPs fail not because of technical flaws, but because the team's mindset is misaligned with the realities of building and scaling a product.

Product-centric to problem-centric

Most first-time founders fall in love with their product idea, its features, the design, and the cool technology. However, successful leaders learn to fall in love with the problem instead. This subtle shift changes everything. Remember, products evolve, but problems remain.

When you are problem-centric, you constantly ask and seek answers to the following questions:

- Are we solving the right problem?
- Is this the simplest solution?
- Is this what the customer wants?
- Will the customer be willing to pay for this solution?
- Can this solution scale to multiple users?

Launch obsessed with learning focused

MVP launch is an important milestone, but remember, it is not the finish line. Stay focused on the launch, but never lose sight of what really matters: how users engage and adopt your product.

The questions that great MVP teams ask are as follows:

- What is the adoption curve telling us?

- Which feature do users love most, and why?

- What is confusing them, and how can we simplify?

Start treating data as the co-founder. Learn the patterns from the user feedback, engagement, and complaints.

Perfectionism to practicality

Each of us wants the first product to be flawless, lovable, and viral. However, that is not how MVPs were built. MVP success comes from speed, simplicity, and focused learning, while perfection is met along the way.

The mindset shift here is:

- Done is better than perfect

- Feedback is better than silence

- Speed beats elegance for early-stage MVPs

Embracing pivots

No product gets it right on day one. Startups that succeed are often the ones that pivot fast and pivot smart. Instead of fearing failure, they reframe it as learning. Instagram, Slack, and even YouTube all started as something very different before they found their true product-market fit. The mindset shift is recognizing that failure is not the opposite of success, but it is part of the journey.

A pivot is not an indicator of a failed product. The following template helps in determining the decision-making criteria for when to pivot.

Pivot investigation template

Growth-mindset teams pivot quietly, realigning their strategy while embracing a mindset shift. However, pivots play a crucial role in ensuring the team stays aligned with evolving market needs, user feedback, and long-term goals. A pivot is an opportunity to refine the approach and drive product innovation.

Product leaders should use this template to ensure every pivot gets documented as institutional wisdom. The key questions to be answered by the key stakeholders are as follows:

- What was the original belief or the hypothesis?

- Who conflicted with the hypothesis, the user or the market?

- What feedback or data point broke this hypothesis?

- What signals did we ignore that could have warned us sooner?

- What mindset shifts would have helped us pivot faster?

- What new hypothesis are we betting on now?

- What will we do differently in the next MVP cycle?

Technology can pivot. Features can change. Even markets evolve. However, the one thing that must stay undeterred is your mindset. Resilient teams do not break when feedback is negative or the market thwarts the product idea. They adapt faster than others, and that is the real strength in the MVP journey.

Mindset of successful MVP teams

Mindset is a survival skill in the MVP journey. Teams that think differently do not just sail through the early turbulence, but they turn challenge into a competitive advantage. They know that the MVP is not about proving they were right all along, but it is about solving the problem in the best possible way.

Let us see what mindset shifts winning teams embrace to build MVPs that resonate with users:

- **Early launch**: Great teams do not wait for perfection because they know real learning starts after launch, not before. The focus is on getting something usable into the hands of real customers at the earliest, even though it is not perfect. *Reid Hoffman*, the co-founder of LinkedIn, says: *If you are not embarrassed by your first release, you launched too late.*

- **Solutions over features**: Stay laser-focused on solving one core problem exceptionally well. Features will grow along the way. Ask questions like: *Does this solve a real customer pain point?* or *Can we do this faster or simpler?*

- **Rapid iterations**: Rather than releasing large updates, adopt an incremental mindset. Keep the release updates small to bring in agility and lower the risks.

- **Pivot when needed**: Keep a check on the market signals and adapt quickly when needed. It could be an architectural change, an experience change, or even a major pivot.

Iteration and feedback

For successful MVP teams, the MVP is first and foremost a learning tool. These teams prioritize rapid iteration over perfection, understanding that early versions of the product will not be flawless. Every release is seen as an opportunity to validate or invalidate assumptions, with the core focus on gathering feedback. This mindset allows them to pivot or refine the product based on real user experiences and market reactions.

Teams value adaptability. While they have a clear vision of the problem they aim to solve, they stay flexible in how they execute it by following practices:

- Data-driven decisions are central to their process.

- Rely on user feedback, performance metrics, and real-world testing to guide iterations.

- Constant learning cycle ensures they focus on what truly resonates with the market.

Collaboration and strategy

A defining characteristic of successful MVP teams is their ability to foster a collaborative, cross-functional environment. These teams understand that building a successful product requires diverse perspectives, so they bring together talent from various disciplines like design, development, marketing, and product management to share ideas and solve problems. By encouraging open communication and valuing every team member's input, they ensure that the product is designed with a broad understanding of the market, users, and technology.

Successful MVP teams strike a balance between conviction and flexibility by adhering to the following actions:

- Stay committed to solving the problem, but remain open to change when data suggests a shift in approach.

- Adaptability helps them navigate uncertainty in the startup world.

- Engage with customers, stakeholders, and advisors.

- Focus on high-impact areas rather than scaling too early, ensuring the right foundation is built first.

Case studies

In this section, we will explore two case studies, *Duolingo* and *Figma*, which had to overcome internal and external non-technical barriers to succeed.

Duolingo

Duolingo started as a research project at *Carnegie Mellon University* in 2009 by *Luis von Ahn* and *Severin Hacker*. The MVP idea was to create a free, gamified language-learning platform that could be accessible to everyone, unlike expensive courses.

The first MVP was a web-based platform with only Spanish and French lessons, built with a simple, text-based translation system. The goal was to validate engagement by assessing whether users would come back daily to learn languages for free.

Launch and early adoption

In 2011, Duolingo launched its beta version, quickly amassing over 300,000 signups without any marketing. The feedback was mixed, though. Users appreciated the gamification aspects, but many found the lessons to be too rigid.

Investors were sceptical of the freemium model, arguing that language learning was not a daily habit like social media and that monetization would be difficult.

Barriers

The founding team came from an academic and research-heavy background, which initially led to slow decision-making and a lack of focus on product-market fit.

There was resistance to shifting from a purely educational tool to a consumer tech product that required aggressive A/B testing, gamification, and monetization strategies.

Growth strategies, such as streaks, leaderboards, and notifications, were internally debated, with some employees feeling that they would *degrade* the learning experience.

Their approach

The team fully embraced gamification, making learning addictive with XP points, streaks, and interactive characters. Instead of monetizing early, Duolingo focused purely on engagement and retention, ensuring users would develop daily habits before introducing ads and subscriptions.

The founders focused on building a data-driven culture where A/B testing dictated every decision. If a feature improved retention, it stayed; if not, it was scrapped.

By 2017, Duolingo launched Duolingo Plus (a premium, ad-free version), proving the freemium model could work. The following figure shows Duolingo MAUs from 2013 to 2024 (mm):

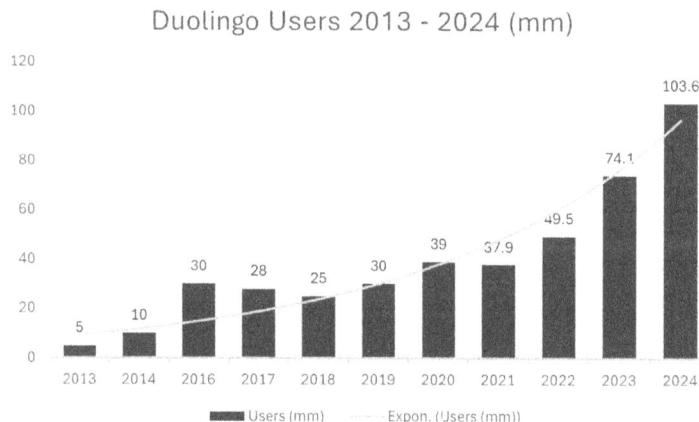

Figure 9.4: Duolingo MAUs 2013 to 2024 (mm)

Duolingo ranks as the most downloaded education app globally and has expanded into math, literacy, and even music learning. The company has built a thriving subscription business, with over five million paid users contributing to its revenue growth.

Figma

Figma was founded in 2012 by *Dylan Field* and *Evan Wallace* with a vision to create a cloud-based design tool that enabled real-time collaboration. At the time, *Adobe Photoshop* and *Sketch* dominated the design industry, but they were desktop-based and lacked collaboration features.

The first MVP was a barebones browser-based vector editor, built using WebGL (a new technology at the time) to enable smooth graphics rendering. The primary goal was to test the following two hypotheses:

- Could a design tool work entirely in the browser?

- Would designers switch from familiar desktop apps to a new web-based system?

Launch and early adoption

The beta version took four years to develop, launching privately in 2016 with a limited group of designers. Early feedback was critical. Users loved the collaboration but complained about lag, missing features, and an unfamiliar interface.

Many professional designers resisted adopting it, believing that serious design work required local software.

Barriers

The biggest internal challenge was convincing their own team that **Web Graphics Library (WebGL)** could handle high-performance graphics. Many believed it was too slow for professional use. External stakeholders like advisors and investors pressured the founders to release the product faster, but the team insisted on perfecting the MVP before launching publicly. The company struggled to hire top-tier designers because most professionals were doubtful of browser-based tools.

Figma focused on perfecting real-time collaboration, making it their unique selling point (*Google Docs* for design).

Instead of competing directly with Adobe at first, Figma targeted students, startups, and product designers, who needed lightweight and collaborative tools. The team prioritized community building, launching Figma Live events, tutorials, and open-source design files to create buzz. In 2018, they introduced a freemium model, allowing free users to collaborate with limited features while businesses paid for premium access.

Figma is now the dominant UI/UX design tool, used by companies like Microsoft, Airbnb, and Uber. In 2022, Adobe announced a \$20 billion acquisition deal for Figma, recognizing its massive industry disruption. The deal was later mutually abandoned in 2023 due to regulatory reasons. The platform has over four million active users, with entire design teams now preferring Figma over traditional tools.

Conclusion

In this chapter, we discussed the usual barriers that MVPs encounter in their growth journey. These barriers are related to people, product, technology, and market understanding.

While building an MVP is about speed and validation, scaling requires stability, efficiency, and long-term strategy. Many products struggle at this stage due to technical debt, lack of market fit, conflicting teams and culture, or poor financial planning.

The key to successful scaling is anticipating and resolving these barriers early and continuously refining based on user insights. The best products evolve by adapting to market needs, strengthening technical foundations, and fostering the right team culture.

In the next chapter, we will cover the ethical considerations of MVP development, focusing on how to balance speed with integrity. We will cover why startups often deprioritize ethics, the long-term impact of early ethical choices on scalability and trust, and the principles every founder must internalize, including transparency, privacy, fairness, and inclusivity.

Points to remember

- **Technical scalability is non-negotiable**: You must address technical debt before it becomes a bottleneck.

- **Market fit evolves**: What worked for early adoption may not be the right recipe for growth. Keep validating and iterating on user needs.

- **Culture shapes growth**: An MVP or a product is only as strong as the team that builds it.

- **Financial sustainability**: A product will need resources to scale seamlessly. Make sure funds are appropriately allocated to the resources to avoid gaps.

- **Scaling is a journey**: Products scale through iterations, market adaptation, and operational excellence.

CHAPTER 10

Ethical Considerations in MVP Development

Introduction

In the last chapter, we explored the barriers to scaling an MVP, from people, product-market fit struggles, to leadership blind spots and execution failures. However, there is one area that often gets deprioritized under pressure from stakeholders and race-to-market urgency. It is an ethical responsibility.

At early-stage startups, when hustling through the challenges, it is easy to prioritize growth over governance, acquisition over accountability, and engagement over ethical design. No, MVP starts with a strategy to exploit, induce bias, or make misleading claims, but a few end up being there because of the sheer ignorance towards ethics.

Some of the biggest product failures of the last decade were not technical failures, but they were ethical lapses that tore user trust and crippled scalability. Whether it is mishandling user data, privacy, features, or ignoring the unintended impact of AI-driven decisions, the consequences of neglecting ethics compound over time; a misstep in the MVP stage can fundamentally break the product's future.

Ethics is not a compliance checklist or a last-minute quick fix. It is a product principle that should be embedded and followed throughout the development process.

This chapter lays down a practical framework for ethical MVP development, focusing on how to balance speed with integrity. It examines why startups often deprioritize ethics in favour of growth, how early ethical decisions can shape long-term scalability, trust, and sustainability, and the approach that every founder must internalize.

Structure

In this chapter, we will cover the following topics:

- Privacy and data protection
- MVP positioning and product messaging
- AI, automation, and bias
- Culture and leadership

Objectives

This chapter enables founders and product teams to perceive ethics as a core part of MVP development and not as an afterthought. In the rush to launch and grow, ethical considerations often get sidelined. But early calls can have lasting consequences on user trust, brand integrity, and product scalability. Through this chapter, you will learn how to identify and navigate ethical risks, build safeguards into your development process, and approach product decisions with long-term responsibility in mind. By the end of this chapter, you will be able to recognize the ethical risks in MVP development and understand how to mitigate them early. You will learn how ethical lapses impact product scalability, from legal ramifications to user retention and brand perception. You will learn to adopt a proactive approach to ethics by integrating responsible decision-making into your product development process, as well. Moreover, you will develop a founder's ethical mindset, ensuring your MVP is not just viable, but also trustworthy and sustainable.

Privacy and data protection

In the current landscape, data is both a currency and a liability. In the early stages, startups are highly focused on user acquisition and outreach, often overlooking a critical question: *Is the user data being handled responsibly?* This is the very first step, and a minor excuse or oversight may lead to security breaches, violations, and, hence, reputational damage.

Regulators are catching up, and so are users. A 2023 *Cisco Privacy Benchmark Study*[1] found that 39% of consumers say they want companies to be more transparent about how their data is used. Apple's privacy-first policies have reshaped the mobile app landscape, forcing businesses to rethink data collection strategies. Privacy is no longer optional but a core differentiator.

The following figure illustrates the distribution of priorities for building consumer trust, as reported in *Cisco's Privacy Benchmark* study:

---

1   Cisco 2023 Data Privacy Benchmark Study - **https://www.cisco.com/c/dam/en_us/about/doing_business/trust-center/docs/cisco-privacy-benchmark-study-2023.pdf**

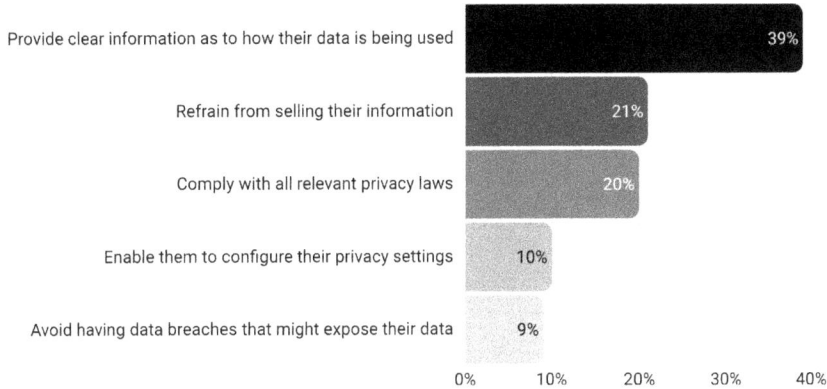

Figure 10.1: *Priorities for building consumer trust are published in Cisco Privacy Benchmark 2023*[2]

Data collection minimalism

Think about an onboarding experience with a new product. If the sign-up flow asks too many questions, users become frustrated and are more likely to exit the process midway.

Most MVPs collect more data than necessary; if more data leads to better insights, stronger monetization, or future-proof for growth. However, over-collecting data increases security risks, legal exposure, and friction in user adoption. Unless legally required, minimizing data collection not only improves user experience but also builds long-term trust.

Startups and even large corporations have learned this the hard way. Take *Meta* (formerly *Facebook*), which has faced multiple lawsuits and regulatory fines for excessive data collection practices. In contrast, privacy-first companies like *DuckDuckGo* and *Signal* have built loyal user bases by collecting minimal data.

Startups must embrace data collection minimalism from the start. The following are a few best practices to note while setting the data capture strategy:

- **Capture what is essential**: If it does not directly improve user experience or product functionality, leave it out.

- **Store responsibly**: The more data you store, the bigger the security risk. Data minimization reduces your attack surface.

- **Avoid just-in-case data points**: Products collect data with no immediate use case, which increases compliance burdens and liability.

---

2   Report - **https://www.cisco.com/c/dam/en_us/about/doing_business/trust-center/docs/cisco-privacy-benchmark-study-2023.pdf**

Use the following template to decide what user data is essential for your MVP and what is good to have that can be left out:

Data type	Justification	Is it essential	Benefit to the user	Retention period
Email Address	Account creation, communication	Y	Login, updates	Until account deletion
Location Data	Personalize experience	N	Better recommendations	7 days
Contact List	Invite friends	N	Network expansion	Not stored

Table 10.1: *Data collection justification table*

Cost of ignoring privacy compliance

While dealing with data laws such as the **General Data Protection Regulation** (**GDPR** - Europe) and the **California Consumer Privacy Act** (**CCPA** - California), startups often view these privacy regulations as bureaucratic or legal hurdles, but they are, in fact, serious growth blockers.

Some of the possible consequences that startups have faced in the past are:

- **Financial penalties**: Under GDPR, companies have faced fines on the scale of one billion dollars in the past two years alone, with Amazon and Meta being among the hardest hit.

- **Investors care**: Due diligence processes now include privacy compliance checks, and startups that ignore this find it harder to raise capital.

- **Consumers demand**: A 2022 PwC study[3] found that 87% of consumers said they would take their business elsewhere if they did not trust a company's data handling practices.

For startups, privacy compliance is about ensuring product credibility, trustworthiness, and hence, longevity. MVPs are built for speed, not resilience, but that trade-off can be disastrous when scaling. When startups move fast, security often becomes an afterthought.

Security debt accumulates just like technical debt. A breach in the early stages can cripple a company before it even reaches product-market fit. In 2021, nearly half of all cyberattacks targeted startups and small businesses, many of which lacked basic security measures.

Common early-stage security pitfalls include the following:

- **Weak authentication:** MVPs often rely on simple logins instead of robust authentication mechanisms like OAuth or two-factor authentication.

---

3   PwC 2022 Digital Trust Insights Survey - **https://www.pwc.in/assets/pdfs/2022-india-digital-trust-insights.pdf**

- **Unsecured APIs**: Startups frequently expose APIs without proper rate limiting or encryption, making them easy targets for data breaches.

- **Hardcoded credentials:** It is still common to see database passwords and API keys stored in source code, a major security flaw.

Startups that embed security into their MVP architecture avoid expensive overhauls later and maintain user confidence as they scale.

Transparency is not optional

Consumers today are more privacy-conscious than ever. They want to know what data is collected, how it is used, and whether they can control it. Companies that fail to provide this clarity lose trust and, ultimately, users.

Many high-profile privacy scandals have stemmed not from outright data misuse but from a lack of transparency. For example, in 2018, *Facebook* faced backlash when users discovered their call and text logs had been stored without clear disclosure. On the other hand, companies like Apple and Signal have built their brands around privacy-first messaging, leading to stronger user retention.

The following are a few approaches to ensure transparency:

- Use clear, user-friendly language. Privacy policies should not read like legal documents; explain data usage in a way users can easily understand.

- Make consent meaningful. Users should have real choices, not misleading *opt-out* dark patterns.

- Provide visibility and control. Let users manage their data preferences, delete accounts, and see what is being tracked.

Privacy and security are not just about checking compliance boxes. They are strategic imperatives that impact user trust, retention, and long-term viability. The best MVPs prioritize data minimalism, early compliance, proactive security, and clear transparency. Startups that get privacy right from day one does not just avoid risks, and they turn ethical data practices into a competitive advantage.

MVP positioning and product messaging

Startups pitch grand visions to investors, promise seamless experiences to users, and rally their teams around the next big thing. However, when the gap between promise and reality widens too much, trust crumbles. The MVP stage is where that balance is most frAgile.

Many founders fall into the *fake it till you make it* trap, believing that early overpromising is just part of the game. However, misrepresentation is not just a marketing misstep; it can alienate early adopters, spark regulatory scrutiny, and even sink a startup before it scales.

In the age of transparency, credibility is your strongest currency. Here is why honesty in MVP positioning is not just ethical, it is essential for long-term success.

The fake it till you make it trap

MVP overhype is real. Startups need users, investors, and media attention, and polishing an unfinished product to appear *market-ready* can seem like a necessary move. However, misleading users has consequences.

For instance, Theranos is a cautionary tale of how extreme misrepresentation can lead to not just business failure, but legal consequences. *Elizabeth Holmes* promised revolutionary blood testing technology that never actually worked. The result was a $700M fraud scandal and a complete collapse.

Another such case occurred when *Nikola Corporation*, an electric truck startup, claimed to have a working hydrogen-powered semi-truck, only for investigations to reveal the infamous *rolling truck* video, where the vehicle was simply coasting downhill. The company's stock plummeted, and its founder was convicted of fraud.

At the MVP stage, selling a vision is acceptable, but selling a lie is fatal. Startups should focus on what they can deliver today, not just what they hope to build tomorrow.

Short term gains lead to long-term damage

Some startups present product functionalities that do not exist yet, to lure in users or close deals. Others deploy dark patterns, like forced sign-ups, misleading free trials, or hidden fees, to create artificial traction.

While these tactics might drive early engagement, they almost always backfire when users discover the reality. Here are a few startups that paid the price of misrepresentation of their products and service offerings:

- *Clinkle*, once the most hyped fintech startup in Silicon Valley, raised $30M for an MVP that was supposedly a game-changing payments app. However, delays, overpromising, and secrecy around what the app did led to skepticism. When the app finally launched, it was underwhelming and failed to meet expectations. The company collapsed.

- *Revolv*, a smart home hub startup, was acquired by *Google's Nest*. The problem was that Google later shut down the app, rendering users' devices useless. Customers had paid for a product they expected to work indefinitely. The backlash was severe, leading Google to change its approach to smart home device support.

- *Juicero*, a startup that raised $120M, claimed its juicer used proprietary technology. The truth was that users could squeeze the juice packs by hand, no expensive machine needed. When this was exposed, the company shut down within months.

- *Fyre Festival*, marketed as an exclusive luxury music event, sold thousands of tickets based on fabricated promotional content. When attendees arrived at chaos and disaster relief tents instead of villas, the backlash was swift and brutal.

While misleading positioning can destroy a startup, authenticity can set one apart. Some of the most successful startups today built trust by being honest about their product limitations in the early days.

We must learn from Figma. Figma started as a limited beta product. Instead of claiming it was ready to replace Adobe, they emphasized that it was a work in progress and actively sought user feedback. This transparency built early loyalty and led to viral adoption. Similarly, Buffer, the social media scheduling tool, gained traction by publishing an open revenue dashboard and blog posts about their challenges. This radical transparency made users feel invested in the company's success.

Key takeaways

MVP success is not about making the size of the product, but it is about driving value with what is there. Here are the key takeaways:

- Do not fake what is not built. Be upfront about what works and what is still evolving.

- Resist the temptation to use deceptive UX tricks. Users do not like being manipulated.

- Lean into transparency. Startups that communicate openly about their MVP's progress and limitations build long-term trust.

AI, automation, and bias

AI-driven products are no longer a futuristic concept. They are shaping everything from hiring decisions to loan approvals, content recommendations, and customer support. However, while AI unlocks efficiency and automation at scale, it also introduces a fundamental ethical challenge, i.e., bias.

Startups building AI-powered MVPs often assume that their models are neutral, objective, and purely data-driven. In reality, though, every dataset carries biases, and every algorithm amplifies them in unexpected ways. If these biases go unchecked, they can alienate users, create legal risks, and erode product credibility before the company even gets off the ground.

The question is not whether bias exists in AI. Yes, it does. The real challenge is how startups acknowledge, mitigate, and design AI systems that are both effective and fair from day one.

Bias mitigation in MVP

Most AI models are trained on historical data, and history is riddled with biases. Whether it is gender bias in hiring algorithms, racial bias in facial recognition, or socioeconomic bias in credit scoring, flawed AI outputs are a direct reflection of the data they learn from.

Let us see some of the biggest AI failures due to the bias in the training data:

- Amazon scrapped its AI hiring tool after discovering it systematically favored male candidates.

- Apple's AI-driven credit card faced backlash when users discovered that it was granting lower credit limits to women than men with identical financial backgrounds.

Startups building AI-powered MVPs cannot ignore the fact that bias is already present in their data. They should take proactive steps to reduce its impact.

Let us explore some of the commonly used steps to mitigate the AI bias:

- Diversify your training data. If your model is trained on a limited dataset, it will only work well for that subset of users. Broaden your data sources to ensure fair representation.

- Continuously test for bias. Bias is not always obvious at first. Regularly audit your AI outputs for patterns that indicate unintended discrimination.

- Incorporate human oversight. AI should augment decision-making, not replace it entirely. Human-in-the-loop approaches help catch bias before it reaches users.

Use the following AI fairness questionnaire to ensure that early-stage AI does not unintentionally reinforce bias or discriminate:

- Have we tested the model on diverse datasets?

- Have we reviewed outputs for potential bias?

- Can we explain how the model makes decisions?

- Are there manual overrides or human review steps?

- Are users informed when AI is making decisions for them?

Data bias is a business risk

AI bias is not a technical problem. The business impact can be critical. Let us consider the impact it can have on the users and, hence, the business.

- **Loss of user trust**: If customers feel they are being treated unfairly by an algorithm, they will leave. *Airbnb* had to redesign its platform after research showed racial bias in booking approvals.

- **Regulatory penalties**: Governments worldwide are tightening AI regulations. The EU's AI Act, California's AI accountability laws, and similar global efforts mean AI bias is now a legal liability, not just a PR issue.

- **Brand reputation damage**: Once bias is exposed, the backlash is swift. Social media amplifies negative AI experiences, and public trust is hard to rebuild.

Explainability in AI-driven MVPs

One of the biggest user-concerns with AI is its *black box* nature, users do not know why an algorithm made a particular decision. If users cannot understand AI's logic, they will not trust it.

For AI-powered MVPs, explainability is not a nice-to-have; it is a necessity. Startups need to provide clear, understandable insights into how their AI models work, especially in high-stakes applications like finance, healthcare, or hiring.

Let us explore the best practices for AI transparency:

- Offer user-friendly explanations. Instead of just saying *the AI determined X*, show why it reached that decision. Google's *Why This Ad?* This feature is a good example of clear AI transparency in action.

- Enable user control. Allow users to adjust AI-driven settings, retrain recommendations, or appeal automated decisions. Giving them control builds trust.

- Disclose limitations upfront. No AI is perfect. Being transparent about what the model can and cannot do prevents over-reliance and frustration.

Companies that prioritize AI explainability build stronger relationships with users and reduce regulatory risks before they become problems.

AI ethics and regulations

Due to the sheer potential of the risk AI carries in its outcomes, regulators no longer tolerate AI as a piece of software that can be tweaked as and when needed. The past few years have seen a sharp increase in AI-specific laws, and non-compliance could lead to fines, lawsuits, or outright bans. The following is the list of major AI regulatory trends startups should watch:

- The EU AI Act (expected enforcement in 2025) will classify AI systems into risk categories, imposing strict transparency and fairness requirements on high-risk applications.

- The U.S. AI Bill of Rights provides guidelines for bias mitigation, algorithmic transparency, and user consent, and future laws will likely enforce these principles.

- China's AI regulations already mandate algorithmic fairness and transparency, particularly for recommendation engines and automated decision-making tools.

AI compliance cannot be ignored. Building an ethical, regulation-ready AI intervention from the start is far easier than scrambling to fix compliance gaps later. AI and automation can be game changers for MVPs, but only when built with fairness, transparency, and accountability in mind. Here are some points to keep in mind while architecting these systems:

- Bias is not hypothetical; it is present in every dataset. Startups must proactively mitigate it.

- Unchecked AI bias is not just an ethical problem; it is a business risk with real consequences.

- Transparency builds trust. Explainability should be a core feature of any AI-driven MVP.

- AI regulations are coming fast; startups that ignore compliance now will struggle to scale later.

Monetization and user trust

Monetization is where ethical dilemmas in product development become unavoidable. A great MVP solves a real problem, but a sustainable product needs a revenue model that benefits both the business and its users. The challenge was that many startups prioritize short-term revenue tactics that, while effective initially, erode user trust and damage long-term scalability.

From freemium models and ads to subscription pricing and hidden fees, the monetization landscape is filled with ethical gray areas. The line between smart growth and exploitative tactics is not always clear, but crossing it can sink a startup before it truly scales.

Freemium models, ads, and pricing strategies

The freemium model has become the go-to strategy for software startups, allowing users to experience a product before committing to a paid plan. When done right, it creates a fair value exchange, free users get functional access, while paid users unlock premium features.

However, some freemium models are designed to frustrate, not convert. Artificial limitations, intrusive ads, and essential features being locked behind a paywall undermine user experience instead of enhancing it. A few monetization tactics that test ethical boundaries are as follows:

- **Pay to remove frustration design**: Free versions that intentionally create pain points (slow performance, forced delays, excessive ads) just to push upgrades.

- **Dark patterns in subscriptions**: Tricking users into paid plans through auto-renewals, hidden cancellation options, or deceptive upgrade prompts.

- **Over-monetized free users**: Free-tier users are being bombarded with intrusive ads, aggressive upsells, or misleading clickbait.

Startups must ask: *Is my freemium model designed to convert happy users, or to annoy them into paying?*

Hidden charges and deceptive UX

Users expect transparency, but quite often, products hide any unintended fees or charges in the fine print, assuming the friction or ignorance will keep users from leaving. But sooner or later, users always discover, and that is when the trust breaks.

Several examples have come to light in recent years. Whether it is Uber's unregulated peak surge pricing or Zomato's sudden platform fee, users eventually notice, especially when they zoom in on the payment breakdown. In fact, Uber faced lawsuits when users realized their upfront fares were not always accurate, and drivers were paid differently than what was shown.

The following figure shows the ethical red flags that may go unnoticed and incur additional charges:

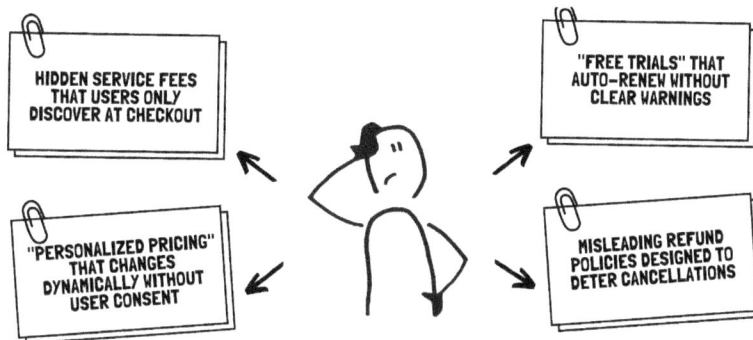

Figure 10.2: Ethical red flags for consumers

For long-term sustainable success, startups must prioritize clear, upfront pricing and provide honest communication about costs. If users feel tricked, they will not just leave; they will also tell others.

Growth hack versus growth manipulation

Every startup wants rapid growth, but not all growth tactics are ethical. Growth hacking, when done responsibly, is about creative marketing, referral loops, and product-led growth. However, when it manipulates users, exploits psychology, or misleads customers, it becomes growth manipulation.

A growth hack respects the user. It creates genuine value, often by rethinking conventional marketing. Think of *Dropbox's* early referral program: *Get more space by inviting your friends.* Simple, honest, and aligned with user benefit.

Growth manipulation, on the other hand, prioritizes numbers over trust. It tricks users into behaviors they did not fully agree with, like auto-subscribing to paid services, dark UX patterns, or masking product limitations.

Some examples of unethical growth tactics are as follows:

- **Viral loop traps**: Forcing users to invite friends before accessing key features (e.g., early Clubhouse invites created artificial scarcity).

- **Fake scarcity and urgency**: Flash sales that restart every day or a countdown timer that resets.

- **Tricky opt-ins**: Pre-checking boxes for newsletters, data-sharing, or premium subscriptions.

- **Data-leveraging without consent**: Using user data for growth experiments without transparency.

- **Auto-renewals**: Hidden auto-renewals or auto-debit linked to a credit card.

- **Forced sign-up**: Forced sign-up before granting access to a feature.

Let us have a brief walkthrough of some cases that have sparked debate on ethical practices:

- **LinkedIn's email import backlash (2015)**: LinkedIn encouraged users to import their contacts to grow connections. However, users discovered the platform was sending multiple, sometimes confusing emails on their behalf without clear consent. The company settled a lawsuit for $13 million.

- **Facebook's psychological testing scandal (2014)**: Facebook ran an experiment tweaking newsfeeds to study emotional contagion without user knowledge. While framed as a product test, it raised massive ethical concerns about user manipulation.

- **Zomato's platform fee (2023)**: Zomato introduced a *platform fee* without upfront notice. Users only noticed after order placement, to which social backlash followed. Platform fee still exists, but more importantly, it is a substantial chunk of their revenues.

If growth comes at the cost of user trust, it is not sustainable. Users today are savvy. They share, they screenshot, they post. If you mislead them, they will find out. And when they do, the viral loop that once brought growth can just as easily bring backlash.

Revenue models with long-term trust

Sustainable monetization is not just about maximizing revenue; it is about aligning business incentives with user success. The most trusted companies monetize in ways that feel fair, transparent, and user-centric.

The best practices for ethical monetization are as follows:

- Make pricing clear and upfront, no hidden fees, no surprises.

- Design freemium models that enhance, not degrade, user experience.

- Give users full control over subscriptions, cancellations, and data.

- Monetize through genuine value exchange, not manipulation.

Startups that build trust-first revenue models, like *Figma's* fair pricing, *Duolingo's* transparent freemium model, or Notion's simple, predictable plans, win because users feel respected, not exploited.

Next, we will tackle the final ethical challenge in MVP development, handling failure responsibly. This is because when things do not go as planned (and they often will not), how a startup communicates, pivots, and learns can define its entire legacy.

Culture and leadership

Ethical startups do not happen by accident. The way a team handles tough decisions, responds to pressure, and prioritizes values over shortcuts is a direct reflection of its leadership. Founders and early team members define the cultural DNA of a company, and if ethics is not built in from day one, it rarely becomes a priority later.

Most startups move fast, sometimes too fast, to pause and assess the ethical consequences of their choices. However, cutting corners in decision-making today can erode trust, attract regulatory scrutiny, and create internal friction that slows the company down in the long run.

A strong ethical culture is not about avoiding mistakes; it is about creating a system where mistakes are caught early, debated openly, and corrected quickly.

Decision-making starts at the top

A startup's values are not what is written on a website; they are reflected in how leadership behaves during difficult choices. When founders prioritize integrity over short-term wins, teams follow suit. However, when leadership turns a blind eye to questionable tactics, even well-intentioned employees justify cutting corners.

Several startups have set examples of embedding ethics into decision-making. A few of them are listed as follows:

- Airbnb took accountability for trust issues by implementing user verification, anti-discrimination policies, and host guarantees, and moves that were not legally required but built long-term credibility.

- Patagonia's leadership drives sustainable choices, ensuring environmental impact is not just a marketing claim but a core business principle.

Founders and product leaders must ask this one question: *Are we setting a precedent that rewards ethical decisions, even when they are inconvenient?*

Startups and ethical guidelines

Regulations like GDPR, CCPA, and AI transparency laws exist to protect users, but legal compliance is a baseline, not a moral compass. Just because something is legal does not mean it is the right thing to do.

Many early-stage startups do not have the resources for dedicated ethics teams, but they can still create clear ethical guidelines on:

- **User privacy and data protection**: What data do we collect? How do we store and use it responsibly?

- **Product honesty**: Are we making promises we cannot keep?

- **Monetization**: Are our pricing and revenue strategies fair and transparent?

- **AI bias and automation ethics**: Are our models trained on diverse, unbiased data?

By proactively defining ethical guardrails, startups avoid the *ask for forgiveness later* approach that has backfired on countless companies.

One of the biggest ethical failures in startups is a culture where no one speaks up. When teams feel pressure to hit aggressive goals, it is easy to rationalize grey area decisions. If questioning leadership is not encouraged, bad calls go unchallenged until they explode into PR or legal disasters.

Successful companies actively create space for internal pushbacks, as shown in the following examples:

- Netflix uses a culture of *radical candor*, where employees are expected to challenge decisions openly.

- Stripe's leadership encourages dissenting opinions before major product and policy changes.

- Atlassian has an internal ethics committee that reviews product and business practices.

Transparency, accountability, and continuous review

Ethical startups do not just make responsible choices once, but they review and refine their approach as they scale. What worked at 10 employees might fail at 500.

Some best practices for keeping ethics at the core of decision-making are as follows:

- **Build ethics into OKRs**: Make ethical product design, data protection, and fair pricing measurable goals, not just *nice-to-haves*.

- **Make leadership accountable**: If ethical breaches happen, founders and execs should take responsibility, not just individual employees.

- **Regular internal reviews**: Revisit ethical guidelines every quarter, just like financial goals.

Trust is not a one-time achievement. It is an ongoing process. The startups that embed ethics into leadership, team culture, and daily operations do not just avoid scandals; they build brands that consumers and the workforce genuinely believe in.

Conclusion

Ethics in MVP development is not a luxury but a necessity. Startups that embed ethical considerations from day one build trust, avoid costly pivots, and create long-term competitive advantages. Whether it is data privacy, product transparency, AI fairness, or ethical monetization, the decisions made in the early stages shape a company's reputation and future growth. Ethics is not about slowing down; it is about scaling responsibly.

Points to remember

- Trust is a competitive advantage. Ethical startups do not just comply with regulations; they earn user loyalty.

- Privacy-first design is the future. Collect only what is necessary, be transparent, and avoid security debt.

- Honesty in positioning is critical. Overpromising and misleading users may yield short-term gains but cause long-term damage.

- AI and automation require responsible design. Bias is a business risk; mitigate it early and ensure transparency.

- Fair monetization builds sustainable growth. Hidden fees, dark patterns, and manipulative pricing backfire.

- Culture defines ethical resilience. Founders and leadership must set the standard, encourage open discussions, and prioritize long-term impact over short-term wins.

- By treating ethics as a growth strategy rather than an obstacle, startups can move fast, without breaking trust.

Join our Discord space

Join our Discord workspace for latest updates, offers, tech happenings around the world, new releases, and sessions with the authors:

https://discord.bpbonline.com

Index

www.ingramcontent.com/pod-product-compliance
Lightning Source LLC
Chambersburg PA
CBHW061809210326
41599CB00034B/6934

* 9 7 8 9 3 6 5 8 9 3 3 3 5 *